THE SERENITY PRAYER

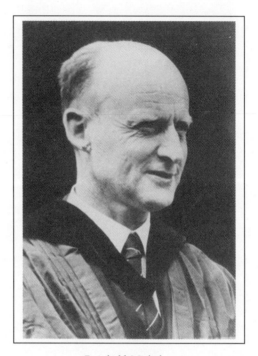

Reinhold Niebuhr

THE
SERENITY PRAYER

*Faith and Politics in Times of
Peace and War*

Elisabeth Sifton

W. W. NORTON & COMPANY

New York • London

For information about permission to reproduce selections from this book, write to Permissions, W. W. Norton & Company, Inc., 500 Fifth Avenue, New York, NY 10110

Manufacturing by The Maple-Vail Book Manufacturing Group
Book design by Charlotte Staub
Production manager: Anna Oler

Library of Congress Cataloging-in-Publication Data
Sifton, Elisabeth.
The serenity prayer : faith and politics in times of peace and war /
Elisabeth Sifton.— 1st ed.
p. cm.
Includes index.
ISBN 0-393-05746-1
1. Serenity prayer. 2. Niebuhr, Reinhold, 1892-1971. 3. Christianity and politics—
United States—History—20th century. 4. Liberalism—Religious aspects—
Christianity—History—20th century.
I. Title.
BV284.S47S54 2003
242'.4—dc22

2003013973

W. W. Norton & Company, Inc., 500 Fifth Avenue, New York, N.Y. 10110
www.wwnorton.com

W. W. Norton & Company Ltd., Castle House, 75/76 Wells Street, London W1T 3QT

1 2 3 4 5 6 7 8 9 0

In loving memory of my grandmother
Lydia Hosto Niebuhr,
and for my granddaughter,
Hallie Elisabeth Sifton

God, give us grace
to accept with serenity
the things that cannot be changed,
courage to change the things
that should be changed,
and the wisdom to distinguish
the one from the other.

—Reinhold Niebuhr

Preface

Americans call it the "Serenity Prayer," which is how it's known to those who encounter it as a mantra of Alcoholics Anonymous. The reassuring calm of the word "serenity" is soothing, though to call it the "grace" or "courage" or "wisdom" prayer might better emphasize the demanding spiritual effort it recommends. People usually presume that it's very old, for its stringency and spiritual clarity seem unusual for our soupy, compromised times. It's surely rabbinical in origin, or Stoic, derived or translated from Latin or Hebrew, maybe Scottish? All too often a facile postmodern skepticism prevails as to its authorship: Even if some latter-day pastor thinks he composed it, the reasoning goes, it's more likely that he pulled it from his ragbag of accessible holy thoughts first set forth in a century with a better prose style than ours, like the seventeenth, and rejigged it for all of us now.

In Germany false confidence about the prayer's venerable antiquity has gone further. And it is superbly centered on the presumption that of course the prayer is German. Not long after Hitler's final defeat in 1945, not long after the four victorious Allied powers had divided Germany's ruined provinces, when its destroyed economy, never mind its spirit, was slowly being rebuilt, the prayer began to be cited as a wonderful eighteenth-century Swabian Pietist guide to wisdom. Within a few years of the founding of a new democratic German state in the old British, French, and American occupation zones, politicians quoted it as a German prayer in morale-building speeches, and a half century later they still do.

How dramatic the irony, then, that the actual author was an American of German descent who wrote the prayer in the United States in 1943, at the height of the war against Germany; whose family for generations had kept a sometimes strict, always careful distance from the fatherland; who thought that German Pietism was often "shallow" and "irrelevant," as weak as the bland hypocrisies of religion in his own country. He was a teacher and writer who had been strenuously opposing much of Germany's religious and political life for decades, all the more so when National Socialism poisoned both; who early on had spoken out, loudly, against Hitler and against the implicit support or condoning of his regime in Europe and the United States. All his life he fought against conservatives because they usually disregarded the imperatives of social justice, but he was also skeptical of liberals because they usually radiated implausible optimism about the likelihood of social betterment. He was an American pastor who found himself at odds with Protestant and Catholic church leaders because he thought that they, like many other public figures, had failed and were failing to give heed to the hideous threats posed to democratic freedom everywhere by totalitarian and fascist forces. Before Pearl Harbor, he preached and lectured and wrote in opposition to his own country's isolationist neutrality; by 1943, he and like-minded colleagues were already debating and planning for the structures of postwar democracy, which they rightly believed would need to be strengthened. A deeply devout man, he wrestled daily with the problem of how to relate his innermost religious commitments to the public life of the community.

So the historical meaning of this quite modern American prayer is bound up in the war against one of the greatest evils posed during a violently evil century. Yet like all ageless prayers it speaks to many generations and of course to good and peaceful people in tranquil times. It reminds us of the virtues we must call on in our private lives, and it also concerns the qualities needed to act in the intricate social networks that connect us to others. In our new century, with its new evils, when we should surely pay attention in new and better ways to our conduct as citizens of the world, the Serenity Prayer can mean even more to us than it has in the past. The circumstances under which it was composed and the reasons that it took on such a life of its own are in themselves inspiring, and knowing them might help us to appreciate its consoling, challenging power. The Serenity Prayer is not just a familiar, agreeable cliché. After all, its instructions are tremendously difficult and puzzling to follow.

What does it mean to ask God to grant one grace? Millions of Christians express this petition every week around the world, but they have never agreed on what it means. Perhaps that's no surprise. Nor do Christians seem especially graceful—there are those who have found them quite the contrary. And of course millions of people in other faiths express comparable petitions, asking for the grace or power or fullness of heart that will endow their lives with meaning. What is this about? Amazing grace! Is it a freely given bounty of God's love, bestowed on all His creatures, or does one have to prepare one's soul for it, and if so how? And how do you know if it's been granted you? In the early years of the American colonies, this became, as it had been in Europe and England for centuries, a hotly contested *political* issue.

The Serenity Prayer presumes that it's hard to accept "what cannot be changed." It reminds us of the human truth that no pain, death, or irreversible loss is easily managed. Yet acceptance must come serenely or not at all, since anger or resentment hardens the heart and makes acceptance impossible. On the other hand, all too many of us seem able, even ready and willing, to accept inhumane and cruel situations that we could ourselves do something to improve. Surely we should find it intolerable to endure them.

If instead we find the courage to change "what should be changed," how far will our decision take us? Do I act just for myself, or for my family, society, country? Does *praying* for the courage to make changes suggest that at morally ambiguous and dangerous junctures, let alone ordinary everyday ones, summoning up the strength to do this may require divine intervention?

And then—wisdom! The prayer says nothing about the moment of discernment when, if we are wise, we shall see which category is which. How do we tell? Most prayers thank the Almighty for having bestowed understanding, wisdom, and good fortune upon the faithful. Or they imply that the religious commitment itself, or God Himself—higher powers, anyway— will somehow generate the wisdom we mere mortals need to get on in life. But this prayer does not. Many prayers in many faiths petition God to show the way to right action. But this prayer asks only for wisdom to discern the right way on our own. It presumes that it's within our powers to accomplish this.

Still, it is a prayer, and I cannot imagine its message in a different mode.

Why is that? Whether Christian or not, why would anyone *pray* about this, not just *think* about it? What, indeed, does it mean to pray? I myself believe it's an inner activity natural to all humanity, and I'm certain that atheists and secular people pray, too, even when they scoff at the very idea. The reassuring truth is that the mode of hope in which prayer is cast is inevitable for all of us, and the habit of true prayer can develop easily. Yet, beyond the contemplative religious communities whose members devote themselves to this subject, not enough of us have thought about what prayer really is or might be.

AS IT HAPPENS, my father, Reinhold Niebuhr, composed the Serenity Prayer in a place and context I knew well and remember vividly, and I grew up knowing his answers to some of these perplexing questions: his daily work acknowledged their importance. There's an ironic connection, too, between the Serenity Prayer's composition and the strange way it was later misattributed in Germany. For me, the Serenity Prayer distills the essence of hope and effort that animated my father and some of his closest friends in their lifework. These people were far-flung allies in many different struggles against economic and social injustice, against bigotries of all kinds, against the evils of unrestrained capitalism, against fascism, against wars; they lived and worked in Missouri, in Germany, in Mississippi, in Detroit, in England, in Washington—and they are the protagonists in the dramas I write about here. Some of them were agnostics or atheists, some of them were Jews, and quite a few of them were Protestant ministers. I think of them as people who understood how to relate their faith to their lives, the world of the spirit to the world of the here and now. They are heroes and heroines to me, but I think they are heroes and heroines for all of us. Their story—the back-story, as it were, of the Serenity Prayer and of its afterlife—was not just about politics, not just about religion in public life, not just about war and how to avoid it or how to fight it. It was a drama about our life as citizens.

It's easy enough to see that the Serenity Prayer came out of, and was affected by, the challenges and dangers of a very difficult, fractured time. Now, sixty years later, our lives are darkened again by grim foreboding about new threats, and civil society seems ever more fractured and frantic. Trust, hope, and courtesy in the public sphere have radically diminished, and this naturally affects our inner lives, too: how can it not?

Yet we are not facing a new spiritual crisis: this is the same old crisis in a new form. Living in history, living in full, always offers as much despair as hope, as much danger as possibility. So it is no wonder that so many millions find daily strength and resolve in praying for grace to accept with serenity that which we cannot change, courage to change what we should change, and the wisdom to discern the one from the other.

THE SERENITY PRAYER

I

For about twenty years, from the mid-1930s to the mid-1950s, my family spent our long summer holidays—from Memorial Day to Labor Day, if we were lucky—in Heath, a farming village in a remote corner of northwestern Massachusetts. In Heath's Union Church, July and August Sundays often found visiting clerics in the pulpit, and my father was one of these; the rest of the service was in the hands of the parish's familiar year-round figures. Mrs. Burrington played the organ as she always did; the great anthem "Holy, Holy, Holy" was the processional hymn as it always was; Miss Dickinson and Mrs. Gleason and Mrs. Stetson arranged the flowers in the chancel— peonies and hydrangeas from nearby gardens and mountain laurel from the woods; Charlie Packard passed the collection plate. I can't remember which of the men joined him in circulating the wooden trays for the monthly communion service, but I remember the cubes of fresh-baked white bread, the little shot glasses of grape juice, and the wooden racks on the pew backs where you put the empties, next to the shelves for prayer books and hymnbooks. Light streamed through big rectangles of clear glass windows into the spare, monochrome hall: this was quintessential rural New England at its Sunday best. It was in an ordinary Sunday morning service at the Heath Union Church in the summer of 1943 that my father first used his new prayer.

I can hardly claim to remember the season when the Serenity Prayer was composed (I was only four then), but Heath didn't change much in the early postwar years when I was growing up there. Children accept as a given the contours and colors of their family world, and it didn't occur to me at the time to wonder why the Heath people were the way they were, how the town had come to be as it was. I took our companionable neighbors for granted. It was a long time before I found out about their stories, since Heath people didn't talk about themselves. And it wasn't until after I'd become acquainted with other communities that I appreciated how special Heath was. It wasn't like anywhere else—yet somehow the place well expressed certain all-American truths.

Heath was very beautiful—on that we were agreed. Much of its hilly, forested terrain had been cleared over the previous two centuries for meadow and pasture, and from the open, windswept hilltops one could see for miles. Its isolated farmhouses, dating from the late eighteenth and early nineteenth centuries, were handsomely plain in that lonely, heartbreaking way that is the distinctive mark of American frontier architecture. But its most striking quality, beyond the physical beauty of the land and buildings, was the relative absence in Heath society of all those banal hypocrisies about money, status, power, and authority that regularly contort and distort social behavior in most places.

It wasn't that Heath folk didn't have views about wealth and poverty, say, but that their views didn't seem to affect the way they actually treated their neighbors and acquaintances. The usual currents of affection or dislike or curiosity coursed through the town's bloodstream, and the usual reflexes of approval or disapproval could be observed. Nobody's perfect—there were personal difficulties of many sorts. But money or social status was honestly of little interest. This may sound banal, but to the Heath people character was everything, and they scarcely had to say so. Country reticence made it plain. This isn't as rare an attitude as you might think, and its benign effects are interestingly infectious.

The social tone of Heath was cheerfully informal—and this despite many of the summer residents' happening to be clergymen. Priests and parsons are famous for generating an atmosphere of pious self-regard among themselves and muffled hypocrisy or edginess among others, but this wasn't the case in Heath. The summer clergymen had no time or respect for religiosity and cant, and certainly no time or respect for biased intolerance. They came from diverse religious backgrounds, and it was among them that I first learned about the often unpleasant quarrels punctuating the history of Protestantism in America. But they were pledged to overcome these squabbles. Most of them had known one another for some time; they shared a complicated, many-layered history of combat against virtually every bigotry you can think of, including plenty of religious ones. They had become friends because they all had the temperament and political commitment to fight for social equality and economic justice in the American communities they cared about; they were equally alive to international dangers. I don't know whether their open hearts and minds were the cause or the effect of their political and religious priorities—probably both.

One or two of the summer people in Heath came from very privileged backgrounds, but most of us lived in genteel poverty; some of the summer visitors came from working-class families and hardscrabble worlds where nothing had been easy. The Christian priests and teachers among them had thought long and deeply about the relationship of their faith to the world around them; their public commitments were bolstered by a confident trust that the Gospels expected this work of them. But they did not believe they could or should do this work on their own: they had the sense to realize that Christians should not set themselves off from other human communities when seeking peace, or justice. They didn't think any human group should do this: they didn't believe in the moral value of group identities, though they certainly saw that many people suffered because of their being in, or being put in, disadvantaged categories—whether of race, religion, or economic standing. They believed in individual responsibility and merit.

Of course Heath's fundamental tone was set not by the summer people but by the year-round residents, the farmers and their families, our neighbors and friends. These were people of real consequence. They went about their work not only with a lively concern for the health, profitability, and continued viability of their family-owned farms, but with a due sense of the fair allotment of community tasks and due attention to the larger world in which they had to sell their produce. About the wider social nets by which they were interconnected—to one another, to the county, to Massachusetts, to the nation—they were alert, well informed, and shrewd. We summer people knew that in Heath we were enjoying the healthy benefits of a vibrant agrarian community to whose strength we only marginally contributed. We also knew that farming in New England was perilously difficult, that our friends worked on a knife-edge of uncertainty and poverty, like so many of the people in our wintertime worlds, too. The agricultural base of Heath's energy and beauty was severely eroded in subsequent years, as happened all over America, and the closing in of its reforested landscape expresses the social changes that had already begun to alter it during the Second World War.

The fact that the Heath township was not a pretentious summer enclave made a big difference. It was off the beaten track, it had no amenities or conveniences of the kind that attract rich urbanites, and there weren't any activities or clubs around which the summer people might have been tempted to focus their social lives. If some well-heeled seasonal outsider, misunderstanding the tenor of the place, had tried to initiate something of the sort, his proposal would have been killed off with polite neglect, I'm sure. We knew the real agenda. We knew what was going on in the township as a whole, knew who would be elected town selectman, what bids were in for resurfacing the town roads, how the town library would raise new funds, or what had happened in the latest school crisis. So Heath wasn't a "summer place." We liked it for its beauty, for its sympathetic human tone, and for still having the physical contours of a classic New England town, with two centuries' worth of New England views about self-governance and self-reliance showing in every hill and valley.

Among the summer clergymen in Heath were shared associations that went back to the years during and after the First World War. The traumas of the war had exacerbated ugly social and ethnic hostilities that were already simmering and bubbling in the great melting pot of American society. Many Americans had responded defensively on the home front, allowing their fellow citizens' liberties to be constrained, their lives restricted, in the interests of security and safety. Especially after the Bolshevik Revolution, fear and reaction counseled, even encouraged, capitulation on the civil-liberties front: they always do. This reflexive nastiness seems regularly to appear among us in stressful times, and it is with us again today. It always hits hardest at those who are unprotected and unable to defend themselves—poor working people without safety nets, often recent immigrants, people considered "alien" and therefore perhaps hostile, people who question the powers that be. Suddenly they are the targets of cynically imposed law-and-order maneuvers, torrents of hate speech are flushed in their direction, and they are threatened with the loss of the very freedom the United States is pledged to assure them. Today this means Arabs, or Muslims, or South Asians, or Mexicans; in the early years of the twentieth century it meant the laboring poor from whatever land, but especially Germans and southeastern Europeans.

To my father and his colleagues, this was all wrong. It was certainly un-Christian, and it was surely unconstitutional. Threats to civil liberties had to be opposed, and opposed vigorously. Americans should not have to accept infringements on their constitutional rights as the price to pay for their supposed safety—and in any case we have all learned and relearned at great cost that none of us is ever truly safe. So they wanted— and worked hard—to curb xenophobia, to defend the rights of immigrants, to end the exploitation and inequities that made life so harsh for so many working people, to insist on the rule of law, to make things freer, not less free.

After the carnage and deathly horrors of 1914–18, it also seemed important to many Protestant clergy to propose socially responsible arrangements in which the churches would work together to make the world safer and more just. They differed greatly among themselves, but the activists with whom my father worked shared a deeply grounded belief in the relevance and essential value of the Christian faith in dealing with the human crises of the time, as of all times. It was vital, they thought, to get Christians to join across national or denominational borders and make their faith universally relevant. Since civil and secular politics in the giddy 1920s were unpleasantly divisive and bigoted, this work was not easy, but the pastors and church leaders who devoted their lives to it considered it urgent: they wanted to help assuage the social injuries, to cure the racist and nationalist malignities, that had contributed to causing the Great War in the first place.

For one thing, the tone of Christian talking to Christian, and of Christian talking to any kind of non-Christian, had to change, and they had to encourage people to make the change. They did their best to develop some measure of cooperative goodwill among Protestants, who were then unpleasantly divided: all kinds of sharp-shouldered attitudes kept Methodists and Lutherans and Presbyterians and Episcopalians from giving one another doctrinal or social respect. The many Pentecostalist and evangelical sects then exploding across America didn't have anything to do with these efforts, any more than they do now. Their hostility is part of the story. And there was nowhere near enough contact among Christians in the different nations— America, France, Germany, England, Serbia, Greece—that had been so recently at war.

It was equally important to improve relations—or simply to *have* relations—with Catholics and Jews. To a degree that people today might find almost implausible, ugly anti-Catholic sentiments were expressed freely—in polite drawing rooms or bawdy bars, in country meeting places or city halls, in schoolrooms and pulpits. In a multitude of ways you could vent your anti-Irish, anti-Italian, or anti-Polish feelings and assert doctrinal snobbery and class prejudice about "papists." "Nativist" anti-Catholicism had many faces. Not to mention the viruses of anti-Semitism and white supremacy, which infected Protestants and Catholics alike. Though political expediency and "political correctness" give the appearance of patchy improvement, these diseases are with us still. Not only have pastors not eradicated them but some have actively encouraged and spread them. The Heath clergymen were benign characters, but I think it's fair to say that they truly despised these bigotries.

So another way of describing Heath was as a hive of integrationist, ecumenical, and international church activity. Small wonder that later one could find four Heath men as delegates to the founding meeting of the World Council of Churches in Amsterdam in 1948, and two as observers to Vatican Council II in 1962. These were men who had learned how not to have needless liturgical or doctrinal disputes, and they were good, conscientious people. I thought of them as typical American clergymen: how wrong I was! Little did I know how unusual was their sturdy broad-mindedness, how atypical their devout modesty. I grew up completely insulated from the barbarous, self-congratulatory sloth of what journalists call Mainstream American Protestantism, and it took me decades to realize this.

All too many leaders of American churches, like their secular counterparts, cherished their privileged position in the status quo, however inequitable or cruel that status quo might be, and they paid no attention to the things my father and his friends thought should be changed. They did not care to examine whether or how their own attitudes had actually been implicated in the dynamics of the Great War. They didn't want to see that the world was rapidly evolving in yet unknown ways, they feared the new forces of modernity while they embraced the modern capitalist mechanisms that enriched them, and they did not lend a hand to improve the terrible conditions that made life so hard for the millions of people less fortunate than themselves. They especially disliked fellow clergy who pointed out the social and economic disparities or, worse, wanted to do something about them. Claiming that the churches were and must remain above the fray, they prayed with their congregations to sustain the churches just as they were, bastions of achieved safety that could reassure and comfort them and their flocks in their old ways. Their ethic was based, as hard-line ethics usually are, on fear, not love.

Still, the Heath clergymen were representative of a small but active sector in the Protestant church that *was* committed to addressing the new problems of twentieth-century America—with all its wealth, its inequities, its racial tensions, its ugly greed, its capacity for greatness. The problems changed and evolved as the century wore on, but many of the worst (they would have said sinful) among them—segregation, the unjust treatment of workers, ethnic tensions and hostilities in a mongrel nation, the increasing vanity and rampant greed of the business classes—metastasized. They believed that a democratically elected government must correct these gross injustices, so most of them welcomed the New Deal when it came, but they certainly didn't think that government alone could or ever would accomplish the genuine improvement they prayed for. The work was never easy, but they never gave up on it.

My father, who started out as the minister of a church in a small Illinois town, realized early on—as priests everywhere have always realized—that pastoral obligations of even the most ordinary, personal kind can pull one into intractable social and ethical dilemmas. Some ministers decide that since the underlying cause of much of a society's pain is so deeply rooted, the situation can't be changed and therefore must be accepted. These are sufferings of this world, they say, and we must learn to bear them, if only to be rewarded in the hereafter. But Pa didn't see it like this. We cannot ignore the sorrow and injustice of today, especially when visited upon others, on the simple expectation or hope of future redemption. To take such a position is willfully to seize a safe high ground and cling to it as the waters rise around you. It is to ignore the New Testament! The whole idea of the Christian community is that it breaks the bonds of the old distinctions and ranks, that in joining one you enter into radically new human relationships of absolute equality.

Moreover, the Niebuhrs—my grandfather and his two theologian sons, who were all pastors—seemed to have an appetite for the fray, the gift to express the heart of these human dilemmas. I know they cherished their pastoral work, but each in his own way extended it from the parish to the larger world beyond. In the case of my father he ended up doing a million things at once—he talked to student groups and YMCA meetings, he threw himself into community betterment projects, he became a pamphleteer, lecturer, journalist, book writer. Eventually he left pastoral work and became a scholar and teacher of Christian ethics, and he joined and organized commissions and committees that lobbied on behalf of the causes he believed in: social and economic justice, industrial democracy, civil liberties, and a church responsive to the deepest needs and hopes of its community.

Other clergymen denounced him for this "political" activity; he got used to that. Conservative, well-placed people like to construe their devotion to their own well-being as a neutral, "unpolitical" thing while insisting that change or disagreement is "political" and destabilizing. This is transparent nonsense, of course: protection of one's wealth, status, power, or authority has just as much intrinsic political meaning as any challenge to it does. The activists among whom I grew up understood that the political label could not be avoided, and they were inured to the routine mudslinging, though in the 1940s and 1950s it was not pleasant when the Justice Department and the FBI, following tips given them by unprincipled reactionary snitches, tried to impugn their patriotism and loyalty.

All over the world in the 1920s, the economy had suffered massive crisis and bloodletting. War had torn apart the world for four horrific years and threatened again. Injustice and wide-spread poverty scarred the very substance of Western life. It was easy, for people who feared change or who were privileged in the circumstances, to call any critic or oppositionist a Bolshevik or a Red. True, the Soviet Union's purportedly Marxist regime presented an alarming challenge to the established political and economic powers in the capitalist, Western democracies. But the heroic friends I'm thinking about were never Red, and only a few of them were scarcely or intermittently socialist. They had a healthy dislike of unfettered capitalism, that was true—and why not? No one, not even the most bullheaded businessman, claimed it as an economic system of unalloyed virtue. And like many men and women they wanted to carry into the future the moral dedication and sense of renewed democracy for which so many had fought in 1914–18. That was work that called for challenging social reconstruction.

But their political work was not party-political and never focused on a single issue, as many so-called Christian efforts are today. In fact the Christians among the group I have in mind would have considered single-issue Christian political-action groups obnoxious and un-American. It was to debase and pervert your spiritual commitments if you smelted them down into the common coin of civil society's markets, into bargaining chips to be wagered in deals to gain or keep political power. True faith had greater value than this.

The idea, rather, was to express one's commitment to the principle of just relations with all people, and to express it across the entire range of one's life. The radicals I am thinking of were interested in socialism not as a system of governance, but as a way of thinking about how the structures of modern society might be adjusted to make economic, political, and social relations among people more fair. This was politics in the largest possible sense, and the Americans among them believed that only a secular republican democracy allowed fully for it.

The people who agitated for social and economic transformations after the First World War were an internationally minded group, and they entertained a healthy skepticism about any nation's pretensions to perfection. But the Americans among them were proud of their country, proud of its founding principles, proud of the enlightened American idea of a civil democracy governed by elected officials deriving their authority from the people themselves. Cruel inequities abounded in the United States, as they still do today, but its constitutional law was respected and could be enforced, so improvements were possible. They kept their devotion to the American way even as the fragile health of democratic institutions elsewhere in the world was subjected to rude shocks and malign incursions. They knew that democracy was threatened not only in Germany, Spain, and Italy. And they supported their beleaguered social-democratic allies in Europe, under assault from both the Communist left and the fascist right, when the forces of reaction led the world toward war once again.

Authoritarian, repressive governments were insidiously popular in the 1930s, and citizens of the "Western democracies" were hardly immune to their appeal. Nor could one count on the churches to oppose National Socialism and Fascism. On the contrary, many Christian leaders encouraged their flocks to accommodate themselves to the dictators' new formations and warned only against the evil Red menace of the Soviet Union. So one knew what one was up against: opposition to tyrannous constraints on human liberty is and must be unwavering; the economic power and military means available to the tyrants were strong then, as they are today, and could grow stronger.

There was another way of seeing it. As Christians are supposed never to forget, the sinful impulses that give rise to the suppression of liberty are rooted deep in every human heart. The threat of oppression is ever present, for it is within each of us. So one dangerous component in the life mixture, which one must pray to have either the grace to accept or the courage to change, is the condition of one's own soul.

And the condition of one's own soul is put to the most severe test in war. The Serenity Prayer was written in 1943, after four years of brutal, total war, after several decades when malevolent forces had worked to destroy the very basis of civilized life. In 1943 it was not yet clear that the Allies would win the war against the Axis powers, either. Not only soldiers but resisters to the fascist dictatorships and foes of violence everywhere were facing choices of action that may seem unimaginably difficult to those of us who've been lucky enough to dwell in peace. The decisions that my father and his friends made during the war are also part of the Serenity Prayer's story. And then, by the time the prayer was published and becoming famous in the prosperous postwar decades, they were responding to yet another stupendous danger—and ethical dilemma—when the advent of nuclear weaponry transformed the welcome years of peace into anxious seasons of distrustful uncertainty.

IN THE YEARS after the victories of 1945, many of the same weaknesses that marred the national fabric after 1918 remained. And part of my story about the Serenity Prayer concerns the views of my father and his friends about those enduring difficulties, which have persisted into our own time—the continuing crises in racial relations, in economic inequities, and in the unstable fluctuations that mark America's relations to the rest of the world. Also, the Christian pastors among them had to cope with the many unhappy disputes about church-state relations that continued to bedevil both believers and unbelievers.

How, indeed, is religion supposed to operate in American society? How does religious faith (or the lack of it) relate to citizenship? Confusion on this subject is perhaps endemic in American life. Put it the other way around and it is just as hard to parse: how can citizens of a secular republic best comprehend the effect and meaning of religion in their communities? It's not just a matter of whether we pledge allegiance to one nation indivisible or one nation indivisible under God, whether we should give public funds to church school programs, or whether we should ever let religious doctrines affect our laws—although all these questions matter greatly. There are deeper, harder conundrums. It is well nigh impossible to solve them, however, when the terms are set either by secularists who even if they are not aggressively hostile to religion are ignorant of its terms, or by self-righteous religious demagogues and their followers. It is not only in China or Turkey or Kazakhstan that religion, state, and civil society seem at odds—they live in unsettled disequilibrium in our own fifty states.

What one needs, I should have thought, is the leadership of men and women who are committed equally to their faith and to the principles of civil democracy—and such were the people I remember from Heath. Yet the traditions of liberal Protestantism that they represented have been eclipsed, and that is another aspect of the story behind the Serenity Prayer. Nowadays it is to very different authorities—to Catholics, Jews or the "Christian right" of "evangelical" Protestants—that the media usually turn to get "the religious angle" on American life. That's all very well, but it was in fact Lutherans, Methodists, Anglicans, Presbyterians, and Congregationalists who over the centuries worked out the most innovative, varied, and challenging new perspectives on the issue of how a person's spiritual and civic obligations might be discharged in a secular world. The plausible, humane voices of the heirs to these diverse Protestant traditions, voices such as those I recall from my Heath childhood, are mostly missing from the national conversation in America today.

Protestant doctrine from the beginning—encouraging as it did a new and more independent attitude toward spiritual authority, suggesting as it did that assent to a faith should be given freely only as one became convinced of the saving effect of its dogma—called into question the old power of religious leaders over their flocks. And Protestants from the beginning proposed new church-state relations, defining them without recourse or reference to supranational allegiances. In rejecting the old arrangements, some early Protestants believed that their new, purified churches should logically be responsible for civil governance, but others renounced this line of thought completely. Some of the early Protestant initiatives seem abhorrent to the modern eye, while others were and are noble. Some of them were perverted early on, while others grew in strength and wisdom over the centuries, and one can discern their relationship to the great Enlightenment theories that led to the world's first republican democracy. In any case, for various historical reasons Protestant ideas about church and state have been woven into the historical fabric of American civic democracy whether you like it or not.

Americans take for granted the principle of church-state separation enshrined in our Constitution, but militantly atheist ones go on to insist that all religion, all expression of religious belief, all spiritual practice, must be kept "private." They seem to want a kind of wall around the dangerous stuff to keep religion from seeping not just into the government, where it does not belong, but into any public space. Yet for any even moderately faithful person, not just a fundamentalist or theocrat, this attitude creates real difficulties, since religion almost by definition cannot thus be contained. Was such an absolute requirement presumed by the Founding Fathers? Surely they imagined a more humane and legally more enlightened solution to the paradoxical problem—

a solution that does not threaten either the secular fabric of our national life or the spiritual lives of our citizens.

One hopes to hear the voices of people who acknowledge how hard it is to understand the operations of faith in history, who approach the chaotic mess of modern life with a degree of humility. My father and his friends, facing these thorny difficulties more than a half century ago, did not pretend to have the answers, but they were at least struggling to sort out the dilemmas, and they could see that old solutions were constantly mutating into new problems needing new solutions. Their religious modesty did not desert them and their steadfast commitment to civil democracy did not wane.

It angers and saddens me, on behalf of the spirited men and women in whose company I first encountered these issues, when I see the very term "religious" hijacked all over the world by political forces who claim a godly right to organize society as they deem it best, acting out their often deranged "faith-based" fantasies in ways I had been taught to find not just shocking but ungodly. The selfless courtesy and kindness that I associate with true devotion—Jewish, Buddhist, Christian, and Muslim—have all but vanished from public life around the globe, and we are the poorer for it. I am grateful that I have my Heath memories, which keep alive my hope that America can regain the innate and lively decorum of a truly secular community that respects truly religious people.

What kind of church was the Heath Union Church? The Heath parishioners were Congregationalists and the summer people, as it happened, mostly Episcopalians. The churchgoers in town, scarcely in the majority, seemed to have no difficulty worshiping together: this was rare, I was to learn. It didn't even last long in Heath, and I should have paid more attention to the ground rules that made it possible at the time. In any case we Niebuhrs were neither Congregational nor Episcopalian, or we were both, depending on how you looked at it. You couldn't fit us into a class scheme, either.

My father's German-American family had been in the United States for only a few generations; born in 1892 in Missouri, he'd been brought up in the Middle West, where his father (and one of his grandfathers) had been pastors in the Evangelical Synod, a largely German church; in 1928, after fifteen years as a pastor himself in Illinois and Michigan, he'd moved to New York to teach at Union Theological Seminary, which as its name suggests offered inclusive instruction to divinity students from many different backgrounds. Some time after he wrote the Serenity Prayer, the Evangelical and Reformed Synod merged with the Congregational Church, which is why I construe Pa as a quasi-Congregationalist.

It's usually presumed—by a mostly ignorant secular press with no sense of history—that to be an evangelical in America is by definition to be a rigidly fundamentalist believer in the literal words of the Bible. And alas it's also true that most evangelical churches today are hostile to modern intellectual inquiry, indeed to intellectual life of any kind. But fundamentalism was once but a fringe position in the evangelical movement, which overall had a vibrant, wholehearted enthusiasm that attracted millions of progressive, up-to-date Americans who didn't necessarily cotton to the fundamentalists' oppressive anti-modernism, their judgmental severity, their keen eye for doing business, and their hunger for political power.

The Evangelical Synod to which the Niebuhrs belonged, for

example, tried to be intelligently responsive to the modern age, and it was capable of intellectual vivacity. Plenty of its pastors—like pastors in other Protestant churches—held firm for a faith that centered on what they believed were the revealed truths of the Gospels but that also welcomed the new worlds of modern science and learning. Like all churches it was divided within itself, and conservatives and modernists struggled with one another as they did in other denominations. So for me the background story to the Serenity Prayer is also entwined with the struggle for the heart of the evangelical movement.

My English mother was quite different: she was an Anglo-Catholic who came from a world quite other from rural Missouri and Illinois. When she met, fell in love with, and then in 1931 married my father, she left behind her English family in Southampton but not the Anglicanism of her youth, which she carried with her in her heart. She also happily left behind the obsessional concern with class that marked English life at mid-century and against which her spirited doctor father had inoculated her. To Americans showing their usual prurient fascination with the English class system, she'd explain in her elegant Oxford voice, patiently, self-mockingly, that she came from the social stratum that George Orwell had delineated with such fastidious precision (it was his own) as the lower upper middle class. Begone to all that! American life and religion were in contrast thrillingly open. Some of its vistas were familiar to her, others appalling and bizarre. The German-American Evangelical scene was unknown to her except as filtered through the Niebuhr family, since she never lived in the Middle West, but overall she knew a lot about American religious life in the melting pot of New York and in the chaster, purer air of New England.

My mother saw to it that my brother and I were baptized and confirmed as Episcopalians, not because of any interest in American Episcopal wealth or class, to which she was foreign, but because of her theological commitments to Anglo-Catholicism. My father went along: his excellent Evangelical mother had already taught us at Bible lessons and Sunday school. Anyway, the whole family attended "Nonconformist" or interdenominational services as often as not. To boot, most of our closest family friends were cheerfully secular atheists or even somewhat anti-religious, or they were Jews or Catholics. Still, I think my mother was often homesick, and so may my father have been, for the worlds they had left behind.

Yet all of us felt completely at home in Heath, and at Heath's church. Why was this so? I grew up believing in, because I grew up experiencing, an America that included prayer and non-prayer, belief and non-belief, stranger and kin. That the distinctive courage of the Heath people was related to their ready grace in praying together, and a source of their spiritual energy, I realized only slowly. That it had a lot to do with their robust humor I think I knew from the start.

II

_____

The Heath part of the Serenity Prayer story begins long before 1943, and it doesn't even begin in Heath. Let us say that it starts in Phoenix, Arizona, in 1909. I've learned that now, but I wish I had known it in my childhood, when I first came to know my father's best friend, with whom the tale must begin.

William Scarlett was a merry, pink-cheeked gentleman who in my childhood years was Episcopal bishop of Missouri. I don't remember his coming to see us in Heath, though he may have. But this genial avuncular figure—who would materialize in our New York apartment straight off the plane from St. Louis bearing gifts and gossip, full of news and questions, with his boundless energy and radiant goodness, his delicious chuckle, and his intense power of listening—this magical person is a central figure in my Heath carpet, woven into its pattern most intricately. Many threads of many colors connected Will Scarlett to the Niebuhrs, to our friends in Heath, and to everything my father cared about. He and my father also exchanged prayers.

Literary readers may note that Will Scarlett is a dedicatee of Mary McCarthy's novel *Cannibals and Missionaries* (1979), which features a snowy-haired, bright-eyed retired bishop of

Missouri just like the wonderful old man she had come to know in Maine, where they both lived in the 1970s. The novel conveys his almost mischievous goodness and calm fearlessness, but McCarthy knew only the elderly Scarlett, and she didn't know how he'd started. I didn't know, either, for a long time, and I didn't find it out from him.

In 1909, when Scarlett was a feisty young Episcopalian prelate working in the famously progressive precincts of St. George's Church in New York, he was called to be dean at Trinity Cathedral in Phoenix, then a small parish in the capital of the territory of Arizona. He was not yet thirty. Shocked by the disparity between the well-to-do Anglos and the impoverished workers in his flock, Scarlett soon became known for his ministry to the poor and the dispossessed. He made an early, unsuccessful effort to mediate during an unpleasant standoff when local waiters and cooks called for a strike and the employers, refusing to budge, were ready to use force against them. The experience taught him a valuable lesson: all the goodwill in the world gets you nowhere unless governmental intervention brings the proper legal sanctions to bear. Civil society needs a rule of law even more than it needs compassionate priests. And the episode taught the people of Phoenix a lesson about Scarlett, too: His conduct showed that he was one of the few clergymen in Arizona who did not fear the all-powerful copper-mine owners, big shots who were among his parishioners.

In June 1917 the tensions in the fledgling state of Arizona increased when thousands of workers in the copper mines near Bisbee went on strike. The Arizona mine owners were enjoying gigantic profits with the higher prices copper commanded during the war, and they were also mindful that continued production was essential for the war effort. (President Wilson had to warn them not to use the words "profit" and "patriotism" in the same sentence.) They dismissed the strikers' legitimate grievances, as set forth in a petition filed on their behalf by the Industrial Workers of the World, and instead brutally fired them all for being "pro-German" agitators. This slimy tactic was available to them only because among the miners were some recent immigrants from the Balkan edges of the Austro-Hungarian Empire. The mining executives loathed the IWW and stirred up the press (which they owned) to publish alarming articles about these dangerous radical outsiders.

Then the business became physically violent. Vigilantes routed more than a thousand of the striking men out of their beds in the isolated little desert towns where they were forced to live in deplorable penury and squalor, shipped them out of state under armed guard, and dumped them in New Mexico without adequate food or water. The vigilantes were led by an Arizona buccaneer named Jack Greenway, who was close to Theodore Roosevelt's family. Like all cities Phoenix naturally had a power elite, the Greenways were natural members of it, and naturally the elite church was Trinity Cathedral, where Scarlett was dean. He had his work cut out for him.

The mine owners hated the very idea of trade unions and thought that even to meet with IWW representatives was to legitimate a principle they had vowed to deny. This contemptuous fear and ignorance of working people were standard in the higher echelons of corporate America, as they still are, though management can no longer maintain, as it once did, that workers have no rights—some things *have* been changed.

The owners' intransigence meant that negotiations to end the strike and reopen the mines required the physical presence of government mediators. By the fall of 1917 President Wilson had created a federal body to deal with such war-related industrial disputes, so he sent a lawyer representing the Mediation Commission out to Arizona to resolve the Bisbee crisis. The lawyer was a then scarcely known young professor who had left the Harvard Law School to work in Washington during the war; his name was Felix Frankfurter. He was as feisty as Scarlett but in a different way; if they were animals you'd have said FF was a bantam rooster, Scarlett more like an indefatigable, cunning Border collie. And they got along famously.

It took ages for Frankfurter to get his work done in those mining hamlets—endless hearings, sleep and meals in a railway car off on a siding, constant negotiations with the miners and Wobblies on the one hand, the angry company officers and their cold-eyed lawyers on the other. Eventually the miners returned to work, but the terms of employment had not improved, and Frankfurter was obliged to rule, for a number of technical reasons, that no federal law applied in the Bisbee strife, though perhaps it should have. But he managed to calm the waters somewhat, and he always said he couldn't have gotten anywhere without Scarlett's help, which was readily forthcoming; they became fast friends for life. Frankfurter and Scarlett each went his separate way—but it seems to me they were traveling on the same broad path.

Scarlett stayed in Arizona for a few more years, then went to Missouri in 1922. The kinds of dispute he was used to dealing with in Arizona were familar in St. Louis, too, and his social activism continued unabated. He and a Jewish ally formed St. Louis's first Social Justice Commission, which offered unbiased third-party mediation and face-saving conflict resolution in otherwise tense sectarian disputes. To have it staffed by Christians and Jews together!—this was unheard of. Everything from squabbles over milk prices and threatened strikes by streetcar conductors to hostilities between mine owners (once again) and the Progressive Mine Workers of Illinois were submitted to the successful mediation of this Jewish-Episcopalian brainchild.

Scarlett also flung open the doors of Christ Church Cathedral, where he was dean and then bishop, and held an interdenominational celebration of Holy Communion there, which shocked many of the parishioners. He resisted their opposition and continued in his ecumenical efforts, which even today would be considered pretty remarkable. (It was because of him that St. Louis has St. Luke's, an Episcopal-Presbyterian hospital.) Soon he and my father met—in Germany, of all places— and became friends: they were together on a study trip arranged for American clerics to visit the Ruhr, the heartland of German industry, which had just been occupied by France. A place of even greater strife and danger.

Meanwhile Scarlett's new pal Felix Frankfurter was off on a different tack, yet set on the same course: for the remaining war years he continued his Mediation Commission work, which sent him from Arizona to the oil fields of Southern California, thence to San Francisco to arbitrate a threatened strike against Bell Telephone. After that there was trouble in the Pacific Northwest logging industry, and on his way back to Washington, D.C., Frankfurter stopped in Chicago, where meat packers were striking against Armour and Swift. He couldn't even persuade the company lawyers there to meet in the same room with the workers' representatives, so he didn't get very far. The companies were complicitous, he thought, in the general failure to use the wartime crisis to adopt promptly the industrial and economic reforms that were needed to help America modernize—and to win the war.

Over and over again Frankfurter warned the companies that it would be far better to change—i.e., improve—their workers' terms of employment (reducing the workday from twelve to ten or eight hours, for example, and introducing plausible safety procedures in the mines, slaughterhouses, and mills) than to face fractious, dangerous, crippling strikes. If they had the notorious Wobblies to deal with, he told them, they had only themselves to blame. But the companies didn't want to listen. My father wrote in an article a few years later, "The changes that are necessary in our economic order will require the sacrifice of many privileges and rights on the part of the holding classes. They will make such a sacrifice willingly only if their vision is broadened and their conscience sensitized by such agencies as the church." There were no such sensitizing agencies doing that kind of work in Chicago in 1918, evidently.

You can't go up against Bell, Armour, Swift, Phelps-Dodge, the oil companies, and U.S. Steel, even in the interests of a government policy to keep industry productive during wartime, and not get a reputation as a troublemaker. The tone of rancorous hostility to Frankfurter was set right away by ex-President Theodore Roosevelt, who wrote to him in a fury after reading the "Report on the Bisbee Deportations," in which Frankfurter condemned the illegalities committed in the name of patriotism by Jack Greenway and his copper buddies. Roosevelt suggested that Frankfurter was taking "an attitude which seems to me to be fundamentally that of Trotsky and the other Bolshevik leaders in Russia." Wilson's man in Arizona replied carefully, regretting "what a great sadness it is for me to find disagreement between us on an important issue. . . . You are one of the few great sources of national leadership and inspiration for national endeavor." But he did not back down.

Frankfurter's continued work for the Mediation Commission and the War Labor Policies Board, of which he was chairman, ensured that corporate, capitalist America would surround his name with obloquy for decades. (Scarlett escaped the net, but only for stupid social reasons: in the higher reaches of rich America, you'd have to be an idiot to take on an Episcopalian "prince of the church," but a Jewish law professor was considered fair game.) In well-bred Cambridge, to which Frankfurter eventually returned, the estimable Mrs. Charles Francis Adams was to worry out loud whether he wasn't "a dangerous Communist." But the Washington work had been rewarding, and Frankfurter forged alliances with wonderful new associates— principal among them, perhaps, the then young assistant secretary of the Navy, TR's cousin Franklin Roosevelt.

Soon Frankfurter was to become nationally famous for his views on yet another notorious, divisive class issue, and soon he came to Heath. These two important developments in his life were connected, actually, and the link was a marvelous old lady whom I knew in my youth as Aunt Ethel, though we had no family connection. She was our link to Uncle Felix, too. The pattern of the Heath carpet now becomes clearer and brighter.

ETHEL PAINE MOORS was a splendid Bostonian who had been summering in Heath since early in the century, and we Niebuhrs came to Heath because of her, as Felix did. Descended

Ethel and John Moors in their home in Brookline, Massachusetts, 1919

herself from an old New England family, she was married to the impeccable John Cabot Moors, Nonconformist and banker, one of the five men who made up the Harvard Corporation, which ran America's oldest university. He was a friend and classmate of A. Lawrence Lowell, who from 1909 to 1933 was president of Harvard. The Moorses were definitely a power couple, as we might say today, though they would have hooted at the idea.

Mrs. Moors presided over a grand house near Boston and a huge seaside "cottage" in Cohasset, on the South Shore, which her husband preferred to Heath. (Pa said, after visiting it, that the Moorses' house there was "a great stone palace" where the neighbors were "all millionaires with General Grant mansions of unbelievable proportions." I suppose it had the virtues of familiarity and comfort for its wealthy owners, but it was hardly congenial for many of their friends.) She had a special fondness, though, for what was called the Manse, the eighteenth-century farmhouse a hundred miles west of Boston, on a remote hillside just north of the Deerfield River, which her father had bought for her in 1906.

In Heath a different angle on the Moorses yielded different insights. Mrs. Moors was right to love the place: its high meadows and pastures, its long views out over the Berkshire hills, its deep snowy winters and brilliant summers were superb. During the 1920s and 1930s she encouraged friends to come to Heath, too; the abandoned old houses dotted along its winding, hilly roads were then just barely affordable as summer places for the impoverished pastors and scholars she favored. But unconventional iconoclasm and a radical devotion to social justice were the unspoken requirements.

I don't know the circumstances under which my parents met Ethel Moors, but they surely involved left-wing politics and surely concerned Harvard, where my father preached several times a year and Mr. Moors was a major force. Mrs. Moors was fiercely radical-progressive, and she approved of my father's politics: critical from the left of the New Deal until after the 1936 elections, then warily supportive of FDR's challenges to political and economic conservatism; emphatically philo-Semitic; vigorously internationalist as against the routine pacifism of the left and the bigoted isolationism of so much of America's political classes.

It is important to recognize just how entrenched and wary those prewar political classes actually were, whether in Boston, Phoenix, St. Louis, Chicago, or New York. Their heirs are still with us, after all, and they are still hostile to change, indifferent to social justice, and devoted to class privilege. In their context Ethel Moors's warmhearted, effervescent enthusiasm made her a rare, blithe presence in a grim landscape. Her tone was ebullient, she seemed always to smile. I loved her for her unwavering friendliness and open spirit. Peonies scented her drawing room, where they filled a big china vase on the old black piano; but you remembered the conversations more than the décor, the people more than her food, and the talk was vividly down-to-earth.

People laughed a lot in the company of Aunt Ethel. She seemed free, which is rare in any social milieu, and she was merry. I have no idea how she came to her radical political views, but they seemed expressive of her liberated spirit and generous social manner. She never forgot how dangerous and difficult it was, and would be, to challenge the status quo; her immense respect for people who devoted their lives to changing the class system of which she was a beneficiary lacked all hint of condescension. "Yes, yes, I suppose she approves," my father once conceded when told that this aristocratic lady praised his work, but, he chuckled, "she'd like me more if I were black and Jewish and socialist." Aunt Ethel had every good reason to believe that among blacks and Jews and socialists she might well find brave, decent people willing to risk their lives to improve the world.

Mr. Moors was an enlightened progressive, though not so radical as his wife, and people who knew him were struck by the ease and constancy of his expansive, principled way of viewing the world. It's such a fashion nowadays to mock privileged white Anglo-Saxon Protestant men, to call into question their value to the American tradition, to imagine that they must be by definition selfish and small-minded. But it's pretty hard to find people like John Moors in any social group—rich or poor, white or black, male or female. In the patrician circles in which he moved so surely, his disdain for conformity and cant, his dislike of sloppy thinking and narrow-mindedness, were component parts of a well-known and now vanishing upper-class Boston tradition.

In 1923 the Moorses befriended Felix Frankfurter, who by then was back at the Harvard Law School. What interested them about him was not just his intelligence, not just his principles, but his spunk. This counted for a lot with the Moorses, who valued it as much as Frankfurter's commitment to improving the world. It was no surprise to anyone that soon Frankfurter and his wife, Marion, could be found every summer in a pretty white house by the waterfall in Dell, a cluster of dwellings near an old mill on a brook road that led down from the Heath hills to the nearby town of Charlemont, on the Deerfield River. They were to stay in Heath for decades.

Frankfurter met the Moorses during the immense national uproar following the prosecution of two Italian laborers who had been charged with the murder of a paymaster in South Braintree, Massachusetts, in April 1920. Nicola Sacco and Bartolomeo Vanzetti, who were barely able to understand English, protested their innocence vehemently, but they didn't have a chance: anarchist propaganda literature had been found in their possession, and however juvenile and innocent those pamphlets were, feelings ran high against immigrants, against "Reds," against grubby workers with no understanding of their place in the order—especially in these years after the Bolshevik Revolution, when conservative elites everywhere fanned the flames of the Red Scare. The trial judge referred to Sacco and Vanzetti as "those anarchistic bastards" and was satisfied with the guilty verdict; he sentenced the two to death.

Aunt Ethel believed that Sacco and Vanzetti had been wrongly charged and wrongly convicted, that they had been targeted because of their acknowledged political views and their working-class, immigrant status; she quickly embraced the cause of reversing their conviction. Many women, as it happens, took up this cause, while the men of the Commonwealth of Massachusetts thought by and large that justice had been done. Frankfurter, for his part, had been abroad when the Sacco-Vanzetti case was tried, but when he got home he reviewed the trial transcript and quickly turned up the heat on the case. While countless motions on behalf of the convicted men were being filed and denied, he brought his considerable talents as a political spin-master to bear on publicizing what he considered were its gross injustices. His impassioned criticism of the state's prosecutorial and judicial powers for their bigotry and lawlessness, as he saw it, made the Sacco-Vanzetti case a national *cause célèbre* and earned, as well, the Moorses' admiration. They knew it was a continuation of the work to which he'd already been committed during the war years.

The entire proceeding had been, Frankfurter claimed, a flagrant miscarriage of justice from the start, poisoned and deformed by unacknowledged class and ethnic animosities. That he was arguing on behalf of bomb-throwing, working-class anarchists naturally opened him to the charge that he was himself a destabilizing extremist. All the more likely, his posh detractors added, since he was a Jew and an outsider. Judge Webster Thayer, in charge of the case, pleasantly called him Professor Frankenstein. He disregarded this irrelevant slander, since it distracted from the real issue, which, he insisted, was the right of all Americans to unprejudiced and proper legal procedure.

"I suggest that you consider what law really means," he wrote to a correspondent who worried that he was overdoing it.

"Anybody can give law to his friends. It's the essence of law to give it to our enemies." Democratically authorized law must be protected and strengthened, for "that's all we have standing between us and the tyranny of mere will and the cruelty of unbridled, undisciplined feeling." Unbridled feelings were running high in well-bred Puritan New England then, and certainly they ran high against immigrant workers with political attitude. But, Frankfurter continued, "The great way to vindicate the greatness of the Puritan tradition was to show that 'a good shoemaker and a poor fish-peddler' were not real threats to the security of the Commonwealth."

Frankfurter's exposé of the bigotry and weakness in the Sacco-Vanzetti prosecution earned him praise among liberals and progressives and Italian Americans, and definitely with John and Ethel Moors. But it pitted him against heavy, eventually victorious opposition that was personified above all by Harvard's formidable President Lowell, who chaired the commission that the governor of Massachusetts set up in 1927 to advise as to whether clemency was appropriate for the by now notorious convicts.

Frankfurter argued, in a famous *Atlantic Monthly* article that same year, that "the temper of the times made it the special duty of a prosecutor and a court engaged in trying two Italian radicals before a jury of native New Englanders to keep the instruments of justice free from the infection of passion or prejudice. In the case of Sacco and Vanzetti no such restraints were respected. . . . [T]he District Attorney invoked against them a riot of political passion and patriotic sentiment; and the trial judge connived at—one had almost written, cooperated in—the process." But President Lowell, along with most of America's opinion-making upper classes and their imitators in the safety-obsessed bourgeoisie, did not agree. Nor did most of Harvard. Even Frankfurter's hero, Justice Oliver Wendell Holmes Jr., like other Brahmins, thought FF was going too far. The Moorses were with him all the way, though, and Mr. Moors remarked astringently of his classmate that Lowell was "incapable of seeing that two wops could be right and the Yankee judiciary could be wrong."

Mr. Moors might have added that Lowell was especially vehement precisely because Frankfurter was on the other side of the Sacco-Vanzetti dispute: they had engaged in a vitriolic exchange of letters in 1922–23, when Lowell had tried to impose a quota on Jewish students at Harvard; relations between them were frosty at best. Given the bigoted and casually superior anti-Semitic attitudes of the time, a high-minded person was supposed to prefer the overt quota of 12 percent that Lowell wanted for Jewish students (who then numbered about 20 or 25 percent of the student body) to the covert one that President Nicholas Murray Butler rigged in New York at Columbia University, where Jewish students were even more in evidence but where Butler didn't want them predominant. FF and the Moorses thought both were disgusting.

Sacco and Vanzetti's appeals had already been denied, the Lowell commission recommended against clemency, and soon the date was set for the Italians' execution. "I never knew, never heard, even read in history anything so cruel as this court," Sacco said. On the scheduled evening, Boston was in a state of high alert, heavily patrolled and anxious. Frankfurter and his wife walked through the dark city restlessly. When the signal came at midnight that the execution had taken place, Felix was "beside himself," Judge Learned Hand reported. Edna St. Vincent Millay, a good New England poet, was devastated and wrote a rather muddled poem:

> Let us abandon then our gardens and go home
> And sit in the sitting-room.
> Shall the larkspur blossom or the corn grow under this
>   cloud?
> . . . .
> Evil does overwhelm
> The larkspur and the corn;
> We have seen them go under . . .

MY FATHER DIDN'T yet know Frankfurter in the 1920s, or the Moorses, either, but the intolerant, anti-democratic forces against which they were aligning themselves were familiar to him, and he was well acquainted with the anti-Semitism and xenophobia that distorted the public face and the private heart of America. Heath, Massachusetts, was still far off in the future for him—there wasn't anything remotely like it in his life then, not even the dream of such a place—but the community of interests and spiritual commitments that eventually drew him to Heath was already forming.

At the time of the Sacco-Vanzetti case, my father and his widowed mother were living and working in Detroit, where as a young pastor he was facing new tasks in a parish there. Detroit was the locus of tremendous strife, racial tension, and class misery boiling up around the new automobile factories, and the shadow of the mighty, much-praised Henry Ford fell across the entire city. Ford was notable not only for his famous factories and Model Ts, but for being an admirer, indeed distributor, of the *Protocols of the Elders of Zion*, the notorious anti-Semitic tract concocted by the Tsarist Russian secret police that he and others slanderously purported to be a Jewish document of sage antiquity.

The churches of Detroit did little or nothing to help their parishioners find their way in the hectic confusions of new American industry, and they certainly didn't discourage their predictable anti-Semitism or change their hostile hearts in regard to the blacks flooding into the city in search of employment. (Ford was considered enlightened merely because he at least hired them.) In 1915 Ford had cleverly co-opted the city's clergymen by getting his personal pastor, who happened to be dean of the Episcopal cathedral, to be the chairman of his company's welfare bureau. Nobody spoke up or out about conditions in the Ford factories, which were better than at Bisbee, but not by much.

Pa felt powerless to give real aid. What was a pastor supposed to do in these circumstances? "Beside the brutal facts of modern industrial life, how futile are all our homiletical spoutings! The church . . . isn't changing the essential facts of modern industrial civilization by a hair's breadth. It isn't even thinking about them," he wrote. Yet the churches gave ample time and room for the expression of the old hatreds. Soon the braying voice of Father Charles Coughlin, the brazenly bigoted Catholic "media priest" of Detroit, could be heard on weekly radio programs all over the country; his overheated populist rants about the Jews who were out to destroy America rose in crescendos of anti-Semitic rage, and the Church did not silence him until 1942.

How different was this inferno in Detroit from the farming town of Lincoln, Illinois, where my father had started out—and where, by the way, the biblical training he'd received from *his* father had taught him to revere and learn from the Judaic tradition as part of his own. He surely already knew that social discord was endemic in even the most peaceful communities, and he had already experienced himself one kind of bigotry which, although we forget it today, was once directed against millions of white Anglo-Saxon Protestants and Catholics in the heartland of America.

When he had succeeded his father as pastor of St. John's Evangelical Church in Lincoln, one of the first crises Pa faced as a twenty-one-year-old newcomer in the pulpit arose over the issue of what language to write, speak, or worship in. With the outbreak of the Great War in the summer of 1914, the patriotism and decency of citizens in bilingual German-American towns all across the Middle West began to be questioned, and the hostility grew over the next years. By 1917, when the United States finally entered the war, it was deemed subversive to preach or pray, write or teach in German.

My grandfather had followed the custom of using English and German in alternate weeks in the church services at Lincoln; this clumsy but well-meant compromise had been the norm for decades. But my grandfather was gone—stricken with diabetes and dead within weeks of the onset of symptoms in April 1913—and his young second son, new to the pulpit, saw that the old arrangement might have to be abandoned. German Americans everywhere were being forced to change the very texture and sound of their daily lives, and it wasn't easy.

One could survive the mockery of one's German name, the reviling of good-tempered dachshunds, the labeling of sauerkraut as "liberty cabbage," but there was no denying the unpleasantness of the taunts. Quick-blooming xenophobia was and still is a famous American habit in times of stress. Everybody seemed to play in the game—there evidently was no racial or ethnic impediment to joining a crowd of outspoken bigots. So Irish, English, Scotch, and Scandinavian Americans—the pink-cheeked majority—were as nasty as they liked about their German-American compatriots in 1917. The venom could go in any one of three convenient directions: you could attack German Jews, Catholics, or Protestants—whatever slant suited your habit of prejudice. (Felix Frankfurter, whose very name elicited derisive sneers, brought public attention to a star-chamber proceeding in which the University of Minnesota fired the chairman of its political science department, a German American—of which variety I know not—when he opposed U.S. entry into the war. The man's politics would not have been agreeable to FF, but they were nothing like so bad as the absence of due process that had taken his job away.)

The German-American problem cut two ways, though, as my father found out when he moved to Detroit in 1915. He was dismayed that the parish to which the Synod had assigned him was even more Germanic than the one in Lincoln, which meant he wouldn't get far in his efforts to distance himself from the old culture and perfect his English. Worse, the mostly middle-class parishioners were wallowing in long suppressed and now weirdly intense spasms of pro-German enthusiasm. He disliked their professed affection for Kaiser Wilhelm II, they held old-fashioned provincial views, and they shared a senti-mental enthusiasm for out-of-date "customs and ideals long since discarded in Germany itself," as he put it. He preached faithfully to these German sympathizers every Sunday, in both

German and English, and—no surprise—found himself, in reaction to their views, becoming in an all-American way "more than ordinarily patriotic during the war." He was twenty-three years old. German was not completely abandoned as a language of worship at Bethel Evangelical Church until 1919.

Very few Americans could imagine that their closed minds and constricted behavior were wrong. Prejudices are pervasive and invisible to those who have them—but that's not news. The point worth stressing is that the churches did nothing to open up their parishioners' spirit to something freer and braver. One of the few priests who did was Michigan's Episcopal bishop, Charles Williams, the first of several good bishops whose friendship my very un-Episcopalian father enjoyed. Williams was notable because he did not flinch from addressing the larger social illnesses of which the bigotries were but symptoms. He encouraged people as best he could to develop some compassion, to extend their ethical concerns beyond their immediate circles, but it was an uphill battle and he did not get far. "If a bishop with all his prestige could make no bigger dent upon the prevailing mood of the city, what chance is there for the rest of us?" my father asked.

It was no easier, Pa soon learned, in that other infernal city of modern American industry: Pittsburgh. The Methodist bishop there, Francis McConnell, was a clearheaded, brave man who cut his political teeth trying to help the Pennsylvania steelworkers during their famous strike in 1919. (He was sniped at from the left by the Communist leader William Z. Foster and from the right by the steel-industry titans, of course.) The 300,000 striking steelworkers were broadly supported by a sympathetic public, and aid was offered by many of the churches in which social activism of this sort was customary, notably the Methodists. But the strike was broken with the assistance of troops working in concert with company snitches and scabs, and the workers were forced to return to the steel mills on the same terms as before, the same twelve-hour days and the same absence of protective provisions about which Frankfurter had warned the companies in 1917. Pittsburgh's better-off citizens gave Bishop McConnell no more respect and assistance in helping the strikers than Williams got in his work in Detroit.

By the early 1920s McConnell and Scarlett and my father had become friends, and you can see why: they shared a common curriculum of social justice and as fellow Christian clerics found a ready bond. (I wish I knew what they said to one another about their denominational differences: a Methodist, an E & R, and an Episcopalian would approach certain issues from different angles. Yet they didn't seem to let it get in their way. As I can't say often enough, this itself was a telling sign of their generosity of spirit.)

Most parsons and priests in Detroit were keeping themselves busy, meanwhile, with the predictable agendas they preferred. The simple dramas of placid, Harding-age America were what they liked to manage, and they smiled, as the administration in Washington smiled, on the concentration of power and wealth in the hands of greedy business. They had little to do with the real crises in their parishioners' lives. They didn't want to think about hunger or fear, about job losses, about the "human problems on all levels of weal and woe," as my father put it. Instead, they polished up what they thought of as their own spiritual excellence, kept themselves in good odor with one another. Pa decided that William James had it right when he observed that the Christian enterprise looked like nothing so much as "an effort to lobby in the courts of the Almighty for special favors."

The righteous lobbyists were correspondingly keen on the trivial nonsense that preoccupies self-confident people. Since most of the pastors in Detroit found it unseemly to challenge their congregations' set ways, they preferred rather to indulge them. Pa noticed one preacher who "never deviated by a hair's breadth from the economic prejudices of his wealthy congregation," for example, but then perhaps he'd misjudged him: the preacher "recently included in his sermon a tirade against women who smoke cigarettes, and lost almost a hundred of his fashionable parishioners. He is evidently not lacking courage in matters upon which he has deep convictions."

Bishop Williams himself, who was forced to "offer his resignation in the face of increasing hostility to his social views," was hamstrung by his parishioners' devotion to irrelevancy. "A young preacher asked him to participate in a Christian Laymen's League," Pa told us. " 'What will the League do?' asked the Bishop. 'We plan a campaign to close the movies on Sunday.' 'I thought so,' said Williams. 'If you would undertake a Christian program on industrial relations you wouldn't be so successful. For my experience is that in those issues there are only two Christian businessmen in the city and they are both Jews.' "

When Bishop Williams died unexpectedly in 1924, my father was stricken. To the Episcopalians of Detroit he wrote,

Your diocese has lost a great bishop, but the church universal has lost infinitely more; it has lost a prophet who had the courage to challenge the complacency of a very self-righteous civilization.

The most outstanding characteristic of Bishop Williams' life was his utter fearlessness. Had he been without this virtue, he could never have insisted so relentlessly upon the social implications of Christ's gospel. . . . Nowhere have I seen a personality more luminous with the Christ spirit than in this bishop who was also a prophet. . . . His fearless protagonism of the cause of democracy in industry won him the respect and love of the workers of the city as no other churchman.

Historians easily praise or condemn the record of radical opposition to American capitalism traced by the Wobblies, or by those who believed that the Soviet Union had the answer, or by others on the secular left wing of protest politics. But they should not neglect beacons of light like Scarlett and Williams and McConnell, churchmen whose objections to the excesses of American economic life, like their views on the ethical need for social and economic change, was based not on Lenin, not on a commitment to solidarity among the world's workers, but on the Gospels. They were unconvinced by the formulas of Soviet Marxism, yet they knew that capitalism didn't have the answers, either. They could see that the basic structures and attitudes of American society were grievously wanting, that the shocking violence and greed of rich owners and entrenched power elites reinforced its failures. They thought the churches had the moral obligation to help their flocks correct these misguided, unethical, indeed sinful patterns. This was the general tenor of belief in the Fellowship for a Christian Social Order, for example, an interesting activist group of progressive pastors where my father first met Williams and Scarlett.

Other initiatives emerged during the 1920s. In New York City, a group of farsighted Catholics, Protestants, and Jews joined together to diminish sectarian hostility and encourage interfaith cooperation. The National Conference of Christians and Jews—founded in 1927 by an energetic Yale man named Everett Clinchy, who roped in Newton Baker, Woodrow Wilson's secretary of war; Roger W. Straus, a leading Reform Jew; and the Columbia University historian Carleton Hayes, a well-known Catholic layman—did what it could to discourage anti-Catholic and anti-Jewish bigotry all over America. It couldn't do very much. I imagine that a single novel by Sinclair Lewis or John Dos Passos may have shaken up more Americans about their own racist shortcomings than any well-intentioned non-governmental group could.

In Britain and Europe, too, the many radicals and activists, Christian pastors among them, who had pledged themselves to work against the social evils that had contributed to the Great War in the first place were dismayed when the moral determination of the early postwar years melted away in the despairing chaos of the 1920s. In England the Anglicans and in Scandinavia the Lutherans had already in the spring of 1919 sent out feelers to the Reformed and Orthodox churches of the Balkans and the Levant. Nathan Söderblom, the Lutheran archbishop of Uppsala, thought there should be an international Christian council like the League of Nations, and his efforts resulted in something called the Life and Work movement, which was strongly influenced by American proponents of the "social gospel" like Williams and my father. It wanted to encourage churches to attend to the social and economic factors that made for unjust and unfair living and working conditions. Another group, largely Anglican, worked in parallel (and not always in agreement): the Faith and Order movement hoped to develop some kind of worldwide organic unity among all the churches, an evolution toward a transcendent global Christianity.

A key figure in Faith and Order was the remarkable William Temple, archbishop of York, another prince of the church whose commitment to social and economic justice could not have been stronger. He and my father were to become friends and allies during the toxic 1930s. In the early years of Faith and Order, Temple and the other European members were offering a needed corrective to the sometimes pigheaded enthusiasms of the American delegates, who were prone, as Americans so often are, to equate their version of the enterprise with the global version. American triumphalism—always a disastrous menace, then and now—had its missionary aspects in the 1920s: influential people like J. P. Morgan and John D. Rockefeller thought that the years after the Versailles Conference were ripe for the spread of *American* Christianity around the world, and earnest proselytizing was in style. For every young American in Paris partying it up with the "lost generation," another one at home was ready to ship out to Asia, Africa, or the Middle East bringing Christianity, modernity, and American values in one convenient package to an otherwise "lost" world.

My father was just about to be pulled into these international waters, but he had his parish in Detroit to look after, and the situation in Michigan continued to be dire. An English observer of the American scene—the great economic historian R. H. Tawney, a friend of Temple's who in due course will reappear as another important figure in the Serenity Prayer story—might well have had in mind the conditions faced by working-class Detroit people in the 1920s when he acidly commented, "Whether the black lists, yellow-dog contracts, company unions, spies, under-cover men, armed guards, gas-bombs, revolvers and machine-guns, and the rest of the American apparatus of coercion . . . contributed greatly to the emancipation of the workers of the Land of Liberty, it would be presumptuous for a foreigner to enquire." Most of Detroit's pastors thought it was presumptuous to inquire, too. They went along with the whole oppressive show, and so did their parishioners—blocking decent improvements not only in the present but for the future. Bishop Williams had believed in collective bargaining for industrial workers—as Frankfurter did, as Temple did in England—but Ford managers and their well-paid flacks had regarded Williams as beyond the pale, and now he was dead.

Even labor organizers themselves seemed to be losing their moxie. The big strikes of 1917, 1919, 1921, and 1922 were followed by seasons of anxious retraction. But it wasn't just the labor movement's own internal stagnation: as Tawney rightly said, the labor movement was everywhere opposed, and opposed with violence, while the courts, in the words of Arthur M. Schlesinger Jr., "gave business sentiment the force of law." The working people of Detroit, fighting for job protection and safety in that city's principal business, were pitted against corporations that seemed bent on extracting their labor with as little recompense, respect, or regard as possible. In the absence of legal safeguards or cultural sympathy, you'd have thought they'd have gotten some moral support, at least, from their spiritual leaders. But no. Few people seemed up to the task. Even the American Federation of Labor spokesmen whom Pa invited into his church to talk up the parishioners didn't cut the mustard: he thought they had "about the same amount of daring and imagination as a group of village bankers." It was to be years before the unions got anywhere in Detroit.

There was another critical social issue that should have been faced by the Detroit pastors, and instead they tragically ignored it. They should surely have offered moral leadership in trying both to improve the lives of the blacks newly arrived from the South looking for work in the automobile plants and also to alter the unacceptable hostility that whites showed toward them. This was a task of Herculean difficulty, Pa was finding. After riots broke out in 1925 over a racial issue, he agreed to chair a commission that the mayor of Detroit appointed to report on what might be done to improve things. The commission's plausible, matter-of-fact, and conciliatory recommendations for racially integrated housing, policing, banking, and schooling went largely unheeded.

In the churches—his own was as white as the others—Pa knew that the people "were committed to the ethical ideals of Jesus" and believed that Christians were "the sole or at least chief agents of redemptive energy in society." But it was "very difficult to persuade people . . . to consider the meaning of that ideal in specific situations." The racial crises of Detroit were a glaring example of this painful disconnect. What, in this bustling new industrial economy, would induce people to resolve their differences when they seemed, if they had any kind of stability or security, anxious merely to protect their settled way of life? How could one formulate a progressive, humane response to the challenges of industrial life, and vanquish the enemies of industrial democracy, when those enemies held all the cards? How was one to counter capitalism's ruthless inhumanity, its greed-power nexus, which that mediocrity Henry Ford so well represented?

I don't know when my father composed the many prayers of his that are preserved in print, but I can imagine that this one could have been written in Detroit:

We give you thanks, O Lord, for life and love and the joy of existence. . . .We confess that we are not worthy of the riches of life for which the generation of men have labored that we might enter into this heritage. We confess the sorry confusion of our common life, the greed which disfigures our collective life and sets man against his fellow men. We confess the indifference and callousness with which we treat the sufferings and the insecurity of the poor, and the pettiness which mars the relations between us. May we with contrite hearts seek once more to purify our spirits and to clarify our reason, so that a fairer temple for the human spirit may be built in human society.

WHEN MY PARENTS eventually got to Heath, a few years after Pa left Detroit, they met there yet another Episcopalian priest for whom that prayer would have been congenial—he wrote quite a few himself. Howard Chandler Robbins wasn't a firebrand like Felix Frankfurter, or a social-gospel proponent like Charles Williams, and his principal interests were not necessarily the immediate problems of industrial relations or the threat of fascism. Still, his spiritual concerns were congruent with these political ones, and he knew they could not be separated. His wife knew it, too, and she was just as important to us in Heath as Ethel Moors, if not more so. And her politics were even more outspoken.

Howard Robbins had been a rector of various Episcopalian churches in or near New York since the beginning of the century and had taught pastoral theology at the General Theological Seminary there. He was a quiet, contemplative man, gifted with words, with plenty of civic experience and pastoral wisdom. He wrote hymns and prayers, he edited and organized liturgical volumes of many kinds, and in the 1920s, as dean of the Cathedral of St. John the Divine, he attended to many of the same issues that engaged Will Scarlett in St. Louis and my father in Detroit. It was because of him that eventually the Serenity Prayer became so famous.

Robbins was a New Yorker by virtue of his career, but he came from a Yankee family with deep roots in the northwestern corner of Massachusetts, so he was the most at home in Heath of all of us. His Chandler ancestors had been among the Deerfield residents carried off to Ontario by the Algonquins who raided the valley in 1675 and massacred many of the settlers—one of the terrifying incidents in the fearsome season of King Philip's War; Robbinses and their Landon cousins had lived all over Franklin County for centuries. We called Dean Robbins Uncle Howard, as we called his wife Auntie Lou, and we spent a lot of time in his wonderful old house with its big, dramatic garden.

Louise Robbins liked building and rebuilding places: I don't know whether she was rich, but she was certainly propertied. She had houses in California; at Sneden's Landing, on the Hudson River above New York City; and more than several in Heath. A circle of friends who learned of Heath from the Robbinses, overlapping with the Moorses' circle, slowly filled up these nice dwellings. I thought her a marvel for having fashioned or discovered such character and wit in all of them, but my mother cautioned me about their damp cellars. "Louise has a gift, but a curious weakness about water." She also, more important, had congenial political convictions.

Like Aunt Ethel, Louise had no time for platitudes or for routine indifference to social justice. Neither a professional career woman nor a conventional volunteer lady, she gave her time and considerable means to causes that were dear to her—and these included aiding progressive political friends, especially when they ran afoul of America's well-financed, right-wing thought police. I heard about this often enough, and later I had the chance to watch it in action.

In 1933 Auntie Lou designed and built a little guest house right next to the Robbinses' own beautiful place. A sloping, flower-filled field lay between the two houses; it was bisected by a brook, which gurgled out from a culvert under the road and ran plashing and burbling through beds of wild watercress to one of three ponds that Uncle Howard had contrived along its course. My parents, having come to Heath on the encouragement of Mrs. Moors, first rented this minute house from Louise and then bought it in 1941. We added to the Stone Cottage, building on a small but badly needed extension (in plain wood), and we lived there happily for fourteen more sunlit summers. I loved my little bedroom next to the back garden, where morning sun came through the pine trees near the road; in the afternoon the western sun glinted across the pond and into the living-room windows, which overlooked terraces leading to a mysterious, fragrant forest.

I never quite understood why the Robbinses had needed a guest house in the first place, since their own house was big enough for the two of them and their friends, but I didn't worry about whether it caused them difficulties to lose their *dépendance*. My visits to Auntie Lou—on the still, hot summer mornings when sometimes she'd ask me to come and help her out with some household chore—would reassure me: the rambling, brown-shingled house was filled with enchanting extra bedrooms, secret passageways, ancient attics, spacious sunlit upper chambers, and its gorgeous old kitchen next to the garden had a huge stone walk-in fireplace. Auntie Lou would tell me stories about how the house had been built and used two centuries before, about her husband's work and life, about how she liked to cook and garden. But she never *ever* talked about herself or dwelled on her own accomplishments; like Will Scarlett's exploits I had to find out about them elsewhere—a pattern that was often repeated with Heath people. They deflected inquiry; legends and gossip withered on the vine. It wasn't easy to get at them.

The Stone Cottage was set into the meadow hillside on two levels and surrounded by the terraces that my mother and Auntie Lou together turned into a lovely garden. Stone steps between flowering shrubs led down to the duck pond, and on the back side of the house huge arborvitae and big lilacs sheltered a little courtyard. Since Auntie Lou had characteristically built the Stone Cottage right on top of a spring, the downstairs living room was always damp and moldy, so we used it for Ping-Pong and for storing bicycles, and lived entirely on the upper level. Its rather clumsy but charming design featured a westerly view toward Mount Greylock, twenty miles away. The middle-distance prospect from our windows, like all those dutiful American copies of Claude Lorrain, had forest on the left, a few big trees on the right, and water in the center—the first of Uncle Howard's ponds, where my brother and I raised ducks to show at the Heath Fair. It was a gloriously pretty place to spend the summer—

"the most gorgeous spot in the world," Pa wrote in a letter once—and we loved it dearly.

The presence of Felix Frankfurter down the hill from us, in Dell, ensured not only gaiety and a stream of interesting summer visitors, like his law students and favorite law clerks, but timely attention to the causes he cared about. Whenever you ran into him he'd be sure to quiz you on the latest news bulletin and what you thought of it. "Well, are you for it or against it?" he'd ask briskly, eyebrows waggling, finger jabbing at the headline about some national or international development, firing his questions at whomever was the youngest person around. This somehow had the effect not of freezing but of emancipating the victim, as one of his friends wrote in a memoir. It was fun to spar with him, as we children of his friends knew, and as the Heath deans and bishops knew.

A good part of Dell, including the house where the Frankfurters spent their summers, belonged to yet another Episcopalian bigwig who summered in Heath: Bishop Charles Gilbert of New York. It was odd to have so many bishops and deans all in one place—it can't have been as odd for me as it surely was for Uncle Felix—but they weren't in the least bishop-y. If they had been, we'd never have stayed: my father and mother had no patience with parsonic pieties. But Bishop Gilbert, for example, was an amiable unpretentious gentleman who was kind to dogs, children, and strangers, and loved to do woodworking. (It was the woodworking that had attracted him to the Dell mills in the first place.) A most conservatively mannered cleric, he was in his own sturdy way another social progressive who favored the laboring poor. No surprise in Heath. And he was broad-minded enough to have once welcomed the

Patriarch of Moscow at his cathedral—another unusual sign. The upper crust of disapproving New York Episcopalians considered him out of line. So many so-called Christians intolerant of "alien" believers! So many eager to ignore the scriptural injunction to "fill the hungry with good things" and send the rich "empty away"! It was ever thus.

Bishop Gilbert took care of his family and his friends and his several houses with the quiet administrative skill that was one of his hallmarks. The Frankfurters liked him for that, and for his card-playing talents. I still have the pretty china teacups my mother bought at an auction in the early 1940s that Bishop Gilbert organized to sell off the belongings of yet another bishop, who had recently died, the kind of chore he excelled at fulfilling with no fuss at all. "No, not Bishop White's china," she'd explain. "It's episcopal china from Bishop Gilbert's white house." The plethora of bishops could be confusing.

In 1939, when President Roosevelt appointed Frankfurter to the Supreme Court, replacing the revered Justice Benjamin Cardozo, the Frankfurters left Cambridge, but their Heath summers remained unchanged. Uncle Felix would arrive in Dell, promptly after the Supreme Court term ended in late June, along with his wife, Marion—fragile, handsome, clever—and many book cartons. Boxes of Court papers were couriered to him all summer long, which I thought quite grand. Like many of the summer people, he worked hard in his study, enjoying Heath's solitude and beauty, recharging his batteries. There were bridge games with the bishops, long walks along the woodsy lanes and abandoned cart tracks through the high hilly meadows. He liked the sharp, richly flavored local ginger ale so much that he ordered cases shipped to Washington in the winters; we all agreed it was far superior to any old Canada Dry. Our family didn't go so far as to get the ginger ale in New York, where we lived during the academic terms in a big faculty apartment at Union Seminary, but every winter square cartons arrived from Heath with reinforced brass corners and "Fragile" stamped in purple on the top, each with seventy-two eggs within in cushioned gray cardboard stacks and rows; we stored them on a cool shelf in the back pantry, along with our Heath jams and my mother's Anglo-Indian spices.

In his unique way FF epitomized the Cambridge–New York–Washington axis in summertime Heath. All over New England you could find clusters of judges and doctors, clerics and bankers, in villages that were seasonally marked with the distinctive colors of some rich city, university, or profession. Up and down the coast of Maine, all over the mountains of Vermont, and next to Connecticut's best trout streams, pockets of posh New Yorkers, Philadelphians, or Bostonians were casually ensconced in summertime gardens planted generations before. There were, for example, Yale clerics who spent their holidays farther south—like the president of Union Seminary, Henry Sloane Coffin, in Lakeville, Connecticut, a most refined and pretty town with many connections to Yale. But Heath wasn't like these places in any way whatsoever. Thanks to Aunt Louise and Aunt Ethel, Heath was dominated by Harvard pedigrees or by no pedigrees at all.

In tone Uncle Felix was proudly law-professorial years after he'd left Cambridge, proudly Viennese Jewish a half century after his arrival at Ellis Island, and proudly Washingtonian in his mastery of high-level analysis of government and law. He fizzed and bubbled. He argued and asked questions. He hadn't lost the huge appetite for political dispute that had animated him as a Lower East Side kid at City College. He snorted like a schnauzer when he laughed, which was often, he chortled when he told stories, and he literally slapped his thigh at his own jokes. He liked edge, and precision, and seriousness, and he hated solemnity. One summer after the war, when Archibald MacLeish and his wife came over for tea from Conway, Uncle Felix trounced him at badminton on our lawn, and then, I'm afraid, we gently trashed the visitor, of whom we were all fond, in a postmortem after supper. MacLeish took himself too seriously, wanted you to recognize his Significance as a Poet, had poor political judgment. None of this went over in Heath.

Uncle Felix, being decisively agnostic, was amused to find himself in a nest of clergymen, but he knew they were atypical men of the cloth. You could trust Aunt Ethel's instincts on this, and anyway the town had none of the social infrastructure that pious snobs usually require for their summer play. So there they all were—not only Bishop Gilbert in Dell, not only Dean Robbins and my father in Heath Center, but a contingent of parsons on the road to the even more remote community of North Heath. Not to mention Mrs. Drown.

If you walked uphill and north from the town center, the first place you came to on the outskirts of the village was a handsome old white clapboard house that belonged to Mrs. Pauline Drown, the outspoken, antique widow of a scholar who had taught at the Episcopal Theological Seminary (ETS) in Cambridge. Here she commanded the slopes of Plover Hill—"my pasture," she called it—all summer long, with her spaniels, her maids (unusual in Heath, if not unique), and her opinionated bluestocking ways. I believe she's the only nineteenth-century person I ever met who actually wore *blue* stockings. She had hairs sprouting from her chin, but you noticed first her feminine wiles, her old-fashioned silk print dresses, her pearls.

I learned much later that Mrs. Drown had been her husband's *second* wife and that when they married in the far-off years before the Great War, Cambridge society had been scandalized: it was bad enough that a nice young lady had chosen to enroll in a divinity school, but to snare her professor! We used to have Sunday lunch with her after my father preached; she'd argue with him over fine points of New Testament interpretation, complain if the strawberries were soggy, and generally carry on in a spirited, eccentric Bostonian way. Behind the swinging door to the kitchen, I could see the maids parking the porcelain plates on the floor so the spaniels might enjoy the leavings before the dishes were taken to the sink. It was said that Mrs. Drown was tactful when it mattered.

Farther along the road came yet more theologians and church activists. William Wolf, who as an ETS student had been one of Mrs. Drown's "boys" who drove for her and then became a professor there himself, was a marvelous rangy man with an infectious sense of the hilarity in most things and a shrewd, energetic intellectual style. William Kirk, another man of the cloth who directed a settlement house in St. Louis and then moved to New York to run another one, rented a place on the nearby road to Colrain, where he lived with his wife and three daughters. And there were Sydney Thomson Brown and her husband, the fine theologian Robert McAfee Brown; in 1943, this missionary's daughter had come with us to Heath as a kind of au pair for the summer, while Bob, a student of my father's, was working that summer on a Heath farm; the Browns married under Heath auspices and became regular summer residents. In addition there were Sherman Johnson, also from ETS, and Worcester Perkins, rector of the Church of the Holy Communion in Manhattan, which is now a nightclub.

Last, Heath enjoyed the serene, powerful presence of Angus Dun, yet another theologian from ETS in Cambridge, who in 1944 became bishop of Washington. Like almost everyone else in summertime Heath, he was an ecumenical activist and decorated soldier on the social-justice front. "Black Angus," the reactionary Episcopalians called him, sneering at his efforts to integrate Washington Cathedral. Early in the 1920s Auntie Lou had built a cottage across the road from the Robbinses' own brown-shingled pre-Revolutionary house, a barn-red little home with a porch facing west like ours for the best mountain view (this was frequent in Heath) and overlooking a swimming pool. Eventually she lured Angus and Kitty Dun to the Red Cottage, knowing the pool would be a beneficence for the bishop, who was painfully paralyzed by polio.

Somehow the Heath people endured all these men of the cloth. Others would have found it too ecclesiastical. W. H. Auden, a good friend who came to see my parents in Heath in 1946 while he was teaching at Bennington College, not far away, wrote later to my mother, exchanging theological views as he regularly did, and commiserating about the unpleasant respiratory illnesses from which she suffered because of seasonal allergies. Perhaps it wasn't the meadow pollen, he asked in his brotherly way, "but too many clerics?"

It didn't seem like that to us, mostly because we saw more of overalls than we did of dog collars; when we thought of our friends in Heath, we thought of the farmers. Ethel Moors knew them best, since she'd been there longest. Her father's Norwegian coachman had loved the Berkshire hills, and the Paines had settled him on a farm there; his son Oscar Landstrom had married one of three daughters in a long established local family, and by the 1940s the farms of that interlocking family—Dickinson, Landstrom, Gleason, Burrington—dominated South Heath; lucky Aunt Ethel had them all as neighbors. For me those four farms, spreading out over the slope of Charlemont Hill facing down to the Deerfield River, were the center of the universe.

The Robbinses, too, knew everyone. Uncle Howard's nephew Dana Malone farmed year-round in Heath: son of a Deerfield lawyer who had been Massachusetts' attorney general, he lived first in the Creamery, up behind the church, then in yet another capacious, white clapboard farmhouse with a handsome porch, this one on the South Heath road, close by the Dickinsons' farm. He had unconventional new ideas about dairy farming that he liked to put into practice, but science or no science people raised their eyebrows at his milking his cows at 9 A.M. and 9 P.M. instead of the standard early hours.

No exclusive social functions or patterns defined the summer group—that would have been frowned on—and we all joined in regular town activities, though there weren't many of these during the summer. The very season that we city people cherished for maximum relaxation, for picnics and long afternoon naps and evenings of games and music, was, of course, one of maximum labor for the farmers—planting, haying, putting up preserves, filling the silos, and a thousand other summertime tasks. Still, plenty of events kept us in touch with our friends.

Charlie Packard, an accomplished man-of-all-trades who

"kept an eye on the place" for some of us in the winter, lived down the road from us, and he was an essential neighbor. He prepared our plots so we could plant our vegetable gardens as soon as we arrived in the spring, throughout the summer tried to drum sense into us, and fixed our ailing cars. If our "victory gardens" thrived during 1941–45, then we owed much of the bounty to Mr. Packard's wizardry. I remember him, wrinkled and darkly tanned, like a walnut, trying to be patient with our stupid questions—about the vegetables, about carpenter ants, or snakes in the well, or busted iceboxes, or the history of Heath.

We borrowed books from the village library every Tuesday and Friday—for me it was yards and yards of Albert Payson Terhune and Gene Stratton-Porter and Frances Parkison Keyes and how many other three-named popular novelists? Next door to the library, in the back of the building that also housed the town grocery store, reigned Miss Dickinson, postmistress, queen of our connections to the outside world. The stamps! The little red and green sponges on her counter, dampened with the water in their round glass dishes so you didn't have to lick! The wooden mailboxes on the slatted wall between her realm and the store in front! I was happy that my parents sent and received so much mail: it gave me the chance to visit her often. At church, my Niebuhr grandmother, an accomplished teacher of small children, helped out Mrs. Landstrom in the Sunday school, Eleanor Wolf spelled Mrs. Burrington at the organ, the Kirk girls and I sang in the choir. We bought our milk and eggs not from valley stores in Charlemont or Shelburne Falls but from our neighbors, and we all pitched in to prepare for the Heath Fair, in late August.

The rhythm of farm and roadwork during the short, intense

New England summers kept Heath men so busy that only some of them were regularly seen at church. I recall my father easily accepting their grave, polite regrets that rain or sun, planting or haying, dispersal or retrieval of pastured heifers would command immediate attention that Sunday and require their absence. But of course. Still, my father knew—after all, he'd been a working pastor for fifteen years and was the son and grandson of pastors—that women, not men, are often the ligaments that hold parishes together, and that plenty of men, like these fine friends, tick the box marked "Christian" on any poll inquiring as to their religious affiliation yet most of the time simply tip their hats to their wives' devotions.

It's impossible, though, to be precise about such matters, since Americans in a patchwork amalgam community will rarely be specific about their spiritual motives or habits. Nor need they be. For the church congregation in Heath, the summer services—and communal attitudes—gave plenty of space for the necessary vagaries of the heart at the same time as they offered order and structure for the spirit. I know that a discipline of regular worship rewards the congregant with untold bounty, but on the other hand I was taught in my family to be respectful of anyone who had doubts or difficulties with religious faith or with the habits of communal worship, so we weren't doctrinaire about this, and no one else was, either.

Once, Uncle Felix came up the hill from Dell to hear my father preach, despite his marked distaste for going into a church. He found the service rather cheering and not offensive to his skeptical, agnostic ears—he even joined in singing the hymns—and said to Pa afterward, "May a believing unbeliever thank you for your sermon?" to which my father replied, "May an unbelieving believer thank you for appreciating it?" So you could say that the Heath farmers were in the usual spiritual pickle—either my father's or Uncle Felix's. "Belief," mused my mother once, "what a weasel word."

The farmers' politics were also paradoxical. Heath had sent a few dozen men into the Union Army the century before, and like all good Massachusetts country people since the Civil War, they were staunch Republicans, invoking the predictable clichés of New England individualism to inveigh against FDR's "socialistic meddling" in the economy. Yet the New Deal's social and economic programs (the Rural Electrification Administration especially), as well as later postwar programs, like the GI Bill, initiated by Democratic administrations, immeasurably improved their situation. Moreover, my father noted, the actual structure of their working lives was far from individualistic. "They're communists, actually," he'd say cheerfully, wondering how they might react if he said so out loud. Pre-1848 communists. For much of the year whole sections of the township pooled resources—financial (to rent extra equipment in the summer or to lease ice-locker space in the winter) and human (when all hands went into the fields together to bring in the hay and to process the corn harvests)—and they couldn't have managed otherwise.

High spirits marked the most exciting of Heath's festivities, the annual fair and its parade, held across from Dana Malone's place, next to an oak grove above the Dickinsons' farm, half under the shade of the dark, high trees, half in an open, mowed field. Yeasty, sugary fragrances suffused the milk-white air in the canvas tents, where tables arranged in a spacious oval displayed constellations of cakes, pies, breads, and cookies; others glowed

*Niebuhr the "circus barker" and his friend the farmer Ken Stetson
as the Fat Lady in a play in the Town Hall at Heath*

with a rich tapestry of jellies and jams, pickles and relishes, gigantic flawless vegetables, perfect fruit. Outside, under the oaks, the
calves and piglets, chickens and ducks (my brother's and mine
among them) fussed and preened in their pens. All morning
Susan Kirk and I would mill about, admiring the displays, eating
snacks—no fast food here! no imported generic carnival junk
from non-Heath hands!—and drinking root beer or celery tonic
in bottles pulled from the sloshy metallic depths of big red Coca-
Cola iceboxes. Our mothers chatted with Mrs. Landstrom and
Mrs. Stetson, and tried to decide which of the beguiling hand-
made rugs to buy—braided or rag? Or the padded dress hangers
covered in gingham? Or cross-stitched table linens? Quilts? Soon
the ox draws began, and the hammer-throw competitions.

As the fair wound down, the parade started up, and here the summer and winter people collaborated in truly deranged nonsense. On the farmers' familiar flatbed trucks or horse-drawn hayricks marvelous floats were mounted depicting all kinds of wondrous scenes: Bishop Dun was a big hit one summer as the Wild Man from Borneo, hairily nude from the waist up, waving his powerfully muscled arms about, munching leaves and bellowing nonsense syllables in a lusty, booming voice that usually carried across vast cathedral naves; one of the Gleason boys was his "keeper."

In the evening we all went to, or acted in, a play at the Town Hall. I have a picture of my father in a star role as a circus barker, with a shiny top hat and striped red-and-white pants; skinny young Ken Stetson, whose vegetables always won blue ribbons and whose farm was famous as a statewide gold-star winner, played the Fat Lady, flirting goofily with the barker. A few years before, about the time he wrote the Serenity Prayer, Pa had the lead as the "toff" of a jewel-thieving gang: I can't remember the play, but I recollect how much he enjoyed memorizing its salty Runyonesque lines. The greatest triumph came the summer when we did Thornton Wilder's classic 1938 *Our Town*—Mary Kirk directed; Bill Wolf played the Stage Manager; Susan Kirk had a lead role and I had a little one; Mrs. Burrington was the hero's mother. Everyone thought the production was ace, and Uncle Felix claimed that Wilder himself would have preferred it to more famous ones.

Thus the summers passed in a blur of sun and rural festivity, or so my romanticizing childish memories would have it. Visiting divinity students were my baby-sitters. Pearl Landstrom taught me how to swim in the Duns' cold, cold swimming pool.

I practiced for my winter music lessons on the piano in the Town Hall. My father and mother went to and fro, as business in New York or elsewhere called them away, leaving me in the care of my beloved grandmother, Mütterchen, or with the Landstroms. My pals and I went on bicycle trips organized and led by Bill Kirk while my father wrote his books. At the Kirks' house, too, we had feisty weekend hymn sings. And from the Stone Cottage we walked every Sunday morning to the Union Church in the village center.

III

Two centuries after its founding, Heath retained its sparse, spread-out, hilly-frontier feeling, so the village green wasn't one of those willed architectural announcements that New Englanders make when they feel truly settled. But it had an austere, windswept sweetness, this isolated, brave place, with its library, its town hall, its grocery store with the post office in the back, and the steepled white clapboard church which, like so many public buildings in New England, one approached on broad, shallow flagstone steps made of local granite. Bishops Dun and Gilbert, my father, Dean Robbins, Mr. Perkins, Professor Johnson, and the Bills (Wolf and Kirk), along with various young student seminarians, all helped to conduct services in that church—an astonishing summer invasion. It was there, in this quintessential New England village—as well as in various liturgical adventures in pagan, wintertime New York—that I began to savor the differences among all the various Protestant denominations.

Modern, secular people who are proud of their innocence— or ignorance—of religious practice are missing out on the fun in this. The inadequate shorthand used to label a church as merely fundamentalist, reform, evangelical, or orthodox doesn't get the half of it. The rich sectarian textures of religious, social, and political meaning may now be thin and frayed and forgotten, but for centuries they formed the warp and woof of daily life for millions of Europeans and Americans. And to know a Protestant Christian's denomination was one of the ways to understand him, as I think it still is. It could also be a fairly reliable way to mark various layers of the social pie, though this was hard in Heath, where people didn't pay much attention to a person's class background or financial wherewithal. It took me time to realize that a pastor in the E & R Synod lived on a different planet from, say, an Episcopalian bishop in New York or a Congregationalist Massachusetts farmer.

Leaving aside the social message, I learned subliminally, both in Heath and in New York, how to recognize the strong opinions about spiritual and civil authority that are built into the different modes of Protestant worship, into the shape of the services, the music, the prayers, the sermons. You have to pay heed to this kind of thing in America, for although the Founding Fathers roundly and rightly insisted on separating church and *state*, churches both amplify and perpetuate all kinds of chasms in American *society*, and they exude opinions about how that society should comport itself. Every community of faith goes about its business in its own way, that's clear, but their varying styles point not so much to what they think about "God," or what they think a prayer is, as to their ideas about the real source of divine authority and the real meaning of civil authority, about the right relation to have with nonbelievers, about how to live in the world, about sin.

In the drastic dark years of this new century we are all relearning what none of us should ever have forgotten: that we must pay heed to the outward signs exhibited by each community of faith—how their members walk, stand, kneel, and pray, how they dress or eat. For one thing, it's a good way to learn something about their views on sex and politics, on men and women, on sin and salvation. The signals of behavior concern not so much the inner core of their faith as the outer arrangements they think are needed to safeguard or improve their situation in the secular world. For an anthropologist or disbelieving "rationalist," a religion's behavioral patterns are supposedly signals that something primary, something "spiritual" or "religious," is going on, but in truth they are usually only secondary clues. They tell you about the regulations and habits that a given church or temple has laid down for its people to adhere to when swimming in the sinful sea around them. The mystery of faith itself remains unmarked, which perhaps is as it should be.

This came across even in Heath's Union Church, despite its services being as modestly devout and unpretentious as any I have attended—or perhaps because of this. Going to church at Heath was simplicity itself, but it wasn't casual. That was itself a signal. Like our neighbors, we dressed for church more formally than we did during the week—anyway not in work clothes— and I tried to emulate their cheerful dignity for the Sunday morning service. I, too, polished my shoes, my grandmother made sure I was shipshape, my mother combed my "hopeless, hopeless" hair, and I tried not to skip and cartwheel as we walked up the hill to the village.

In the church itself, there were no rich man's pews saved for wealthy parishioners who bought their way to box seats for the holy show—an obnoxious arrangement that in later years I was shocked to find in plenty of other American churches. And certainly no relegation of women to a balcony or curtained side space, as with Muslims and Orthodox Jews. The rationale is supposed to be that the sight of women might divert or distract the men from the central activity of praying. The injunction against a female presence is deranged, in my book, and it's amusing that it presumes—as so many male chauvinist rules do—inevitable masculine weakness.

The pulpit in Heath was not a high and mighty prow thrusting out over a sea of medieval seats below; the sanctuary was only a small step up from the main floor of the church, and the altar wasn't far from the front pews. The pastors, inevitable intermediaries in the God business, could be seen up close for what they were: people like us. No *imagined* intermediaries, of course—no virgin mothers or saints hovering in the windows or above the altar or on the walls. No ancestor worship implied in brass and stone displays on the floor or walls. No hierarchy of place or position, no gussied-up displays of wealth and power passing off as reverential devotion. No art. It was just a plain room, and the simplicity focused your heart. No overt or theatrical mystery: the mystery was inner. The space itself insisted on the democratic, devout truth that is or should be at the core of every church or temple service: the communicants are all equal among themselves and before the Lord.

To me this was a quintessential Protestant meeting hall, its tone quickly recognizable wherever it might be encountered. Once in the Swiss mountains I wandered into a beautiful little seventeenth-century church, all pink stone and white marble, with a beautiful bell tower; the village was only a mile or so from the Italian border (in fact, the township had once been in

Italian territory, with the border farther north), and it was distinctively Italian in architectural, linguistic, and culinary culture, so it never occurred to me that the church would be anything but Roman Catholic. The moment I was in the door, though, I felt a difference. The whitewashed walls were perfectly bare; the dark wood of the pews and modest altar shining in the Alpine light afforded the only visual luxury. The pulpit was plain, the cross (not crucifix) hanging behind the altar was plain, and the choir balcony set at the back was plain. No surprise to find a plaque by the door explaining that this was "the Evangelical Protestant Church of Switzerland in the Italian Language," that the town had been *"riformata da gli errori e superstizione"* in 1520. I felt right at home.

Yet I couldn't help noticing, even in Heath, the different ways people disposed themselves physically to do this worshiping business. One never saw the Heath farmers praying *except* in church, and so one couldn't imagine their religious comportment in daily life. It does not occur to a Christian to fling himself to the ground several times a day, as Muslim men all over the world do, but, one might ask, why not? The heart of the prayers may well be comparable, after all. I have a suspicion that many Christians don't pray often except when in church or at moments of dire stress, but perhaps I have that wrong. So much Christian behavior, if that's what to call it, seems reserved for Sunday mornings. When I was little I was taught to kneel at the side of my bed every evening before climbing under the sheets for the night—"Lighten our darkness, we beseech thee O Lord, and by thy great mercy defend us from all perils and dangers of this night, for the love of thy only son our savior Jesus Christ"— but I never sank to my knees otherwise, and I didn't know anyone who did, except in jest. Strict fundamentalists might conclude that we were godless sinners, but in truth the absence of kneeling doesn't, and didn't, mean the absence of sacred meaning in ordinary life.

So in Heath there were few clues, and the Heath people held their cards close to their vests. In church on Sundays, I'd see the Congregationalists praying as they stood or sat, looking slightly downward—at the shoulder blades of the man in the pew in front, say. Correct and forthright, as Congregationalists generally are. Not so far off their similarly composed behavior at any serious public gathering, like a town meeting, except the neck was fractionally tilted. The bowed head could be accounted for by the plain act of reading the hymnbook or prayer book. Where was the religion? Episcopalians lurched to their knees and bowed their heads, but they didn't genuflect as they entered the pews, as Catholics do, or cross themselves, a gesture they considered both superstitious and show-offy; they didn't saunter in casually, either, as Jews do in temple. And nobody in the Heath church wore that smug look that American politicians arrange across their faces whenever public prayer is called for, a poisonously fatuous expression that puts all religion in bad odor. The idea was to carry yourself with deliberation and composure, and you did.

Naturally everyone enjoyed the release from seated quiet that the hymns brought. Singing at a church service, a Protestant innovation, affirms a joyous popular will. It's a pleasant sound—the rustle and bustle of several hundred people simultaneously standing, stretching, finding the right page in the hymnbook, clearing their throats and letting go. It's nice that most hymns have many verses, so that you can work up through the first and second and third until, with the last stanza, big organ noise thundering and pealing in the air, you can really open out and make something of the alleluias. I loved the hymns we sang in the Heath church, and I loved the fact that they had been sung there for centuries: to sing them was to sing something brave and new each Sunday, yet to share in an expressive outburst of meaning that had been going on for generations.

One hymn was especially splendid, and I now know why. Its stalwart eight-beat lines, foursquare, simple harmonies, and lines repeated at the beginning and end of each verse were devices deliberately employed in the earliest hymns of the Protestant Reformation to make it easy and inspiriting for the congregations to join in, just as similar patterns make sea chanteys or barroom songs such a gas. This particular tune, used in modern services for the hymn entitled "Turn Back, O Man," is one of the greatest of the early Protestant chorales; it comes from the *Geneva Psalter*, composed in 1551, only a short while after Luther began the glorious tradition. The words, written in 1919 by Clifford Bax, a minor English poet (and brother of the composer Arnold Bax), have none of the majesty of the chorale and leave much to be desired. Still, their rising inflection from admonition to penitential hope to triumphal celebration express the best of the Christian spirit in the dark postwar years in which they were written:

> Turn back, O man, forswear thy foolish ways.
> Old now is earth, and none may count her days,
> Yet thou, her child, whose head is crowned with flame,
> Still wilt not hear thine inner God proclaim,
> "Turn back, O man, forswear thy foolish ways."

Earth might be fair, and all men glad and wise.
Age after age their tragic empires rise,
Built while they dream, and in that dreaming weep:
Would man but wake from out his haunted sleep,
Earth might be fair, and all men glad and wise.

Earth shall be fair, and all her people one:
Nor till that hour shall God's whole will be done.
Now, even now, once more from earth to sky
Peals forth in joy man's old, undaunted cry,
"Earth shall be fair, and all her folk be one!"

But the praying part was trickier. Many Protestants—caught doctrinally between in-your-face uprightness and kneeling, which to them feels abject, perhaps even papist—ready themselves for church prayer by shifting to an awkwardly tipped position at the edge of the pew, knees dipping a few inches toward the floor, ankles flexed well beneath, torso angled forward, eyes down. The "Prot squat," Wystan Auden called it. This ugly posture is supposed to indicate a reverent intention equivalent to kneeling but without the implicit subservience. I remember mastering it as a child as a kind of safe compromise that I could resort to whenever I couldn't resolve my conflicting loyalties to Congregational and Anglo-Catholic training, whenever I wanted to fade into the ecumenical woodwork. Or when I was embarrassed.

Only secular hostility masked as indifference can claim, in the name of politically correct tolerance, that this was meaningless nonsense, a weird Wasp hang-up that should be forgotten. My embarrassment was real: behavior signals belief, which one is supposed to respect, and I didn't want my behavior to be construed as offensive. Men and women had once gone to their deaths over such matters, after all, and you had to acknowledge the dangers. Though the midcentury years of my far-off childhood are now painted as having been bigoted and unenlightened, I can certainly remember, and want to credit, Americans of that time for making a conscious effort, teeth clenched and smiles drawn, to manage the clashing styles of different faiths, not to ignore them, which is what we tend to do today. These strains and social awkwardnesses may now be mockingly interpreted, by people with no religious imagination and quite a lot of class hang-ups of their own, as typical Wasp priggery or snootiness, but that's not how it was. The edginess about deportment, like the larger disputes over politics and church doctrine, was part of an at least intermittently honest effort to acknowledge the recalcitrant, obstinate signs of what Perry Miller, a great scholar and student of New England theology, called "the enigma of Christian liberty."

In Christian doctrine, each church, each community of the faithful, when it gathers together is testifying to the presence of Jesus Christ in the communicants' lives, and should be doing so in a way that is meant to be very different from any other form of community expression. The sacrament of Holy Communion, in which bread and wine are shared, as they were at Christ's Last Supper, is the mysterious, intense moment when this sense of partaking in the "body of Christ" is most fully experienced. But the entire order of worship is supposed to give depth and urgency to the congregation's sense of its spiritual unity. All the more tragic if this liturgical moment of grace is lost in disputes about who is allowed to participate, or about how to enact the sacred moment.

Other moments of grace and promise get lost, too, when sacraments are defended with doctrinaire righteousness, as if they were real estate or bank accounts. Rituals that ought to be joyous celebrations become sources of strain, and people suffer. One of my father's regular sideline activities came about, for example, because of his willingness to marry perfectly nice, upright, principled people whose priests or rabbis or families had spiritually disowned them because they'd crossed the line into forbidden, godless territory by falling in love with an infidel and, worse, deciding to spend their lives together.

The couples would arrive on my father's doorstep virtually in tears, in desperate need of spiritual counsel. For people who cherish and respect the faith in which they were raised as well as the commitments made by those whom they love, it is no easy matter to proceed to a new life together whose patterns will differ in many essential ways from the ones they grew up with. It wasn't easy to give the young people advice, but no priest should have just disowned them, it seemed to me, as so many of them did. A routinized, turf-defending cruelty lay at the heart of the priests' and rabbis' and ministers' conventional refusals to offer positive signals to these young couples—a Methodist and a Catholic, say, or a Jew and an Episcopalian, or a Lutheran and an atheist.

We may find it hard to imagine how doctrinaire and absolutist people once were about these "interfaith" matters, since in today's much more secular world, ecumenical clichés have made progress against the most extreme dogmatic hostilities. But the improvement has come about as much through indifference and atrophy as through genuine broadening of the spirit. Another one of Pa's prayers went like this:

Help us each to walk worthily in the vocation wherewith we are called, forbearing one another in love and endeavoring to keep the unity of the spirit in the bond of peace. Teach us to look not each at his own things, but at the things of the other, so that we may impart and receive from one another whatever gift of the spirit you have given to each. O Lord, bind us together in the body of Christ that we may grow unto a perfect man, unto the measure of the stature of the fulness of Christ.

IN THE CHAOS of new-millennium America at its most trivial and self-absorbed, plenty of secular people presume, with a certain vulgar snobbery masking their ignorance, that Christians are either Protestant or Roman Catholic and that's that, and that of the two the second is more "genuine," more truly religious— with its ancient history, its priestly costumes and incense, its confessionals and schools, its strictly enforced doctrines, its vast papal superstructure. They make the same mistake about comparable divisions within Judaism and, for all I know, Islam. How often my breezily anti-religious friends have told me—while in 'fessing up to needing some "transcendent meaning" in their lives, to longing for some old-time security—that if they were to topple over into religion they'd "go the whole way" and become Catholic.

This notion that somehow Protestants are less "religious" than Catholics would be amusing if it weren't so ignorant. Secular people may wistfully admire the ritual rigmarole and the dogma about the supreme authority of two millennia's worth of priestly power, and I suppose that if they want something explicit and worldly to hang on to for greater "meaning," these aspects of Catholicism are reassuring, just as enjoying the colorful display of a religious institution's wealth and geographical reach is no doubt diverting. But the panoply of Roman Catholic worship is only the outer carapace of, and merely substitutes for, what is hiding in plain sight in front of all of us: the invisible, inner life of real faith, which can be found in every human context and certainly plenty of Catholic *and* Protestant ones.

For myself, I have always liked the way the Protestant denominations offer a whole palette of colors in which to paint the dynamics of Christian life from the very start. Even in Sunday school, children can sense that different churches tell the story with different emphases: the versions vary. It's plain that it hasn't been easy, during the twenty centuries of church history, to express well the dilemma built into the very heart of the Scriptures: the disputatious and threatening story of a charismatic itinerant rabbi in Palestine who questions the prevailing orthodoxies taught by his elders in the Jewish establishment— and whom his followers believe to be divine. Altercation over the nature of the faith Jesus preached, over the sins from which salvation is to be sought, over the doctrinal authority that will define faith, over the formal structure of a civil society that does or does not respect it, over the arena of doubt in which the drama of faith is played—these all appear at the very center of the Passion story itself, and for good reason. Naturally enough they have punctuated the entire history of the church: the Reformation did not begin and end with Luther—far from it!

Since my father was E & R and my mother an Anglican, since we lived in polyglot Jewish-Catholic New York in the winters and Protestant New England in the summer, I grew up knowing the basic outlines of sectarian history as well as I knew that you put the fork on the left and the knife and spoon on the right. I certainly knew that Massachusetts was home to many kinds of Puritan and that much of New England history was the history of their "kingdom of God in America," as my uncle's book on the subject called it. For three hundred years God-driven visionaries had dwelled in the frontier villages and towns of what had been the Massachusetts Bay Colony, where "the enjoyment of economic and political liberty fostered the desire for similar privileges in religion" (my uncle again).

New England's austere Dissenters from the prevailing powers of the Anglican Church included the Congregationalists, of course, who had renounced the English Catholic church's hierarchy of bishops and archbishops and the claim of "apostolic succession" going all the way back to Saint Peter that was used to justify it. They believed in entrusting church authority to the congregation itself. No wonder their services felt so different from Anglican or Episcopalian ones.

But rather quickly, in the New World, the Congregationalists became, as churches are always in danger of becoming, complacent and doctrinaire. Already in the seventeenth century they were known to tolerate theological dissent poorly, and it was in part the Pilgrims' own intolerant orthodoxy that induced their Nonconforming, Dissenting children to head west and south rather than wrangle with them in Massachusetts. One disaffected or reforming impulse after another propelled group after group to found new Puritan communities, which, they hoped, would be even more faithful and free than the Pilgrims' foundational ones. They left their traces as they trekked on to their Promised Lands in the "burned-over districts" and wildernesses to the west. The Ranters and Diggers and Shakers! They recalled American settlers to Protestantism's old but still vital doctrine of inner experience as the source of spiritual authority, and also to its central commitment to programs of social reformation. This was the Puritan tradition to which Frankfurter had recalled the Massachusetts lawyers and judges, reminding them and the American people of its high standards for the sober practice of equality and fairness. It had influenced the Founding Fathers, it had influenced Abraham Lincoln, and it was part and parcel of the American ideal.

Not to mention the enthusiastic Methodists, followers of the evangelical reform movement that the Wesleys (John, Charles, and Samuel) had led in a storm of emotional fervor sweeping across England and America in the late eighteenth and early nineteenth centuries. Methodism had begun, like most Protestant sects, as "poor man's Christianity," and proudly so. Yet since its focus was on sin as individual vice, on individual "good works" as a means of redemption, it tended to neglect society's oppressions, maladjustments, and injustices, and this led it—like so many other Protestant groups!—to favor the middle classes and to tend toward conservatism. Here we go again. There was something fine in Methodism's intensity and color, but one didn't like its politics. Naturally there were exceptions, like the heroic Bishop McConnell. But you can always find truly Christian behavior in single individuals; it's the institutions and public forms that cause such trouble.

I used to associate Methodism with businessmen, but since I knew scarcely any businessmen or their families when I was a child, this prejudice developed without any social information to support it, which happens all too often. Eventually I found plenty of Methodists, usually in cities, not villages, and few of them were in business: I liked them for their energy and forthrightness.

And I loved their ecstatic hymns. They were even more fun

to sing than the early German and Swiss Reformation ones. By now every benighted American who has ever gone Christmas shopping in a mall knows the most famous Wesley hymn, though they may not realize it—"Hark, the Herald Angels Sing, Glory to the New-born King"—and even mere Easter-service Christians know the beautiful anthem "Jesus Christ is risen today, Our triumphant holy day, Who did once, upon the cross, Suffer to redeem our loss." Sarcastic, knowing, Internet-educated children would never stomach the once popular "Gentle Jesus, meek and mild, Look upon a little child; Pity my simplicity; Suffer me to come to thee." I couldn't stomach it myself. But there were others:

> Come, thou long-expected Jesus,
> Born to set thy people free;
> From our fears and sins release us;
> Let us find our rest in thee.

> By thy own eternal Spirit
> Rule in all our hearts alone;
> By thy all-sufficient merit,
> Raise us to thy glorious throne.

I like the clear, bright, eighteenth-century liberationism of this fine Wesleyan hymn.

But the flavor of the Christian churches in America came mostly from long simmering broths set on the stove by Continental and Celtic churches. Though statistically Anglo-Saxon Protestants accounted for a huge proportion of the population in my childhood, I saw eventually that most of the American world wasn't English like my mother or German-American like my father—or even Jewish, like everyone I knew in New York.

Take the Scotch-Irish Presbyterians, with their austere, plain church ways laid down by John Knox, mighty Calvinist of Edinburgh. They were quite a different kettle of fish. These quintessential frontier Americans, scrappy and judgmental, were found all over New England. Sometimes they became part of a village amalgam of Presbyterians and Congregationalists called "United Brethren"; one saw them in plenty of Massachusetts towns.

But the very name "Presbyterian" gives off warning signals: the presbyters are elders of the church (the canonical Gospel reference is to elders, or *presbyters*, of the Sanhedrin), and Presbyterians believed their elders should run things, certainly run their churches and if possible their communities. Budding theocrats, they had been in Scotland, and they were fierce and bossy in the New World. The importance of maintaining strict lines of authority was central to their psychology—presbyters are mullahs, really. This tone was absent from the Heath style of Protestantism, but American life quickly acquaints one with it. To be fair, spirited, community-minded energy was equally a Presbyterian marker. And of course every church displays this sinful tendency to bossiness, once well established—all religious organizations are prone to it. No wonder that secular people fancy the stereotype of Christians as power-obsessed people who want to run things their way. Presbyterians seemed, to my unruly childish heart, especially dour and self-righteous. I distrusted their pursed mouths.

In the New England experiences of my youth I didn't learn much about the Continental European Protestants, but I already knew something about Martin Luther, and any foray into Pennsylvania or farther into the Middle West told you plenty more.

I had the impression that the Niebuhr family had good inside info on all the German-American ways of being Protestant (and knew about German Jews and Catholics, too, for that matter). Naturally I preferred to believe that for Americans of German descent, the Evangelical and Reformed Synod was the best alternative to Lutheranism, though there were other options, better represented in America than in the fatherland. Mennonites and Bohemian Brethren and Amish! For centuries, dissenting Central European Protestants who had been unable to live in freedom or safety in their own countries had chosen flight to the New World over oppression and injustice at home. River Brethren (among them the Eisenhowers)! Anabaptists! Unitarians, even!

The Evangelical Synod, which my German grandfather had been active in developing, was largely to be found in the Middle West. It was an offspring of the German Evangelical Synod of North America, born some time after the failure of the 1848 Revolution in Europe had sent huge influxes of German immigrants to the New World. Once again freedom to worship had been compromised by political difficulties, and once again political turmoil in Europe shook the kaleidoscope of civil life in America. E & R, being the American child of the Church of the Prussian Union, combined devotion to Scripture (the sacramental, evangelical, Lutheran part—bless Luther for having translated the Bible out of Latin on behalf of ordinary people) with pared-down, democratic ways that emphasized the direct relation between the congregant and his God (the reformed, more Calvinist part, though goodness knows Calvin was no democrat).

E & R's archrival was the Missouri Synod of the Lutheran

Church—stolidly bourgeois in the ultra-conservative prudence of its German doctrines, carefully adjusted to accommodate itself to the structures of local power. Lutheranism does that. The Missouri Synod is still, a century after my grandfather did battle with it, rigid and unfriendly to everyone who deviates from what they consider the true way—even their cousins among the United Lutherans and Evangelical Lutherans, who constitute the Lutheran majority.

It was the Missouri Synod that suspended one of its ministers because he participated in an ecumenical service of mourning at Yankee Stadium after the tragedy of September 11, 2001: the good man had appeared with Muslim, Catholic, Jewish, and other Protestant clergy, and he was expelled for having thereby violated a whole mess of Biblical injunctions to abstain from worship with "infidels." It turns my stomach, this loveless dogmatic absolutism. Sad but true: the Missouri Synod is but one of many spiritual groups that insists on the priority of its punitive powers over a genuine ministry to suffering people.

E & R, in marked contrast, was ecumenical in its inclinations and progressive in its social policies. My father's and my uncle's revered Evangelical teacher Samuel Press, for example—who "always took the Bible seriously," Pa wrote (though not in the "absolutely literal way some Biblicists take it and kill the spirit by the letter")—had "a generous understanding for the great social problems of the world," never failing to relate his Christian beliefs to the "terribly complex and . . . tragic facts of world history." Press was among the Evangelical leaders who worked for the synod's merger in 1934 with the Reformed Church and then, in 1957, with the Congregationalists to form the United

Church of Christ (UCC). The Union Church in Heath was, basically, UCC *avant la lettre.*

Though the Evangelical and Reformed Church loomed large among German Americans and large in my corner of America, it wasn't a big national group. Conversely, there was a gigantic Protestant denomination that was all but unknown to me when I was growing up. I don't think I knew any Baptists in Heath, but I knew there were millions of them, especially in the South, and I knew their basic theme concerned the essential importance of total-immersion adult baptism. I thought it was rather exotic, this business about getting wet all over in order to establish that you were a real Christian, and in a real river if possible, but I could see the appeal.

I learned quickly enough that the question of when and how one became a true member of a church was one that Christians of all persuasions took very seriously, and Baptists especially so. At least they had clear-cut views on it. I also knew that atheists found the whole issue absurd. But the cheap mirth that secular people enjoy when faced with terms and experiences that are foreign to them—terms which by the way Baptists are forthrightly comfortable in using, terms like being born again, sinning in one's heart, dying to live—this jeering mirth is well-known, not only to Baptists like Jimmy Carter.

Whether a community of faith welcomes you when you are a mewling infant in a lace dress, or a well-trained thirteen-year-old, or a fervent college kid wet all over, or a repentant person of pensionable age—this is a difficult question, answering which requires you to decide what you think being a member of a church or temple means. This is, of course, in essence a political issue, and when no civic or political rights are attached to church membership, it should not be a dangerous one, as it has been so often in worlds and centuries past.

Protestants have been arguing about the meaning of baptism for centuries, and I like the candor of their dispute. I like their having declined to cede the decision about such a central life experience to a priestly tradition. A billion other Christians prefer to imagine that two millennia of self-appointed, celibate, hierarchical priests can better lay down the law for them on this point, but I don't agree. True, the various Protestant denominations have long since gotten stuck in their ways—adult baptism for Baptists, infant christenings for Lutherans (and adolescent "confirmation" thereafter) and so on—but at least their liturgies acknowledge the variations. "Truth is many-sided, even Christian truth," my father wrote. "We ought to be tolerant with people who see the truth a little differently than we do and who worship with slightly different forms."

Baptists were a good example of the sorry Christian trajectory, so oft-repeated: they started out as a sect of fiercely egalitarian and true believers, many of them from poor and neglected parts of society, who wanted to be Christians as they judged real Christians should be. They sturdily rejected the whole structure of ecclesiastical authority that gave Anglicans, Lutherans, and even Methodists a priestly bureaucracy that you'd have thought Protestants might have jettisoned. Baptists wanted lay preachers, communicants baptized as adults who knew what they were doing, and each local church enjoying autonomy within the sect as a whole. This makes sense to me— or it would if the Baptists hadn't lamentably failed to develop a liturgy and theology to go along with their plans, and if they hadn't kept their power structure strictly in the hands of *men*.

(Not that they were alone in that regard.) In any case the eighteenth-century powers-that-be considered Baptist doctrine outrageous, and surely it was splendidly subversive.

But as the Baptists settled down and made some money in America, their churches began to practice the very exclusions from which they themselves had once suffered. At the time of the Revolution, Baptists abominated slavery (Congregationalists and Episcopalians evidently did not), but after their enrichment by King Cotton they became staunch defenders of the status quo in the South, and by the Civil War they supported it. Southern Baptists became so entrenched and conservative it was hard to imagine they had once been outcasts on the fringe, way to the left of Congregationalists and even of the quietist power people of seventeenth-century England, George Fox's Quakers. They explained their Confederate allegiance as being due to their commitment to states' rights, but their position on slavery itself, and on the racial views of the white majority, had obviously altered to fit their new prosperity. Comforts and rewards had done their evil work, and the Baptists came to believe, conveniently, that the slave system could not possibly—and therefore should not possibly—be changed. Their racial politics were as repellent as that of every other church in the South.

Until quite recently, the variations among these Protestant churches were still socially significant, liturgically self-evident, and politically suggestive, as the novels of Willa Cather or John Cheever or John O'Hara or Sherwood Anderson richly demonstrated. And you could inhale the air of denominational difference everywhere. It changed depending on where you lived. Maryland still had its proud, rich English Catholic habits, New Mexico its austere Spanish Catholic temper. Pennsylvania will never be rid of the modest, ethical Quaker mores of its founders, even though generations of Scotch-Irish frontiersmen, Episcopalian bankers, Polish Catholic steelworkers, Lutheran and Amish farmers from Germany, and Mennonites from Bohemia have made the state their home. Garrison Keillor has hilariously taught us that in Minnesota, a single church can set the cultural and stylistic tone without its ever being even mentioned: Scandinavian Lutheranism colors everything in the Upper Middle West, just as Massachusetts is indelibly stained with the Puritan ink of its founders. Three centuries after John Winthrop came ashore at Plymouth one can still scent the whiff of Congregationalism's bracing independence in any New England town.

How curious it is that over recent decades the Protestant churches in America have been eager to promote mergers among these denominations, without always bothering to reaffirm the marks left by their ancestors' long centuries of struggle to express their precise ideas about the right relation of priest and people to their shared faith, to one another, to the world beyond the temple walls. Everybody and his uncle, including atheists, have opinions (however ill-informed) about how the spiritual world should function and the place of religion in society: Why shouldn't at least some of the hard-won formulas worked out over the centuries be attended to? People actually care about these matters, care to get them right. Yet except for the most rule-bound reactionaries, like the Missouri Synod authorities, few believers today work up the energy to remember what the arguments were about, while atheists insist that the Christian enterprise is either meaningless or corrupt or both. Even the word "theological" has a new secular use that derides the precision that was once prized among believers. Sloppy journalists use it to describe any obscurely fussy doctrine—in business, war, or policy of any kind—that is maintained to the point of irrationality.

Actually, the E & R–Congregationalist merger, for example, makes sense to me, but I nonetheless suspect the pieties that are invoked to defend Protestantism's new homogenized banality. The new-style church services are often weirdly out of tune. They combine details taken from once strongly contrasting styles of worship and meld them together in liturgies concocted by tone-deaf ecumenists unacquainted with the history or meaning of what they're saying or singing. Perhaps it is simple laziness and indifference—another form of spiritual sloth—that determines the shape of those bizarre folk masses with their Baptist call-and-response anthems, their Lutheran prayers, their Roman crucifixes, their Methodist benedictions.

I'd grown up thinking that whether atheist, agnostic, Jew, or Christian, you not only could but should be an ecumenical pluralist about all the once distinct varieties of religion, and at the same time you should recognize the positive values of the old sects, not just their idiocies. Considering that Protestants had once spent, over the centuries, spectacular amounts of time insisting on the purity of their individual ways and making sure that congregations and the public respected their allegedly unique virtues and doctrines, the new banality is almost bitterly ironic. By now too many of the interesting, divisive points have been sidelined as "merely" *theological*, which means that the Christians who once deemed them vital have caved in to the secular view that they are unimportant.

Meanwhile the secondary issues of class, real estate, education, and money come to the fore, where they should never, ever, be. In the old days a church's insistence on obedience to doctrinal rules often masked an anxious fear that if any leeway were allowed, the church's physical being—its buildings, its schools, its funds, its social power—would be compromised. And these issues, not of religious faith but of the churches' arrangements with civil society, were the ones that created their most divisive, bilious behavior, determined their degenerate local politics, and drove their petty social and political ambitions.

In an ever more secular world—and America is much more secular today than it was when I was a child, statistics about churchgoing notwithstanding—in which moral standards and levels of interest seem to be set and adjusted by Hollywood agents or overpaid corporate thugs, these worldly aspects of church life are now given primary, defining importance. Politically correct college teachers tell their students that the "dominant narrative" about religion in our national life is, precisely, shaped by political issues concerning power and money, though they don't put it like that. The "secular humanist" profs ignore or downplay the animating religious or scriptural injunctions that created a sect, then a church, in the first place (except sometimes to stress that Jesus was a dead white male and the whole deal is a patriarchal power play)—which shows that they are idolaters themselves, raising on high the worldly social edifices and the crude sociopathic maneuvers they like best to talk about.

I suppose it is only just. Churches the world over, like mosques and synagogues and temples, have worked to develop their power bases and fatten their treasuries, get along in the world and please their parishioners with their efforts to trump local or national rivals. So if they are studied today solely as engines of social and economic prejudice, one could say they had it coming to them. My father and his colleagues saw the crisis from a different vantage point, however, and Pa prayed about it. Fifty years ago or more, he wrote this entreaty:

> Look with mercy upon this company of your people, the church. You have called us out of many lands and places to serve you in the ministry of your word. Teach us rightly to divide the word of truth. Grant that our love may grow in all knowledge and discernment. . . . We pray, O Lord, for your church, that it may be healed of its divisions by your grace; that it may teach your word with courage to a sinful world, and may mediate with true charity your love and mercy to all men. Strengthen every ministry of reconciliation therein with your spirit. Grant that it may be a true community of grace in which the pride of race or nation is humbled, where the strong and mighty are brought to judgment, and the meek and lowly are lifted up. Make it more faithful to its Lord, and more instant to meet the needs of men.

Only when I had distanced myself from the benign, devout world of my childhood did I see that the secular world accepts the churches' tiresome sectarian warfare as normal and, worse, imagines that the squabbles among or within "faith-based communities" are what much of the game is about. Looked at from the outside, it all seems fairly awful. The famously high proportion of citizens who claim to believe in God and go to church includes far too many people for whom the basic Christian instructions, if they know them, are apparently irrelevant. Not to mention their priests and pastors, who, equally, do not seem to have love in their hearts. But that the churchgoers are fulfilling the predictable social expectations they set for themselves is clear, and that many of them dislike how other Christians go about it is tragically clear, too. I suspect that some of these churchgoers actually enjoy the judgmental exclusions, the stiff-necked pride, the social and spiritual disapproval of other Christians, let alone Jews or Muslims or "infidels."

This pleasure in hostility differs greatly from the understandable wish to draw some kind of boundary around a church's shared life. Which is to say, the spirit in which a congregation is defined can be malign or benign. My initiation into the difficulties of this issue came late, since the services I attended as a child and adolescent were largely in churches that did not have strict membership rules—at Union, at Columbia, in Heath. Innocently enough, I imagined that if you had been christened and confirmed in any church, then any *other* church would welcome you. I was very far indeed from the truth.

I still haven't quite erased the shocked anger I felt as a teenager, a newly confirmed and enthusiastic church member, when I learned that I could not approach the altar rail for Holy Communion in a Catholic church, that any non-Catholic would be turned away from this central Christian sacrament. "Come unto me all that travail and are heavy laden, and I will refresh you," Jesus is quoted as saying (in the Gospel of St. Matthew), and the priestly invocation to this service continues, "Ye that do truly and earnestly repent you of your sins, and are in love and charity with your neighbours, and intend to lead a new life, following the commandments of God, and walking from henceforth in his holy ways, draw near with faith and take this holy sacrament to your comfort, and make your humble confession to Almighty God, devoutly kneeling." Where is the sectarian exclusion in these majestic words?

The judgmental separations still amaze me when I encounter them, though I try to understand the reasoning—just as I try to see why, for example, one of America's most famous black preachers has said he'd prefer not to have white congregants listening to his sermons. How, I wonder, does he preach on the text (I Corinthians 12:13–25) "For in one spirit were we all baptised into one body, whether Jews or Greeks, whether bond or free; and were all made to drink of one spirit. . . . God tempered the body together . . . that there should be no schism to the body, but that the members should have the same care one for another"? Do social conformity, sectarian self-righteousness, and plain hypocrisy always have to win the day? One can feel only anguish, if one has any respect for the founding principles of the enterprise, at seeing how easily Christians forget, ignore, or pervert the gospel of inclusive love supposedly guiding them.

With the new millennium upon us, the Methodists, Episcopalians, Presbyterians, and all the other Protestant denominations I knew so well are said to have been relegated to the ash bin of history—or so the trivializing media report—and much of their tone and color have vanished. Yet the old self-congratulation and willful certainty of doctrine are still with us. The puffed-up inanities have migrated rightward, to the Pentecostal and fundamentalist sects that once at least had the courage of their outsider status and the fervor of true belief, and that are now as bigoted, rich, and ignorant as any Anglican ever was, with much worse church music and an even more brazen appetite for political power. The strobe lights and thrumming movie-theater organs of the mega-churches' televised spectacles give their parishioners a warm wet feeling, but I cannot believe they instruct the soul. They offer, to quote my father, "a magic which gives an unrepentant heart an even cheaper security before the final judgment than any simple moralism." And they practice a loveless exclusionary church politics: you are either with them or against them; either you join their church or you're not a proper Christian.

The fundamentalists' ironclad dislike of other Christians, let alone everyone else, yoked to their "simple moralism," is a telling sign that their hearts are unrepentant, to my mind, though I have no business rendering such a judgment, I suppose. Yet I know they read the same New Testament that I do.

> "Ye hypocrites, well did Esaias prophesy of you, saying, This people draweth nigh unto me with their mouth, and honoureth me with their lips, but their heart is far from me. But in vain they do worship me, teaching for doctrines the commandments of men." And he called the multitude, and said unto them, "Hear, and understand: Not that which goeth into the mouth defileth a man; but that which cometh out of the mouth, this defileth a man."
>
> Then came his disciples, and said unto him, "Knowest thou that the Pharisees were offended, after they heard this saying?" But he answered and said, "Every plant which my heavenly Father hath not planted shall be rooted up. Let them alone; they be blind leaders of the blind. And if the blind lead the blind, both shall fall into the ditch."

Paradoxically, the alleged openness that has made evangelical Christianity so thrilling to so many people is the source of its almost hysterical rigidity of belief, its certainty that it's got the right answers and nobody else does. If you emphasize the spon-

taneous excitement of the worshiping experience and the reassurance of a done deal, then of course you are going to simplify
the doctrine. You will reduce or eliminate the inward-facing,
difficult spiritual exercises that are, in fact, *meant* to try men's
souls. If salvation is assured so long as you walk the walk and talk
the talk, then you will find it hard to acknowledge fear or
uncertainty, confusion or complexity. Soon you will find it natural to disapprove of anyone who challenges you, anyone who
might be honoring God in his heart differently, or silently. This
is to fall into a very deep ditch indeed.

One quality among many that distinguished the Heath people from the unctuous parsons and church monsters I encountered later in my life was their dislike of censorious spiritual
behavior. It went with their tolerance for uncertainty. The
hearts of true believers—Jews and Buddhists, Muslims and Hin-
dus, as well as Christians—are ever open to doubting sinners, or
anyway that's been my experience. You can sense when a person's spiritual condition has the freedom and modesty born of
real humility; his compassion about human fear and uncertainty
will be boundless. The Heath people—and I mean both the
year-round farmers and the summer clergy—seemed to understand that it was not easy to sustain the spiritual effort to live in
the world's chaos and danger and yet not capitulate to it. Like
many veterans of actual wars (which some of them were), they
showed the alert, patient attentiveness to suffering and doubt that
is the fruit of long experience. And they had not lost their spirit.

Pa had a deep attachment to the passage in the Gospel of St.
John about the skeptical St. Thomas Didymus, who won't
accept from his fellow apostles a secondhand account of Jesus's
appearance after His death and resurrection, and "said unto

them, 'Except I shall see in his hands the print of the nails, and put my finger into the print of the nails, and thrust my hand into his side, I will not believe.' " Doubting Thomas's skepticism is so understandable! The impossible standard of believing in the absence of evidence that one's faith is justified is all the more striking when Jesus sets it forth again eight days later, saying, "Thomas, because thou hast seen me, thou hast believed: blessed are they that have *not* seen and yet have believed." The New Testament repeatedly hammers away at what has always been true, human nature being what it is: that it is never easy to grasp the redemptive grace of the Christian message, even when one wants to.

It's not easy for any of us, in fact, to believe that our lives have any transcendent meaning or worth when so much that happens seems to negate this. It requires a huge commitment of hope and trust if you're going to claim, against all the ugly evidence to the contrary, that the loving human effort is worth making. It is all but impossible to know what one should try to strive for, and what one must settle for. Patient vigilance and constant, daily work so as to believe in and hope for the triumph of life over death—these are the ingredients in the necessary (though not sufficient) spiritual exercise. Every great faith knows this, and every great faith recommends practices and prayerful habit to encourage people's commitments to the enterprise.

My parents would often quote the great prayer—or cry—in the Gospel of St. Mark uttered by the suffering father of the boy possessed by spirits and brought to Jesus in hope of a miraculous cure. Jesus instructs the father, "If thou canst believe, all things are possible to him that believeth," and the father replies "with tears, 'Lord I believe; help thou mine unbelief.' " This was something to pray for every day. It's important to remember that Christ does not rebuke the unbelieving father. Instead He explains to His amazed disciples how He saved the little boy by casting out the evil spirit, a spirit of the kind that "can come out by nothing save by prayer."

IV

————

The prayer my father wrote for the Heath church has become so associated with the "twelve-step program" of Alcoholics Anonymous that most people construe it as expressing only what, in our self-help culture, we think each one of us must aim for, day after day, in our personal self-improvement projects. There's nothing wrong with this, I suppose, since daily prayer is in and of itself empowering in a singular way. And we have many reasons to need diurnal reinforcement, after all. The corrosive possibilities include the mere "fatigue of being oneself," as one psychologist has called it, or the repeated inner crises that come upon us all, or—for religious people of any persuasion—a loss of faith or a spasm of unbelief.

But the Serenity Prayer was composed in wartime, and it also addresses the inconsolable pain, loss, and guilt that war inflicts on the communities that wage it; it goes to the heart of the possibilities and impossibilities of collective action for collective betterment—that is to say, to the heart of the possibilities for peace. These take us across a terrain where one cannot walk alone. The first-person *plural* is grammatically conventional for prayers in many Christian traditions, and my father did not use it here by accident. I'm sure it's how his own father—from whom he learned so much about prayer, about the Christian life, about the promises and dangers of American life—would have phrased and interpreted it.

It's a peculiar irony that my German-American grandfather passed on this spiritual legacy to his children only a few short months before the long peace that preceded 1914 was shattered. From the time of his death in 1913 until the summer of 1943, when his son composed the Serenity Prayer, were thirty years of brutal war and near-war, years that saw deadly, vicious confrontations between the two countries he had loved. It was a tragedy for Pa to lose a beloved father and pastor-teacher then at the height of his powers, yet Pa once told me he was glad, in a way, that Grandfather had died before the first terrible global conflict, for it would have broken his heart to see the United States at war with Germany. He didn't have to add that his own constant efforts to reconcile or make sense of the conflicting values of the German and American spiritual traditions were at the heart of much of his own work. It's not far-fetched to say that they're at the heart of the Serenity Prayer.

When Grandfather was still alive, the largest ethnic minority in the United States was the German one, a huge immigrant group from the very nation that was shortly to become the mortal enemy. But in the years of my grandfather's ministry and my father's childhood, Americans had not yet demonized the hated "Kraut" of the Great War, nor dreamed of the horrors to come with the Third Reich, nor imagined the unimaginable horror of a *second* world war. Pa's earliest childhood memories were thus of a benign world that was both surprisingly German and entirely American—that great swathe of the German-speaking, German-thinking, German-farming Middle West whose richer soils allowed people to prosper as few New Englanders could, where the farmers settled agreeably into selling their crops to grain companies that dominated whole counties, where their villages and churches had a strong provincial flavor that echoed back to Saxony or the Palatinate or Prussia.

In Illinois in 1900, about the time the Niebuhrs moved there, the European presence was recent but vigorous in this empty huge landscape. The small-town streets ended in walls of corn, and then, across the infinite flat fields beyond, stretching out to the horizon, one could watch for the horsetails of approaching tornadoes. Checkerboard Ralston signs on grain elevators all across the prairie punctuated the vast spaces; the economic structures were fairly well advanced, and so were the German social arrangements. Within the families, German was the mother *and* father tongue; my grandfather's Saturday-morning Hebrew and Greek lessons for his sons were conducted in German. Local newspapers were printed in old German type. Of course, when itinerant workers appeared from nowhere at the parsonage's back door, offering to "help around the place," and my grandparents gave them shelter and board for a while until they could land jobs, the social transactions took place in English. Still, Pa started speaking English full-time only when he went off to junior high school, and he went on dreaming in German into his twenties.

The jobless strangers, as well as Grandfather's big family and countless guests and parishioners, needed to be fed, and the Illinois meals naturally celebrated the German-American duality. Decades later in New York, as we'd walk the few blocks down the hill from Union to my grandmother's little apartment for our very German Christmas Eve dinner, Pa would tell me about how Mütterchen had managed the cooking when he was a boy. The wife of an almost penniless parson inevitably had a frugal pantry, even in summer, but it was amplified by the bounty of provisions—the hams, turkeys, geese—with which his parishioners paid Grandfather for baptisms, weddings, and funerals (and for his famously expert dowsing, a useful, nicely pagan sideline in a rural parish). And I knew for myself the calm virtuosity with which Mütterchen still turned out the great Middle Western classics; my English mother might not have approved of those wonderful bean soups, the glistening baked pork, the sauerbraten, the infinite potatoes and cabbages, the pickles and sausages, the rye bread and salt sticks, the buttery layer cakes and stollen, the cinnamon stars, but I loved them all. (No surprise to me that *The Joy of Cooking,* once America's best cookbook, was written by a German-American woman from Missouri, just like my grandmother.)

Cooking was women's work, and although Grandfather believed that women's work was central in a parish community, he took it for granted that the primary pastoral work must be done by men, so in the Niebuhr household the heavy theological lifting was undertaken by the father and sons. And here was another way in which the German influence was almost palpable: Pa, like many American pastors of the time, like not only his father but several generations of his mother's family before him, studied for the ministry with German-trained theologians.

Yet very early on he decided that much of what the German scholars had taught him was irrelevant. They were learned exegetes, they knew their Bibles, but few of them related the Gospels to the intractable nasty modern dilemmas he was finding all around him. They taught a carefully honed version of the

Christian story that was considered liberal and up-to-date because it was suffused with benign thoughts about the power of rational man to grasp the truth and improve the world. The sufferings of Jesus, they said, whom they pictured as a very good and rational person as well as being the Son of God, redeemed the world's ills so that virtue triumphed in the end.

How could one repeat this so complacently, after 10 million people had died during 1914–18? The Christian reassurances rang especially hollow in the face of the setbacks to peace and freedom that marked the 1920s. The superficiality of American church life during the flush Harding-Coolidge years was dismaying.

But in Germany itself, where the political and economic situation was more parlous, one could hope that the church was responding more actively. The defeat of the old empire in 1918 had created dangerous circumstances that called for decisive acts of renewal, and the Weimar democracy offered grounds for hope. Despite his reservations about his German training and the German worldview, when my father had a chance to go to Germany in 1923 he imagined he could be at home there, that the intellectual and spiritual cultures of his family's other country might be congenial to him. And he looked forward to meeting his cousins in Lippe Detmold.

The big old farm in Hardissen, whence his father, Gustav, had fled in 1881 to escape the mindless tyranny of an autocratic father, charmed and amazed him. It was a comfy, self-confident place, handsome, effective, dull; no doubt it had been like this for the many centuries the family had lived there. But he could see why the American Niebuhrs had wanted to leave (his father hadn't been the only one). He became uncomfortable with its complacency; it distressed him to see the authoritarian tone with which the farmhands were relegated to a lower table away from the family, with its rigid hierarchies, its pious conventions, its implicit autocracy still.

Things hadn't been at all like this in Illinois. Gustav Niebuhr had come to America a half century before in part because he so admired Abraham Lincoln, and he had developed a great enthusiasm for Teddy Roosevelt's resourceful opposition to the robber barons' predatory greed. Grandfather's pastoral work in California, Missouri, and Utah had confirmed him in his devotion to progressive American politics. The Lippe Niebuhrs, on the other hand, admired Germany's intensely conservative, almost feudal political and business leaders. It seemed that the cousins had responded very differently to the challenges of the twentieth century.

While he was staying with the German Niebuhrs, his Aunt Henrietta gave a reception where my father could meet the local pastor, "a benighted and bigoted man . . . , a 'pietist' in the classical sense of the word," as my father could still remember fifty years later. He found the pastor's political ignorance repellent, not to mention his "sublime knowledge of his own salvation." The conversation took an unpleasant turn when the *Pfarrer* mentioned that he thought Weimar's early woes had been due to the "machinations of a Jew" in the Cabinet, by which he meant Foreign Minister Walther Rathenau, one of Pa's heroes, "a particularly enlightened industrialist who might have saved Germany if there had been more like him." The Niebuhr temper flared "at this manifestation of pious anti–Semitism, and I spoiled my aunt's party," Pa remembered.

The bigotry was especially obnoxious inasmuch as the pastor evidently did not object to the hideous circumstances in which

Rathenau had met his death in June 1922, only a year before this tea party; he had been murdered by right-wing nationalists who were hoping to bring down the Weimar Republic—an ominous premonitory moment in its fragile, brief history. And in only a few short months Hitler was to attempt his National Socialist coup against the Bavarian government in Munich. The Beer Hall Putsch failed, but even before it happened it was clear that German democracy was threatened more by reactionary foes like these killers and the men behind them than by any other danger. To "blame it on the Jews" was unconscionable. (Fifty years later, recalling this pastor and his views, Pa wrote, "I have not had cause to change my mind about the irrelevance of pietistic individualism and perfectionism in all problems of political justice." Not that German Lutheranism, "against the formalism of which pietism was a reaction," was any better.)

During 1922 and 1923 Germany had been rocketing from one crisis to another in an atmosphere of melodramatic instability and fear. The government's reluctance and often its actual inability to repay the huge reparations that the Versailles Treaty had imposed created conditions that fed a turbulent politics of resentment and reaction on the right. Then, six months after Rathenau's death, when Germany defaulted on promised coal deliveries, French and Belgian troops invaded and occupied the Ruhr, taking over its mines and railroads; the German government encouraged a policy of passive resistance to the French and, to defray the costs of supporting the idled workers, recklessly inflated the nation's currency to the point of its collapse.

At this edgy, complex, and dangerous juncture Pa joined a group of American pastors on a "study trip" to see for themselves the situation in the Ruhr. The enmity they witnessed there between French and German seemed palpable, and the Allies' democratic ideals—on behalf of which liberals imagined they had sacrificed their millions of soldiers so recently—had been extinguished. The landscape was blackened with suffering, hunger, poverty, pain, and limitless rage. "The Ruhr cities are the closest thing to hell I have ever seen. I never knew that you could see hatred with the naked eye, but in the Ruhr one is under the illusion this is possible," he reported. For Pa and for Will Scarlett, who together flew from Cologne to London (a first flight for both of them, and the beginning of their friendship), this exposure to the Ruhr was shocking—and neither of them was inexperienced or naïve. Even in London, injurious suspicions seeped into every conversation about the international situation, and they were sickened by the "repetitive exposition of a selfish and nationalistic point of view."

What was a churchman supposed to propose in these circumstances? The German pastors they met in Düsseldorf, Essen, and Berlin, like so many others, could not or would not acknowledge that after the devastations of the Great War, Europe's social, intellectual, and spiritual structures were dead and dying. They would not see that the war's terrible traumas had rent apart nations, families, and communities, and destroyed confidence in many of the cherished verities of Western civilization. For millions of people, this made it easier to argue that modern civilization didn't need religion at all, just as it made it easier to put one's trust in the false religions of communism or National Socialism. The pastors should have been taking account of this.

Only a few of them were. But in Berlin, one young theologian in particular was eager to seize the day. Like my father and his brother, like Will Scarlett and Francis McConnell, the young Paul Tillich believed that the Gospel was ever more relevant, however disregarded, for it expressed the instructions, the "good news," that might guide the perplexed, the wounded, the lost, the oppressed in these dark times. Of course, those in power, those gifted by privilege and position, were as much if not more in need of Christianity's radical, demanding instructions.

Only months after he returned in 1918 from four nightmare years as a pastor in the trenches of the Western front, Tillich had turned up for his teaching assignments at the University of Berlin radiating hope and energy. In their account of this moment, his biographers Wilhelm and Marion Pauck hint at the energy and political forthrightness that was to make this Prussian Lutheran such a tower of strength in the coming years:

> He came to class [in January 1919] dressed in his army greys with the Iron Cross on his chest. ... It soon became clear to his class that Tillich had endured the demons and horrors of war even as they had, but that he seemed unconquered by them. He stood with both feet in the present, wrestling with immediate problems and communicating his certainty that something new was in the making. This expression of faith, together with the favorable attitude toward socialism, was part of his early appeal.

Tillich was later to develop analytically his ideas about the origins and meaning of courage (and grace and wisdom, by the way), but he was already a living demonstration of what he later wrote about as "the courage to be."

With the *kairos* circle of religious socialists in Berlin, Tillich explored his revisionist notions about the New Testament idea of *kairos*—the moment of timely action when the truth of the transcendent eternal breaks into time, the moment when something new must necessarily emerge out of the old, moribund world. The *kairos* socialists believed that the clergy should be engaged with the social and political forces that were working to build the future. But the superintendent of the Protestant Consistory of Brandenburg—a bastion of unrepentant pride in the old Prussia, which scarcely acknowledged that Germany had just been defeated—reprimanded Tillich for speaking at a meeting of Independent Socialists in the spring of 1919, since pastors weren't supposed to engage in politics. As if the superintendent's own support of the status quo ante bellum wasn't political! Tillich was not deterred, which is no surprise. The reactionary church leaders who clung to their memories of the Kaiser's Germany were demonic forces of the evil past, lost in the realm of non-being. Tillich was living in the present—and for the future.

During the mid-1920s and after his first trip to Germany, Pa set to work on his first book, published in 1927 under the title *Does Civilization Need Religion?* In those same years his brother Helmut, still living and working in Illinois, was finishing his doctoral dissertation on the great German historian and theologian Ernst Troeltsch, beginning the translation of a book of Paul Tillich's, and writing a book of his own. In their daily rounds, the Niebuhr brothers were immersed in practical, very American issues of life and work; in their intellectual world they were engaged in German theology and history. It is understandable that the brothers' books were dedicated to the memory of their father.

In *Does Civilization Need Religion?* Pa attacked the presumptions of both liberal Christian theologians and liberal secularists who purported to know how to improve the world. The theologians, he noted, endlessly elaborated their concept of a sweetly perfect, otherworldly Jesus whose teachings could lead mankind to paradise. But they skirted around the contentious New Testament Lord and Savior who "triumphed over the forces of evil," as Pa put it. Where, for them, was the Jesus who cried out, "Woe to you, scribes and Pharisees, hypocrites! For you tithe mint and dill and cumin, and have neglected law, justice and mercy and faith; these you ought to have done, without neglecting the others. You blind guides, straining out a gnat and swallowing a camel!"? Law, justice, mercy, and faith: these were forgotten while the liberal theologians focused on love. But, my father thought, law and justice shouldn't and couldn't be postponed: Christians had to confront, not accommodate, the structures of power that defined society and state, law and justice; a Christian's commitment to the Gospel could not be truly honored otherwise.

And the secular liberal types were equally foolish in their implausible certainty that human rationality and goodness would do the job. Vain expectation! When in human history had that ever been likely? What in the modern world made one imagine it was likely now? Greed, corruption, and vanity were the hallmarks of collective life in the rational, freedom-loving democracies: where could one find reassurance in their grotesque insufficiencies? To the degree that religion had cooperated with secular strategies aimed at making modern progress, it had been co-opted and corrupted. Thus, Pa insisted,

> even the possibility of future usefulness of religion demands the
> largest possible measure of immediate detachment from the

unethical characteristics of modern society. If religion cannot transform society, it must find its social function in criticizing present realities from some ideal perspective and in presenting the ideal without corruption, so that it may sharpen the conscience and strengthen the faith of each generation.

In that same year of 1927, Uncle Helmut opened his fine book on *The Social Sources of Denominationalism* with this implacable passage:

> Christendom has often achieved apparent success by ignoring the precepts of its founder. The church, as an organization interested in self-preservation and in the gain of power, has sometimes found the counsel of the Cross quite as inexpedient as have national and economic groups. In dealing with such major social evils as war, slavery, and social inequality, it has discovered convenient ambiguities in the letter of the Gospel . . . it has found it easier to give to Caesar the things belonging to Caesar if the examination of what might belong to God were not too closely pressed.

I like the inexorable irony of the last sentence especially. Helmut, like my father, was a personally gentle, courteous man, but there was steel in his gaze.

So the question was the eternal one: how did one relate the absolute commands of the religious life to the exigent demands of life in society? "The significance of Jesus for the religious life of the Western world is due to His attainment and incarnation of a spiritual and moral ideal," as my father wrote, and this was an ideal that was not to be compromised in human social existence. But then how was one to try to attain it? Although the modern churches "give themselves to the pleasant hope that time and natural progress will bring inevitable triumph to every virtuous enterprise," the terrible truth was that they were doing nothing about "the brutalities of the economic conflict, the disillusioning realities of international relations, the monstrous avarice of nations, the arrogance of races." This was not right. It was not, indeed, Christian.

The Niebuhr brothers, like Tillich, had for some time been attentive students of Ernst Troeltsch and of his masterpiece *The Social Teachings of the Christian Churches,* which in the Weimar years was a beacon of modern learning for the German clergy. (Troeltsch, dismayed and openly critical of the radical right-wing forces that were threatening Weimar, had died in 1923, just a year after his murdered friend Rathenau.) Study of this important work led them to the works of Max Weber, who had strongly influenced Troeltsch.

The Niebuhrs and Tillich could not have known then that Weber himself had expressed a kindred skepticism about, even a hatred of, the inadequacies of "organized Christendom" in Germany. In an astonishing letter that he wrote in 1906 to the church historian and scholar Adolf Harnack, Weber had contrasted German Lutheranism's abominations with precisely the kind of Protestant reform tradition that was so strong in American life and history:

> As much as Luther towers above all others, Lutheran*ism* is for me, I don't deny, in its *historical* manifestations the most horrible of horrors, and even its ideal form . . . is for me, *for us Germans*, a structure that can exert I am not entirely certain how much force on the way life is lived. It is an intrinsically difficult and tragic situation: *none* of us can himself be a "sect"-person, Quaker, Baptist, etc., *everyone* of us can see immediately the fundamental superior-

ity of the established church measured by *non*-ethical and *non*-religious values. And the age of "sects" or something essentially like them is historically quite gone. But that our nation never went through the school of rigorous asceticism in *any* form is, on the other hand, the source of everything I find loathsome in it (as in myself), and moreover, in terms of *religious* values, I can't help thinking the average American sect-person ranks as high above our established-church "Christians" as Luther, as a religious person, ranked above Calvin, Fox, *e tutti quanti.*

What did he mean by this? Weber found it "loathsome" that Lutheran Germans—not having experienced the "rigorous asceticism," the austere self-questioning, the skepticism about political authority that was endemic among Protestantism's radical sects—lacked the power and freedom to shape their own lives. This was a fascinating, complicated insight, and rare in its time. (In a similar vein, Pa was later to say that Lutheranism lacked the "certain degree of mature disillusionment required for appreciation of the Christian religion in its more classical form.") The great Weber expressed his misgivings privately, and they weren't part of the public judgment of the time, but they were precisely the misgivings that animated good parts of the Niebuhrs' and Tillich's later critiques.

The Weimar years were desperate, but one had to live in hope. Tillich was working very hard in Berlin to create the intellectual structures and social contexts for a truly modern pastorate and an ethically responsible theology, and my father and his brother were hardly inactive in America. So when my father returned to Germany one year later, in 1924, and again in 1930, he searched out interesting Evangelical pastors to discuss with them the future of the church, of Christianity. The German clerics were guardedly optimistic: they weren't quite so opaque and self-righteous as the pastor Pa had tangled with in 1923.

But then one of the best and brightest of them confided to him that nothing would improve until "we get the Jews out of politics." This kind of remark made one's heart sink. My father found it outrageous: he did not believe that there was any serious theological or cultural basis for a Christian to consider such bigotry permissible, however customary it might have been, however condoned or even encouraged. This was the twentieth century, after all, and it was not too much to expect decent people to try to move beyond the murky medievalism of Christianity's worst moments. Granted, such anti-Semitism was widespread and often flagrant, a sign of the moral bankruptcy and tawdry superficiality of churches everywhere, but that made it only all the more important to uphold the central Christian doctrines that found it sinful.

Alas, the theological faculties and churches in Germany were filled—as organized religion everywhere so often is—with banal, corrupted, thoughtless people. And so certain of their own godliness! "These kinds of people are ruining our world," my father wrote. "If the world will go down, it will go down not by the hands of criminals, but by the hands of those who were so conscious of their righteousness." It was dismaying to find the deeply conservative theologians so self-satisfied—and this in the "mother-nation of theological liberalism." If only their sense of things was "more relevant to the desperate moral situation which a modern industrial nation faces!" He thought most of Germany's official church was living as if in the pre-1914 epoch—as if Germany had not been defeated in 1918—

and he compared its "thoughtless identification of *Christentum und Deutschtum*" to the "naive nordicism of our Klan-infested churches in the Deep South." It was sinister, wrong, dangerous.

Ironically, Pa concluded that American church life had at least a potential vitality and attentiveness to ethical and social issues that the German churches lacked. But he also pointed out that "an organization of religious leaders calling themselves 'religious socialists,' in which, among others, the young philosopher of religion Paul Tillich is active, has been working on the problem of religion and labor with a thoroughness and honesty which no American religious organization has yet approached." Would that those brave, thorough, honest efforts in Germany had had time to bear fruit! They were soon struck down, ruthlessly.

I ponder the reasons for the clarity and power of the Niebuhr brothers' insights, as I ponder the reasons for Tillich's extraordinary strength in Berlin. My hunch is that the tough-minded theology and political independence were effects, not causes, of their spiritual strength. These three tremendously different men—one in Detroit, one in Illinois, and one in Berlin—related their teaching and their public work to their Christian faith with a kind of urgent calm and energy which was, for those who knew them, their most striking quality. This was a courage that quite transcended the differences between Germany and America, between Lutheran and Calvinist, Evangelical or Reformed, and it was recognizable anywhere.

However, though Max Weber may have respected the relatively high standards of the average American "sect-person," the sectarian leaders of most American churches shared the German pastors' myopic complacency and anti-Semitism. The parsons were, as to a dismaying degree they still are, rather conventional and tidy-minded bureaucrats with a taste for local power and a badly limited worldview. The same could be said of their Roman Catholic counterparts. As tense, anxious seasons passed in Detroit, my father became ever more impatient with the bland irrelevance of his fellow pastors' "Christian thought," as impatient as he was grateful for the fervent civic energies of a Jewish businessman and one or two other activists who had worked with him on Detroit's race-relations board and with whom he'd become friends.

It's no surprise, then, that virtually no American pastors or priests spoke out on the subject of the Nazi assault on Jews when it came. And naturally, given the circumambient anti-Semitism of American society, neither did many rabbis. The few voices heard were those of scholars at divinity schools teaching only a tiny percentage of America's clergy; while influential in their own way, they did not command ecclesiastical power structures.

It's instructive, and gratifying, to hear the steady tone in the pronouncements of those very few who *did* understand the urgency. They didn't have to wait until disaster struck in 1933 to know how much this mattered. The American theologian Paul Lehmann and my father, to name but two of the few, were outspoken in their denunciation of the theological inadequacy of Christian double-talk about Jews; so was Wilhelm Pauck, the noted German historian of theology and fine Luther scholar, trained in Berlin by Harnack and Troeltsch and since 1926 teaching in Chicago. This had been a key issue for centuries, of course, but in the Weimar years it was even more salient. All three made a point of noting the sinister connection between

anti-democratic indifference and piously anti-Semitic impreca-
tion, whether in Germany or the United States, and they noted
it early on. Needless to say they had no expectation that Germany's "official Christians" would oppose the godless ranting of
Nazi demagogues and terrorists when these terrible people
came to power; they already knew that "official Christendom"
was fatally corrupted and weak.

THE APATHY AND INDIFFERENCE of most clergymen to the
crises of the Great Crash and the worldwide Depression that
followed, not to mention their prejudiced and reactionary selfishness, are not surprising, then. The churches' vacuity and vap-
idity during the Roaring Twenties had given ample warning.
Still, they are shocking. The parsons, having failed to be on
guard against the dangers of unwarranted affluence in the
1920s, were equally unarmed against the chaotic impoverish-
ment of their flocks when the stock market crash of 1929
brought the economies of the West stumbling to a halt.

How did one extract meaning from this? How did one
respond? It was not easy to formulate a coherent answer,
heaven knows. Lulled by the bland nostrums offered by Herbert Hoover, Americans seemed to be losing a sense of themselves as a democratic society, abandoning themselves to
cynicism and indifference. And their pastors, too, snoozed opti-
mistically through the gray years of 1930–32, reassuring their
congregations that soon all would be well. With very few
exceptions the leaders of the American Catholic Church, along
with Episcopalians, Lutherans, Baptists and Congregationalists,
remained silent or evasive about the crises threatening America's spiritual and social life. When the fatuously optimistic

Unitarian Reverend John Haynes Holmes opined in 1931 that Europe was "slowly but surely approaching the longed-for goal of harmony and peace," a Niebuhr rebuke thundered back: "Let Liberal Churches Stop Fooling Themselves!" Among the less "liberal" Presbyterians, Baptists, and Methodists—divided between North and South, the racist Southern wings of all of them being rigidly segregationist—it was if possible even worse. (Alas, the color line in these churches still holds across most of the South and much of the North; neither blacks nor whites seem much disposed to erase it.) In the bitter gloom of these Hoover years, the American people were sinking. Decline was accelerating.

American Protestantism's official leadership group, the Federal Council of Churches of Christ, did its best to throw light into the shadowy corners of American public life, but it faced heavy opposition. Social activism of any kind—which was obviously what was needed at this juncture—continued to be deplored. The fact that in 1930 the resourceful and experienced Bishop McConnell happened to be president of the FCCC attracted not gratitude but reactionary lightning, and my father's presence on the FCCC's masthead didn't exactly help. All the more so since at that juncture he had agreed to participate as a Socialist Party candidate in a legislative campaign on New York's Upper West Side—a single, unrepeated foray into electoral politics born of despair in the nadir of the Depression.

When it was learned that Bishop McConnell favored the reelection in 1930 of the austere reformer Senator George Norris of Nebraska—the splendidly independent Republican politician who had left his party in disgust, who had voted to outlaw yellow-dog contracts, who believed in the liberating possibilities of publicly owned hydroelectric power and public natural resources—the conservative clergy called their business pals into action against him. An editorial in the *Chicago Journal of Commerce* amused McConnell and my father:

> Bishop Francis J. McConnell, President of the Federal Council of Churches of Christ in America, is one of the many radicals inhabiting other states than Nebraska who sent pleas into Nebraska for the renomination and re-election of Senator Norris, member of the coal-and-power socializing committee of the Intercollegiate Socialist Society.... Professor Reinhold Niebuhr ... is chairman of the social service commission of the FCCC [and] candidate of the Socialist Party for member of the New York State Senate from the nineteenth senatorial district in Manhattan. There seems to be no further doubt that the FCCC has gone socialist.

I wonder what the Chicago Chamber of Commerce thought when that scion of a great Ohio Republican family, Mayor Charles Taft of Cincinnati—Chief Justice William Howard Taft's son, Senator Robert Taft's brother—became the first lay president of the Federal Council.

By 1933 fully 25 percent of the labor force was out of work and destitute, its morale and health broken; the economy was in advanced chaos; and most people were living without insurance, without hope, without sustenance. You would have thought they deserved some straightforward clarity about moral "priorities," but it was not forthcoming. Help eventually came in the national political arena; it did not come in America's parishes or local communities.

It's amazing, really, to see what so-called community leaders were up to in 1932–33. In the church, the picture was quite clear. Bishops, archbishops, pastors, editors in the church press, elders, rectors, and wardens—these big shots devoted their energies to preserving their positions, augmenting their safety, insulating their precincts from one another's doctrinal "impurities." Their first obligation was to themselves.

The Scriptures are unambiguous about this dreadful inclination of priests to advance their own cause. One thinks of St. Mark's account of Jesus preaching to "the common people," who "heard him gladly. And he said unto them in his doctrine, Beware of the scribes, which love to go in long clothing, and love salutations in the marketplaces, and the chief seats in the synagogues, and the uppermost rooms at feasts; which devour widows' houses, and for a pretence make long prayers: these shall receive greater damnation." Damnation seems the right word. But the underlying selfishness is an illness to which we are all prone, a disease whose symptoms we always find hard to recognize. And the selfishness breeds indifference. One of my father's prayers addressed this particular sin, from which he did not of course exempt himself:

> We give you thanks, O Lord, for life and love and the joy of existence, for the echo in human hearts to all pure and lovely things, for the promise of life and youth and the dawn of the unknown, and for the hope and assurance of fulfillment. . . .
>
> We confess that we are not worthy of the riches of life for which the generation of men have labored that we might enter into this heritage. We confess the sorry confusion of our common life, the greed which disfigures our collective life and sets man against his fellowmen. We confess the indifference and callousness with which we treat the sufferings and the insecurity of

the poor, and the pettiness which mars the relations between us. May we with contrite hearts seek once more to purify our spirits, and to clarify our reason, so that a fairer temple for the human spirit may be built in human society.

WHEN MY FATHER WENT once again to Germany in 1930, he went not from Detroit, which he had left in 1928, but from New York City, where he had accepted a position on the faculty of Union Seminary. He was in Germany on his way to the Soviet Union, which he was going to visit on a fact-finding mission with Senator Alben Barkley of Kentucky (later to be Harry Truman's vice president). Together they looked at Potemkin villages and incompetently run collective farms, and together these commonsensical sons of Kentucky and Missouri could see for themselves that the promise of Soviet communism was a false promise, that this was certainly not the future. Their disaffection from the actualities of what was still for many the hoped-for revolutionary new world required, my father realized, that he rethink many of the rather conventional Marxist positions he had once espoused. It was a useful and sobering encounter, and it served him in good stead.

Thirty or forty years later, "new left" critics used to claim that early anti-communism of this sort was a sign of a weak commitment to radical politics, or of corrupted careerism, or of a regrettable eagerness to become more "mainstream"—none of which remotely applies in my father's case. In fact it's nonsense. Anyway, I'm not impressed by their judgment about such matters, since these same critics nonetheless have often given credit to those who arrived much later at the same disillusionment with the Soviet Union—after the Moscow show trials, or the

Spanish Civil War, or the Nazi-Soviet pact, or even after 1948, or 1956—as if somehow the delay in coming to one's senses shows a truer radicalism.

Daniel Bell has written that he was saved from this political stupidity by a professor of his at City College in New York in the early 1930s, who discussed with his class the famous uprising against the Bolshevik regime by sailors at the Kronstadt naval base. In 1921 Lenin's regime had put down the mutiny among these "darlings of the Revolution" only with difficulty and after much bloodshed; the brutal repression shocked many who until then had been sympathetic to the Communist experiment, and the very name "Kronstadt" became a code word for disillusion with the USSR. The professor, expatiating on years of enchantment and disenchantment with Soviet politics, shrewdly told his class, "The best answer to the question, 'When was your Kronstadt?' is, 'My Kronstadt was Kronstadt.' "

It was in that same year of 1930 that the Niebuhr brothers in America broke off relations with their German cousins in Lippe Detmold, after receiving letters reporting contentedly on Hitler's early electoral advances there and on the cousins' consequent hopes for a positive, better future for Germany. The American Niebuhrs were aghast at the German Niebuhrs' complacent enthusiasm for National Socialism. My Aunt Hulda, a teacher of religious education, and Mütterchen continued to send Christmas and birthday greetings, keeping up a modicum of family news-exchange, but my father and uncle demurred. They had their hands full, their spirit committed elsewhere.

CLAYTON C. MORRISON, editor of the monthly *Christian Century*, was an earnest, good man who completely failed to see the sinister dangers of which my father and his brother wrote, though he was routinely pessimistic about world affairs. His views had long been at odds with my father's, but he was a shrewd enough magazine editor to persuade Pa to write a regular column for him, in which my father inveighed against *The Christian Century*'s standard pacifist-neutralist (also anti-Semitic) editorial line—this was all no doubt good for circulation. In 1931, Morrison gave my parents some beautiful Chinese embroidered linen place mats as a wedding present—I still use them, thinking of all this as I do—telling them in a note that he admired but could not share their brave optimism at a time so dark and full of foreboding. Such gloom, my father thought, rested on sloppy foundations, on inadequately reasoned Christian faith.

This was a matter his new English bride understood immediately. Ursula Keppel-Compton had turned up in one of his courses at Union in 1930—she was one of two foreign students around that year—and she had a sharp, extremely well trained mind; she had just come down from Oxford with an honors degree (a "double first") in theology and history. (When she won a coveted fellowship to Union for a year, President Coffin had objected to having the honor go to a woman. The Regius Professors of Divinity at Oxford and Cambridge, however, who determined the winner, insisted.) Her clarity of mind, like her intense blue-eyed, blonde beauty, was soon well-known to my father's political, secular friends and to her fellow seminarians. By the end of the academic year the two were engaged, and the wedding was set for the following December, in England.

My mother brought to Pa's personal intellectual life—he

already had a bent for British, especially Labour Party, history and politics—a welcome dose of English skepticism, with her dislike of woozy German profundity and academic pretension. Also, she had interesting friends among English clergy, both Nonconformist and Anglican, whom he was shortly to come to know. Since she was deeply devoted to the liturgy, theology, and music of the Church of England, there were tensions between her views on proper forms of worship and those of my father, who was used to the freewheeling improvisational daily prayers and stem-winding sermons of the Evangelical tradition. This liturgical discord was to create a lively, sometimes difficult ground bass in the music of my childhood.

I never got a clear idea of what my English grandparents thought of their youngest daughter's turning up with a Missouri fiancé, except that they were quite genial about it. (I do know that however conventional they may have been in some respects, they were remarkably open in their enthusiasm for transatlantic culture and global experience: their other daughter was working in Prague for a German-Jewish bank; one son was in Africa, where he spent three decades in the Colonial Service; and the other was studying music in Austria.) Nor can I imagine what they thought of my father's polemical left-wing politics, although I know they forgave him for writing an article entitled "Great Britain in Second Place" just before the wedding.

My parents married in Winchester Cathedral in December 1931, she in tea-dipped ecru lace, he impressed into a morning suit (though he drew the line at spats and refused to wear them). Together they chose the hymns for the service (we sang them again, as they requested, at their funerals): one the beautiful George Herbert translation of the Twenty-third Psalm,

"The God of Love My Shepherd Is," and another the noble anthem "Ye Watchers and Ye Holy Ones." "We stood on either side of the tomb of a Saxon king," my father would tell us. "Can you imagine a yahoo like me from a farm in Missouri in such a situation?"

The other foreign student at Union Seminary in 1930–31 was a German Lutheran named Dietrich Bonhoeffer. During that year at Union, none of his teachers or fellow students could have had an inkling of Bonhoeffer's destiny as "a twentieth-century Christian martyr," as the psychoanalyst Robert Coles and many others have labeled this now famous figure—and not only because the future is always unknowable. The fact was that in 1930 Bonhoeffer's capacity to relate his Christian commitments to his active life was still undeveloped and unclear. It took time for his ideas about Christian action to evolve; his last writings, from the 1940s, show that his spirit never ceased to grow and was still expanding as he faced execution, in 1945, with unflinching courage and serenity.

My mother never thought Bonhoeffer was much of a theologian, though she greatly respected his spiritual and political courage during the last years of his life. Perhaps it would be more accurate to say that she was in a position to witness how much he changed and grew from the conceited classmate he'd been in 1930, when he was snobbishly critical of his fellow students at Union, and with comprehensive European arrogance dismissed the lectures he heard there, along with most American intellectual life, as "shallow." So easy for him to say! He was so much more densely and seriously educated than the other students! He was so well attuned to religion as, in his words, the "transcendent experience of Goodness, Beauty, Truth and

Holiness"! He was proud of being among the first to bring the new ideas of the eminent Swiss theologian Karl Barth to American shores, but my mother and plenty of others noted that he seemed, in the theologically conventional way, indifferent to their ethical inadequacies.

Barth was famous for challenging the liberal orthodoxies of modern European Protestantism with his rigorous insistence on a pure understanding of the Word of God, the only light shining in the darkness, as he believed, acceptance or nonacceptance of it being a pure mystery of grace. This was an interpretation of Christian doctrine that properly emphasized certain ineffable truths about faith vis-à-vis the tragedy of human history—on that my father and Bonhoeffer could agree. But Niebuhr and others were already contesting not so much Barth's precise formulations as his insistence on ignoring the consequences of maintaining a notionally uncontaminated church community, pure and removed from the messy facts of political strife. Barth's spiritual instructions may have been brave and profound, but the widespread habit of declining to relate them to people's political situation could only have baleful consequences.

Barth's position on this point had a tragic irony: he had deplored, indeed hated, the German churches' shockingly nationalistic tone during the blood-soaked years of the Great War, their conflation of Christian goals and values with imperial German ones. So his clarity in denouncing this corruption, in insisting on the absolute value of the Christian commitment, was a welcome antidote to the poisonous distortions he had witnessed during the war. Some years later, in 1934, his refusal to countenance Hitler's ruthless commands that Christian cloth be cut to National Socialist patterns had a similar nobility:

Jesus Christ, as he is attested to us in Holy Scripture, is the one Word of God whom we have to hear, and whom we have to trust and obey in life and in death. We reject the false doctrine that the church could and should recognize as a source of its proclamation, beyond and besides this one Word of God, yet other events, powers, historic figures, and truths as God's revelation. . . . We reject the false doctrine that there could be areas of our life in which we would belong not to Jesus Christ but to other lords, areas in which we would not need justification and sanctification through him.

But was this the only thing to insist on in those difficult years right after the Great War? The soil of German democracy was still thin and ill nourished; pastors and their flocks alike were haunted by death and travail, by fear and mourning. Were pastors simply to ignore these circumstances? Throughout the defeated land, leaders were encouraging the Germans to believe in false notions about their nation's past, including its culpability (or, as they put it, innocence) in the war. To say nothing about these misrepresentations was to collaborate in a great deceit.

It was fatally wrong, my father thought, to advise Germany's pastors to have nothing to do with politics in these (as in any contested) circumstances. In mid-1919, just as the Weimar Republic was being established, at a conference of religious socialists Barth had urged everyone to work through the church, not against it; they must not link the church to any social program or political party, he said. He wanted to repudiate the arrogant marriage of the German churches with the hawkish, warmongering nationalists of 1914–18, but in admonishing the left-wing pastors to abstain from their quite different political activity, he was in effect leaving the field to their fascistically inclined colleagues, who had no such scruples and were ambitious to boot.

Again it comes down to the basic question of how to think about one's religious faith in relation to the rest of one's life. Churches and their congregants perforce are in the world, after all, and one cannot pretend otherwise. No amount of inner commitment to one's personal beliefs can excuse one from the requirement to relate them somehow to one's community life. R. H. Tawney wrote, "Obviously religion is 'a thing of the Spirit.' But the social order is also a thing of the spirit. The forms of economic organisation which a society establishes, the property rights which it maintains, the relations between its members which it sanctions—these things . . . reflect its scale of moral preferences." If you don't link your Christian faith to the social and economic situation, then are you saying it has no bearing on your view of society's scale of moral preferences?

For the Barthians, as my father put it, insofar as his "theology reintroduces the note of tragedy in religion, it is a wholesome antidote to the superficial optimism of most current theology. But it is quite possible that it has the moral limitation that it preoccupies the soul with an ultimate problem of life, to such a degree that it loses interest in specific moral problems and struggles which must be faced day by day."

By the time the 1930s had run their "low dishonest" course and war had erupted all over Europe, my father and his likeminded colleagues were even more outspoken about this tendency to decry political corruption and remain aloof from the dangers as they grew exponentially. Pa became harsher about what he saw as the Barthian mistake. He wrote that Barth "applies a doctrine of total depravity to the political realm, and therefore he cannot deal with the actualities of politics, which represent bewildering mixtures of idealism and self-interest, of the sense of justice and the inclination to injustice. . . . He bids the Church to wait until the issues are clear before it bears [its] heroic witness [to the resurrection], just as he himself waited in witnessing against Hitlerism."

In New York in 1931, Bonhoeffer's teachers and fellow students therefore challenged him on his Barthian theology of witness. The Scottish John Baillie, a professor of systematic theology, observed that Bonhoeffer "was then the most convinced disciple of Dr. Barth that had appeared among us up to that time, and withal as stout an opponent of [theological] liberalism as had ever come my way." Everyone liked Bonhoeffer, but he hadn't yet learned what Aunt Ethel already knew, what some of his "naïve" American fellow students at Union already knew: that to put one's faith to the test of lived experience is to put one's life on the line.

On March 23, 1933, the Enabling Act gave the new National Socialist government the dictatorial powers it demanded. A month later, Bonhoeffer—now back in Germany—opined, good Lutheran that he was, that the church "has neither to praise nor to censure the laws of the state," and much as he disliked the Nazis he kept his head down. But then a few months on, perturbed by the German churches' evident willingness to accept Hitler's policy of imposing "racial uniformity" within their parishes ("The Jewish question troubles the church very much and here [in Berlin] even the most intelligent people have entirely lost their heads and their Bibles over it"), he spoke out eloquently in opposition to the regime. The church, he declared, had the obligation "not just to bind up the victims beneath the wheel, but to halt the wheel itself." But how would this be done? Who would put the stick in the spokes of the Nazi wheel? Would *he*? Bonhoeffer left for a temporary, perhaps temporizing job in London without answering the question.

A year later, in a celebrated speech Bonhoeffer insisted on the Christian obligation to renounce force. But how could you fulfill your obligation to stop the Nazi wheel, the wheel of a well-armed, aggressive machine of terror, if you had renounced the use of force? Bonhoeffer did not have an answer here, either. Like many Christian pastors of the time he considered himself a pacifist. At an international youth conference in 1934 a Swedish student walking on a beach with him asked, "What would you do, sir, if war broke out?" And, it is said, "Reflectively, he allowed the sand to trickle through his fingers, then turned calmly toward the questioner and replied: 'I pray that God will give me the strength not to take up arms.'"

DURING THOSE SAME seasons of 1932–34, the young American pastors who had been in class with Bonhoeffer at Union and whom he had mocked for their naïveté were already risking their lives in another kind of war, and while they hadn't taken up arms, certainly arms were taken up against them. Bonhoeffer had astutely noticed the shocking racism of American society, but he may not have given equal attention or respect to his American colleagues' commitment to changing it. Now some of his classmates were busy trying to help black farmers and white workers in interracial parishes, schools, and labor groups they helped to organize in the South and Middle West.

The tone, the atmosphere, of the radical seminarians who

studied with my father in the early 1930s was wonderfully astringent and clearheaded. Years later they were still my family's dear friends and heroes. Their mix of practical political courage, social energy, spiritual depth, and cultural vivacity was intoxicating, and I miss it. Again, it took me far too long to recognize how unusual they were: I made the happy, stupid mistake of thinking lots of Americans were like them. Alas no. They were a small, embattled minority, albeit in some quarters a respected, honored one. And now? Historical amnesia having reached epidemic proportions, especially about principled opponents of American capitalism such as they, I fear lest their work has been forgotten.

For example, there was Myles Horton, another student at Union in 1930. "I wasn't a typical seminary student, I didn't have the academic background," he wrote in his memoirs. He was, in his own words, a mountain man from Tennessee. "I went to Union because I had problems reconciling my religious background with the economic conditions I saw in society. . . . I wanted to see if I could get help on my ethical ideas. . . . I went to learn things that would be useful when I returned to the mountains." He found other students who cared about the same issues—"I talked about my ideas to everybody I thought would be interested—and some who weren't. Most of us were students of Reinhold Niebuhr"—and after he'd returned to Tennessee he persuaded some of them to join him. By the spring of 1932, he had worked out plans for an interracial school that would serve the impoverished people of Appalachia, and Pa agreed to send out a fund-raising letter on its behalf. Soon Horton and another student named James Dombrowski had the Highlander School up and running.

Modest but effective efforts like theirs to improve social and racial justice in the South were bound to run into all kinds of hostility, which Horton was good at defusing but which never disappeared. Lynchings, Ku Klux Klan rallies, and race riots were, after all, regular ongoing features of the American experience. The violent danger that attended all the issues involving black and white workers came close to being a "war," to use Horton's own word, when efforts were made to unionize industry in the South. Highlander was helping the Congress of Industrial Organizations to do just that. Just how powerful the entrenched corporate interests were in defeating this drive can be measured by noting that even now most southern workers earn their livings completely without the wage, safety, and fiduciary protections that the unions wanted to obtain for them.

In 1933 the president of a local United Mine Workers chapter, Barney Graham, was targeted after he'd led the miners out on a strike; everyone knew that the coal companies had hired professional thugs to rub him out. (Eleven men had been murdered in similar circumstances during a recent labor dispute in Illinois.) Graham "knew he was going to be killed, because that's what happened to people like him in those days," as Horton put it, and he did everything he could to bring public attention to the impending crime. But his efforts were unavailing, and in desperation the angry miners discussed the idea of killing the killers before they struck again. Horton, in principle and practice just as pacifist as Bonhoeffer, pointed out to them that this would "start a war" in which not only they but plenty of other people "would get killed."

Horton was tormented by Graham's murder when it came, and he never forgot his dilemma—having known the man would die and having been unable to keep this from happening. When he discussed the principles of nonviolence with his pacifist friends, he'd talk about the decision that he and the miners had faced. He'd ask them, "Did I do the right thing? What would you have done?" But he was shocked to see that he "couldn't get anybody in the room to say anything other than that they wouldn't get themselves in such a situation." This was not an option! Even Bonhoeffer knew that. Life *put* you in these situations: did they mean they'd run away from the problem? that they'd solve the problem before it arose? that they'd discourage the miners from trying to improve their lot? The choice for nonviolence over violence is easy when you think it's simple, but it's never simple. He wondered if these pacifist ministers were going to put themselves on the front lines in the "struggle to build a decent society that can be nonviolent," as he wisely defined his own efforts.

The brave work continued all over the South and Middle West. Jim Dombrowski, already acquainted with trouble because of his union work in Pennsylvania, moved on to Mississippi, which was even more dangerous. Elsewhere, two other seminarians were jailed on charges of criminal syndicalism. (This arcane fascistic law used everywhere against "socialist agitators" reappeared thirty years later as a trusty weapon wielded by white-supremacist policemen in the South against the next generation of civil-rights workers.) "We cannot save our civilization at all except we change its whole basis, nothing less," wrote my father in a magazine called *The Unemployed*, put out by the League for Industrial Democracy. Unemployed people then counted almost 13 million in the United States, but the point was not just people who were out of work. Change was absolutely required for everyone.

Yet overall very few Americans or Germans went along with my father's radical notions about the need for change in 1931, let alone in 1933 or 1936. And there certainly weren't many like-minded clergy, those wonderful students at Union notwithstanding. Even twenty and thirty years later my father was still viewed in most churches as dangerously "pink," and their pastors didn't want to have anything to do with him. True, exciting new thinkers were transforming classrooms in those interwar years, and a few of them were welcomed in university chapels—my father virtually rode circuit from campus to campus during the academic year—but they were rarely invited into, or respected in, ordinary parishes. All too often, Christians were serenely accepting the idea that since it seemed pretty difficult to change things, it was okay serenely to endure the odious status quo.

Many people who heard my father teach and preach in the 1930s and well into the 1950s have told me how vividly they remember his lectures and sermons, and I remember some of the sermons myself—with their open-ended questions, their proposed answers discarded when seen as inadequate, their challenges to pious certainties, their barbed inquiries that got under the skin of placid self-righteousness. The congregations could tell that the religious and ethical probing was genuinely a personal spiritual quest. Certainly I know how hard, within himself, he struggled to stay clear of what he knew to be an inevitable human sin, about which he preached so often: that of believing that what you are doing is good, is right, is virtuous, when of course you can't possibly judge this yourself.

I think even his voice made the difficulties clear. He sounded like what he had been to start with, a young parson in a community of German-speaking farmers in southern Illinois, so the plain Middle Western, middle American speech had a hint of the kinder vowels and rhythmic intensity you get in the South, along with a certain German precision and majesty. But any listener's attention was caught by the alternations of speed, from a slow, thinking-aloud meditative pace to a rapidly, apparently improvised and accelerating riff at a passage that wound up an important point. The variations were many and dramatic, but the purpose was always to drive home a vexing point, a difficult paradox.

In the handful of college chapels where he preached for thirty years, he excited the students' seriousness, challenged their presumptions, stirred up their faith or lack of it; he was not easily forgotten. The South African Alan Paton, a Christian liberal reformer who was working on his great novel *Cry, the Beloved Country* when he encountered Pa in London shortly after the Second World War, called him "the best speaker I heard in my life; he spoke for an hour without notes, and he had us in the hollow of his hand." But beyond those college campuses where he was a hardy perennial, only two or three churches in America invited him to preach—one in Philadelphia, another in Chicago, as I remember.

The warmest welcome came from St. George's Episcopal Church, on Stuyvesant Square in New York, where for many years Pa preached on the second Sunday in January. Afterward we'd be invited to lunch with the church's chief warden, C. C. Burlingham, a sensational old gentleman who befriended me (we were roughly eighty years apart). Since this annual event fell near my birthday, he made sure to have a fancy, frosted cake for the luncheon dessert and would give me a mischievous little present. But politics and liberal theology were inevitably the mealtime topics—I was used to that.

St. George's was one of the oldest churches in New York, with a long tradition of social activism and community involvement, and while Episcopalians might be the poshest people in the neighborhood, Burlingham thought this meant simply that they had to work harder to be Christian. Here was yet another intrepid progressive with a merry sense of humor and a fearless commitment to social justice. It was impossible to be intimidated by him, any more than by Bishop Scarlett or Justice Frankfurter or Myles Horton.

For most of the twentieth century Burlingham had been not just a Harvard patriot, a fine admiralty lawyer, and an indefatigable social activist, but a true legend in New York City politics, where throughout his long life (he lived to be almost 100) he gave unflagging attention to new developments in the city's social and political life. He liked, as he put it, to "meddle" in politics. Some meddling! For one thing, he helped to put some of America's greatest judges on the bench in New York—like Benjamin Cardozo and Learned Hand. For another, his behind-the-scenes maneuvers made possible the Fusion reform ticket that landed Fiorello La Guardia in City Hall in 1934 and kept him there for three terms. (The irrepressible Jewish-Italian mayor had gained a national reputation as a junior congressman in the 1920s, when he had joined the protests against the Sacco-Vanzetti verdict and earned Felix Frankfurter's admiration. But of course.)

Naturally CCB had many friends in Heath, and my father and he had mutual friends in the lively world of progressive New York politics: a key seemed to be Frankfurter, who always knew everybody. CCB and FF were both legal members, as my father and Will Scarlett were clerical members, of what for me was a magic planetary society of good people. If you added their friends and associates, the allies in England and Scandinavia, the fellow workers in the South and West, you got a sense of ever expanding potentials for reform and improvement. They were all so completely matter-of-fact about their politics, and their tone was so buoyantly upbeat, that despite the odds against them I naturally believed they would prevail in the end. I know better now, as they did themselves then.

People like Alan Paton or CCB or Myles Horton are rare at any juncture of history. How many among us are ready to hear our prejudices challenged, our spiritual sloth disturbed? How many of us are ready, willing, and able not just to argue but to work for a complete restructuring of our postmodern, post-industrial, but alas not post-unjust society? It was unusual then, and probably even more so today.

Many long years later, in the spring of 1981, I happened to turn on the television set one Saturday—it was the afternoon of the Kentucky Derby, and I hoped to watch it—and as the TV flickered on, I saw Bill Moyers interviewing an old gentleman in a rocking chair. I knew that Moyers, who had been President Lyndon Johnson's press secretary before he became a celebrated broadcaster, had trained for the ministry in the Southern Baptist church and was known in Texas for his liberalism. I had no idea who the other man was. The two were sitting on a porch, and you could see behind them a sublime landscape of wooded mountains. " . . . Mah political gaahds?" the old gentleman was repeating Moyers's question in a beautiful Southern voice. "Oh, Ah'd say Shelleh." My Yankee ears couldn't catch this, and I had to listen more carefully. "Yes," he went on, "Shelleh, Mox, and Reinie Niebah."

Tears of happiness bolted from my eyes. It was Myles Horton, bless him! Just to hear his voice touched my heart, but my nostalgia for his robust, unpretentious political courage nearly broke it. This was just what I remembered from my childhood—these intrepid marvelous people! The crucible that was the Great Depression had been an experience that for some had forged real character: as my father always insisted, the important distinction was, or should have been, not between *which* formulas for improvement one fought for, but that one fought at all, since altogether too many people took no position and defended this fatuity as respectable caution.

In adversity, a glaring beam of ethical consequence lights the moment when one chooses action or inaction, and it throws up sharp shadows. This is what Myles Horton had understood. To take no position at such a moment is to be prey to fascism: that's the way we saw it. Blind acceptance of the status quo cannot possibly be called a true choice to "accept what cannot be changed." Anyway, fifty years after he'd been a student at Union, here was this fine Southern schoolteacher naming Niebuhr, Marx, and Percy Bysshe Shelley as his guides to a lifetime of dangerous opposition to entrenched segregationism!

Moyers was interviewing Horton on the grounds of the Highlander School, in Tennessee's beautiful Cumberland Mountains. It was at Highlander in the 1960s that the first workshops were held to train black and white students and ministers in Gandhi's techniques of nonviolent civil disobedience. These were the vanguard civil-rights protesters who went on to challenge the evil racial laws and customs of the South. Horton had always been courageously committed to changing what had to be changed, and mercifully he lived to see some of his efforts bear fruit in the Civil Rights and Voting Rights Acts passed during the Johnson administration. And there he was, reminding us of how he had started.

A direct line ran from his Union classes in 1930 to Birmingham and Selma—that he made clear. He had gone north to Union in the first place because he wanted to study with theologians who were exploring ethical and religious issues that were going unheeded in the white South. My father had written then, "It is hopeless for the Negro to expect complete emancipation from the menial social and economic position into which the white man has forced him, merely by trusting in the moral sense of the white race. It is equally hopeless to attempt emancipation through violent rebellion," which would only "accentuate the animosities and prejudices of his oppressors."

Pa believed that the only possible hope was to employ all the techniques of nonviolent resistance to break the stranglehold of white supremacism, and this was something the churches ought to further. They had much to learn from Mohandas Gandhi, and from his insights into the moral and ethical landscape of public affairs. "There is no problem of political life to which the religious imagination can make a larger contribution than this problem of developing non-violent resistance," he wrote in 1932—a time when Southern churches had long since abdicated their obligations to the Gospel in favor of reinforcing their privileged congregants' worst racial prejudices, their most selfish social attitudes. Horton had worked hard on these themes at Union, and then, back in the South, he had in turn passed on the lessons to the ministers and students who were to found the

Southern Christian Leadership Conference and the Student Nonviolent Coordinating Committee.

And he was still at it—now, fifty years later, with Martin Luther King Jr. and Robert Kennedy dead, with Americans sourly, grimly, yet eagerly having settled for the criminal malefactions of a bigoted reactionary like Richard Nixon. At least Horton could take some comfort from the recent experience—unthinkable earlier—of having a Southern liberal Democrat in the White House. (Jimmy Carter had long supported another interracial initiative in the South that Pa had dealings with, Koinonia Farm, founded in 1942 right next door to Carter in Sumter County, Georgia. *Koinonia* is a beautiful New Testament Greek word meaning fellowship. Whites and blacks lived, worked, and worshiped together at Koinonia—which was enough to have the place firebombed, its staff shot at, and its workers beaten by local KKK people. The fellowship endured, however.) You can bet that Horton's continuing practical optimism, sitting there on his porch overlooking the glorious Cumberland Mountains, was a true reproach. I watched the Derby, but it's Myles Horton I remember.

Horton's valiant hope and confidence—where was one to find their like? The dominant tone in American politics and religion during the Reagan years was a celebration of mediocrity and avoidance of truth. On every airwave and printed page, you could find cynical, disgruntled malcontents posing as "pundits" and cutting their angry deals with fatuous commerce, while craven, smoothly coiffed schemers posing as "evangelists" obscured their greed by quoting from Romans and Corinthians and appealing to an easy-sleazy faith in the "God of Scripture." There had been dangerously corrupt media clergy in the early

1930s when Horton was a student, and fifty years on they were even more prevalent: the greedy religion business, its televisual hegemony spreading, has been metastasizing ever since. Once, Horton's brand of activism had been opposed with force and violence. It still might be today—or, worse, suffocated by indifference and disregard.

CLAYTON MORRISON—he of the pious do-nothing school and the beautiful linens—had frowned upon the political engagement of young pastors like Myles Horton, for he found it distastefully upsetting, unpleasantly radical. He and others like him did not want to acknowledge that oppression and loss of freedom threatened everywhere—not just in far-off countries with dangerous governments and difficult conflicts, but in the United States itself. "Always the enemy is the foe at home." He lingered, in a hand-wringing posture of anguished Christian uncertainty, a distance away from the trouble, decrying the use of force against evil, drawing back from active commitment to a curriculum of true social justice. As for the Jews, they ought, surely, to be more clearly whatever it was they wanted to be, less "hyphenated," more assimilationist, frankly, or else one could not be sure of their loyalty?

This cheap bigotry was lousy theology and ridiculous politics, Pa thought. Such insensitivity about Jews was not only deeply repugnant in itself but a sign of general moral sloth. "The Christian Church in America has never been upon a lower level of spiritual insight and moral sensitivity than in this tragic age of world conflict," my father wrote in 1934. Well, he was right, but things *can* get worse. Fifty years later, Jerry Falwell and Pat Robertson and those who greeted the new millennium with cheers of New Age self-congratulation plumbed even deeper reservoirs of vain inanity. High-decibel religiosity, with its excellent profit margins and growing political clout in the new century, is drowning out true religion all over the country, and the voices of the genuinely devout cannot be heard.

By 1934 two enormous transformations had occurred that changed the political culture from the one that Bonhoeffer, Dombrowski, Keppel-Compton, Niebuhr, and the others had discussed in 1931. Franklin Roosevelt had won the election in 1932 and had given his stupendous first inaugural speech. In the tempest of activist governmental work that marked his first Hundred Days, he had initiated the New Deal. His affirmation of the basic principles of a true democracy and his trust in the future were a bracing challenge to the reactionary vehemence of his opponents.

It is still a marvel to consider the stalwart courage of that amazing inaugural, the tone of which has been lost to much of American politics. Voters responded with a rush of gratitude and hope to FDR's repeated assurances that their safety and security could be restored—not by reaffirming all the old arrangements, which had helped to bring on the crisis, but, rather, by making new ones. Acknowledging the many fears that afflicted otherwise brave men and women and pledging that his administration would assist in banishing them, Roosevelt promised to do the job without endangering their freedom: "In every dark hour of our national life a leadership of frankness and vigor has met with that understanding and support of the people themselves which is essential to victory. . . . We do not distrust the future of essential democracy. The people of the United States have not failed."

Felix Frankfurter, still teaching law at Harvard, energetically went about getting his best students jobs in the new government agencies that were going to help put America back on its feet. (That the now ex-President Lowell of Harvard disliked FDR, "a traitor to his class," even more than he disliked FF gave this work an extra, exhilarating punch.) But my father was skeptical: the progressivism of Teddy Roosevelt hadn't been enough; his cousin's New Deal wasn't going to be, either. The problems seemed insurmountable. Still, it was a great deal better than elsewhere.

In Germany, Hitler was appointed chancellor of a coalition government and in March 1933, only days after FDR moved into the White House, he gained by parliamentary vote the dictatorial powers he craved. Germans cheered or remained silent when he proclaimed his victories. An emergency decree handed down on February 28, the morning after the Reichstag fire, put every kind of restraint upon free political activity, and this Edict for the Protection of People and State was never abrogated during the Third Reich: "Thus restrictions on personal liberty, on the right of free expression of opinion, including freedom of the press, on the right of association and assembly, and violations of the privacy of postal, telegraphic and telephonic communications, and warrants for house searches, orders for confiscations as well as restrictions on property rights are permissible beyond the legal limits otherwise prescribed." Within a year, Hitler had destroyed political opposition to his regime, and by 1935 he was enacting the laws that banned Jews from the German polity.

From the beginning of the Third Reich, Germany's principal church bigwigs showed an appalling eagerness to preserve the structures of power to which they were accustomed. The

Catholics were first off the mark, with the Vatican's early concordat with Hitler's regime. In July 1933, the treaty assured the German Catholic Church that it could continue to operate its schools and societies provided it didn't meddle in politics. Bending its principles of ecclesiastical integrity, which supposedly held it above and beyond the dictates of the state, the Church agreed to submit all its diocesan appointments to the Nazi government's approval. A craven deal, of course. I suppose some of the priests may have told themselves they were protecting the 40 percent of Germans who were Catholic. Others accepted the arrangement as an excellent one on the face of it.

The Lutheran bishops made even more obsequious arrangements with Hitler so as to hang on to what power they already had. The structure of the German Protestant hierarchy was and is complex, but put simply: as privileged, public corporations, its churches had quasi-establishment status in many parts of Germany, and many of them now welcomed the Third Reich. Pro-Nazi pastors were elected to roughly two thirds of the seats in the national synod of the German Evangelical Church. These so-called Reich Christians made horrible pronouncements about what they praised as German Christianity: one Lutheran pastor, Joachim Hossenfelder, proudly announced, "The German Christians are the SA of Jesus Christ."

Yet from the start the Nazis subverted even the tenuous church autonomy that these unpleasant arrangements allowed. The regime tolerated and even encouraged neopagan movements, taught anti-Christian doctrines in the Youth Movement, and subjected countless pastors and priests to Gestapo searches and interrogation.

Not all German clergymen could stomach the grotesque

developments, although virtually the entire German university world and other "intellectual elites" did so. In April 1934 a group of Protestant pastors who had been anti-Hitler from the start, Bonhoeffer among them, united in the Pastors' Emergency League, later called the Confessing Church, and in September they issued a manifesto—the Barmen Declaration (drafted by Karl Barth)—declaring their opposition to the Nazified policies that most German clergy were willing to accept. They did this after attending a meeting of the Evangelical synod at which most of the priestly delegates wore Nazi paramilitary brown shirts and voted to prohibit "non-Aryan" Christians, and even those married to "non-Aryans," from working in their churches. Bonhoeffer's dissenting minority claimed that this virtual abandonment of Christianity was itself schismatic and, therefore, that it was up to them to preserve the real church. This was a political decision of real courage, and who could but welcome it? In the parts of Germany where the Confessing Church was in the majority, its members did what they could to hold the line.

At meetings of Faith and Order and Life and Work, the two ecumenical groups that had been networking among British and Continental churches for years, the delegates did their best to help the Confessing Church pastors. But these were outnumbered and outflanked by their unscrupulous Nazified brethren, who were determined to control the face that the "German Church," or Reich Christianity, presented to the world. The Barmen Declaration was too little, and too late.

Bonhoeffer had already, and bravely, warned of the dangers of the new regime, but his theological position on Jewish-Christian relations was awkwardly occluded, as was so often the case with German Lutherans. They hewed to the old line that

Jesus' kingdom of glory had triumphed over the Jews' old order, that Jews must suffer for having crucified Jesus Christ, that the Chosen People "must bear the curse of its action through a long history of suffering," as Bonhoeffer himself put it in 1934. (What I find fascinating about this piece of Lutheran ugliness, which bedeviled even stalwart anti-Nazis in the German pastorate, is that it was not so noticeable among Scandinavian Lutherans during the Nazi period, and you can hardly fault *them* for indifference to the founding doctrines of the Reformation. Perhaps this has been explained: I should like to understand it.)

In any case, by the time of the Barmen Declaration several seasons had already gone by during which all potentially effective challenges to Hitler's terrorist state had been quashed, and it was late in the day to be fussing over a theory of church-state relations that would satisfy both Calvinists and Lutherans and not rattle the Third Reich. (This was what most of Barmen was about.) The theological underpinnings of the Confessing Church, as well as its realization of the huge dangers about to engulf it, were at best wobbly, accommodationist at worst. Its most heroic heroes—like the Lutheran pastor Martin Niemoller, the famous rector of an important church in Berlin and a decorated former U-boat commander, or Bonhoeffer himself—still did not decisively recognize the urgency, and part of their obtuseness came from their strange difficulty about Jews. Meanwhile the sand was running through the glass.

Many Christians in Germany and America, as elsewhere, glossed their cultural and social bigotries with a patina of churchly double-talk about Jews being, as it were, theologically challenged ought-to-be Christians, people who, if they stopped to think about it for a moment, would surely understand that they were more than halfway on the road to inevitable Christianity. Devout German Pietists especially found one of the most obnoxious things about Jews to be their resistance to conversion, which, they liked to claim, was already an issue in the Gospels.

When still in his twenties, in one of his earliest published pieces, my father had denounced this influential nonsense, and he did so with strong biblical arguments. For Christians, the covenant with the Lord does not begin with Jesus Christ and there is not a break, or crack, dividing the Old Testament of law from the New Testament of love: the covenant for us all begins with Abraham. Moreover it was from Jews that Christians had learned, and should be learning still, that the imperishable moral wisdom of the Prophets has as much to do with the institutions of the nation as with the heart of a single person.

This way of understanding it, which has a long, strong, and distinguished record over several millennia of Christian doctrine, was scarcely attended by Jews or Christians in positions of ecclesiastical authority. And this neglect was among the many factors that fatally slowed down the responses to Hitler among German church leaders. Yet I believe many good people, reading their Bibles, instinctively understood it, as they continue to do today. But when virtually no bishops or deans, not enough professors and pastors, said it out loud, the way was left open for the most degraded kinds of "rationality" to invade debate on these political-theological issues. Those lost, silent months of 1933 and 1934 in Germany are a tragic catastrophe; a swift and pugnacious riposte was needed to the Nazi regime's first declarations about Jews in the Christian Church, and it was not forthcoming.

For my father and his friends, the grotesque efforts made by scholars and theologians in Germany during the Third Reich to argue instead that one could have a de-Judaized Christianity were beneath contempt. The Reich Christians showed a craven obeisance to state authority, a shocking perversion of classic Christian doctrine, and their ideas did not merit discussion. But one had to note that the rise of fascism was bringing out latent poisons in doctrinal disputes all over the place. It was vitally important to be very clear on the theological points, which few pastors were, and not to haggle over minutiae, which all of them did. Reading today about the debates within the churches during this time is dispiriting, if not enraging. The doctrinal issues were not arcana, but matters of life and death, as they had been for centuries and are still.

Hitler's luridly pagan fascism, preying as evil will on human weakness, not strength, encouraged thoughtless Christians in Germany and elsewhere in their social and cultural misgivings about Jews. But this is not to say that Christian Germans, who may have been predisposed to this bigotry, were doomed to promote or succumb to it. (Many of my secular American friends, whether or not they'll admit it, believe that Germans *are* so doomed, I've noticed, an attitude as prejudiced as the anti-Semitism they rightly loathe.)

Take Paul Tillich, that fine "Aryan" holder of the Iron Cross First Class. He had written not only his good book on *The Religious Situation* (which my Uncle Helmut translated) but another on *The Socialist Decision* (which my father admired). He was crystal clear on this issue. Of course, his philo-Semitism was related to his liberal, socialist views, and both set him apart from most German theologians of the 1930s. A profound interpretation of Christian doctrine as it relates to inequality and injustice in contemporary society was not their idea of what a young scholar should be aiming for. Tillich instantly got in trouble with the National Socialists, and not just for his party-political allegiance, which had already annoyed the powers that be for more than a decade, but in good part because of his unwavering philo-Semitism.

Some decades later, Tillich wrote memorably about Jewry in terms that are still relevant today, terms that undoubtedly he had thought about in 1933 and 1934. The "gods of space," he warned, are protean dangers of which we should all beware, mortal enemies of the Judeo-Christian tradition. These gods of space come in many forms, and we know them when we see them, whereas

> the Jewish nation is the nation of time, in a sense which cannot be said of any other nation. It represents the permanent struggle between time and space going through all times. . . . It has a tragic fate when considered as a nation of space like every other nation, but as the nation of time, because it is beyond the circle of life and death it is beyond tragedy. The people of time, in synagogue and in church, cannot avoid being persecuted because by their very existence they break the claims of the gods of space who express themselves in will to power, imperialism, injustice, demonic enthusiasm, and tragic self-destruction. The gods of space, who are strong in every human soul, in every race and nation, are afraid of the Lord of time, history, and justice, are afraid of His prophets and followers. . . . The church is always in danger of identifying herself with a national church, of leaving injustice, the will to power, national and racial arrogance unchallenged. The church is always in danger of losing its

prophetic spirit. . . . [But] synagogue and church should be united in our age, in the struggle for the god of time against the gods of space.

Shortly after Storm Troopers indeed stormed into Frankfurt University in April 1933, where Tillich was chair of the philosophy faculty ("Paul among the Jews," Max Horkheimer called him), he was suspended from his post. This was just before the brownshirts burned books in a great bonfire in the square in front of the Römer—"the ancient building where German emperors were crowned," he noted poignantly, in an aside that hints at his old German patriotism. Students joined the uniformed Nazis in book burnings on May 10 all over Germany, shouting out the names of the authors as they flung the volumes into the flames: Albert Einstein, Walther Rathenau, Heinrich Heine! Thomas Mann, Stefan Zweig, Erich Maria Remarque! Uncertain months passed, so Tillich went to the Ministry of Culture to ascertain for himself what his future might hold. And what did he and the callow young official there talk about? They discussed the relation between the Old and New Testaments, Tillich insisting unequivocally that the Jewish Bible was a fundament of Christian faith.

By June of that catastrophic year my father helped to engineer a job offer at Union Seminary for Uncle Paulus, and by September the Tillichs—brokenhearted but relieved, in anguish but in hope—left Germany. He and his family were lucky to have this escape: he feared that many would not be so fortunate. It was a grim moment, and everyone knew it was going to get much, much worse. His friends noticed that at the train station he "was strained, tense, quiet, almost desperate . . . more concerned about the fate of his Jewish friends than for his own." When the Tillichs reached New York, my mother was at their new apartment to greet them, and my father found a German-speaking Union student to coach Uncle Paulus in English. (As it happens, it was Carl Voss, great-great-grandson of the Johann Voss who first translated Homer into German. He became very active in ecumenical international work over the next years.)

As the persecution of Jews in Germany grew more flagrant, Tillich, like many others, found himself painfully but inevitably breaking off friendships and severing bonds with his former colleagues in Germany who disagreed with his views. In America, though, Wilhelm Pauck was bending the ear of Robert Hutchins, president of the University of Chicago, on behalf of beleaguered and dismissed German academics, as others were (not very successfully) bending the ear of James Conant at Harvard and (with splendid results) Alvin Johnson at the New School for Social Research; many artists, scholars, and scientists did in fact find new professional homes in America. "Tillich emphasized over and over again that not the Jews alone but Christianity and humanism were also being put to death," Pauck said. As the world knows, Germans did not see it that way—or see it clearly enough, or see it in time.

So the loss of freedom and hope in Germany, and the intolerable situation for Jews there, were among the many things that I believe my father thought one should pray to have the courage to change—not just the public policy but one's own heart feelings. That already in June 1933 he had seen that Hitler was "bent upon the extermination of the Jew" and had destroyed the basis for any political opposition to his regime only strengthened this commitment as the decade wore on.

Paul Tillich, Ursula and Reinhold Niebuhr—at an ecumenical conference at Fletcher Farm, Vermont, 1935

But how was one to express the commitment? The means effectively to counter the blatantly anti-Semitic policies of the Third Reich were not easy to identify. Europe's formal public and political life had atrophied in fear and torpor; democracy had been snuffed out in Russia, Germany, Portugal, and Italy, and it was threatened everywhere else. So the people who really cared to do something had to commit themselves to a kind of nonviolent, spiritual guerrilla warfare; they had to use, however they could, the opportunities that came their way in their work and their lives to make ad hoc, improvised advances against the forces of unfreedom. They had to be vigilant, and they had to be ready for the unexpected.

In Germany itself Bonhoeffer and his allies were slowly gearing up for this, though for many seasons they did not or could not do more than engage in a kind of passive resistance to the regime. In France and the Low Countries, socialists, pacifists, and other anti-fascists were wavering, while in England, where the Conservative government was frankly sympathetic to the Third Reich, anti-fascists, too, opposed rearmament against the German threat; there wasn't much room in the national conversation for robust opposition both to the Tories' do-nothing inaction *and* to Hitler.

We are back again at the key question: how does one know when it is the moment to act, and how does one decide to take action? The ability to recognize the absolute danger of violent, armed, and anti-democratic formations was not—perhaps is not—a political skill you could depend on finding in the Western democracies. I suppose it is always rare. Yet the sturdily socialist Tillich, for example, whose steel had already been tempered in the infernos of the Great War, responded instantly to the full danger of Hitler's destructive intentions. So, in a very different context and from a different corner, did the unabashedly imperialist and Tory Winston Churchill, drawing on his vast reserves of trust in the essential genius of British democracy. People like this, famous like Churchill or little known like Tillich, who even in the darkest times do not waver in extending their confidence to their fellow citizens, are giants. They are fearless and therefore hopeful.

Pa did not himself return to Germany and therefore did not report directly to his American readers on the situation during what Germans call the Nazi Time. Though his focus on European events remained steady, the base of action shifted: between 1936 and 1940 he and my English mother spent many months in England, where the anti-fascist battles were being waged with peculiar, deflected intensity. Meanwhile he had second-hand news of Germany from academic and clerical friends and from ecumenically minded pastors elsewhere on the Continent—especially in Scandinavia—who were doing their best to help Jews, indeed all victims of Nazis. Alas, there were so few of them. But he organized or joined many groups devoted to this aim, and continued to write regularly on the fate and nature of Jewry. This theological and political commentary was one of his "most fundamental contributions," as his friend the scholar Franklin Littell has written, "much appreciated by Jewish spokesmen and one that shoots an arrow straight into the golden center of American *Kulturprotestantismus*."

V

By 1935 the Niebuhrs had settled in the Berkshire hills for the summers—my father, my mother, and my brother, Christopher, who had been born the year before. It wasn't Heath or the Stone Cottage to begin with—the family lived in other rented houses, including one in Sharon, Connecticut, with a big lawn and garden. I came to know about it many years later only from faded snapshots and from catching glimpses of the place itself as we drove through Sharon on our way up to Heath every June, or back down to New York in September.

My ignorance, combined with the fleeting glimpse of this mysterious house with its ample, pleasant grounds, allowed me rich fantasies about my pre-babyhood there. Sharon was opulent and spacious parkland compared with the scruffier up-country wildness of Heath's woods and pastures. I presumed I could have been happy there, but of course it wouldn't have lasted: Sharon was full of Republicans. (We got out of Connecticut about a decade before the Roman Catholic William F. Buckley, Sharon's most famous reactionary, wrote his curious book *God and Man at Yale*, a screed about which my father and his Yale friends kept quiet, though they thought they knew plenty about the subject, heaven knows. Their attitude to this book can best be expressed by a remark once made by the great physicist Wolfgang Pauli: he refused to comment on a physics paper concerning a subject he knew authoritatively—his own work—because, he observed wryly, "It's not even wrong.")

In Heath, where the Niebuhrs eventually landed, the political air definitely improved, what with all those ecumenical bishops, all those friends of Aunt Ethel's and Auntie Lou's, all that wonderful uproar of buzzing political commentary coming from the Frankfurters' house. Not to mention the congeniality of the township's farmers. Heath's harshly rocky pastures, its New England fields with boulders and obstructions it had taken two centuries to clear, its old dairy farms tucked into sheltered dales and mill houses perched over tumbling forest brooks (Uncle Felix's was like that)—these were exotic for my Middle Western father and my English mother. But they felt at home in Heath, and they admired the intelligence and deep modesty of their Yankee friends, their stoic liveliness and easy democratic spirit. This was a good place to be in these dangerous, difficult years.

Various rental arrangements preceded the Stone Cottage. The first one was in the woods of South Heath, off Burrington Road, with a wonderful shaded porch and big bedrooms. But wherever he was, my father would clatter away on his typewriter all morning and afternoon, pounding out (in 1920s two-index-finger ratatat style) his torrent of articles, reviews, and books. Summers were more low-key than winters, but the work was always going on, and it was becoming more and more hectic as the national and international situations deteriorated. The Heath interludes shortened as the decade wore on; they were interspersed with long summertime trips to England and constant returns to work in New York. But both at Union Seminary and in England the back-story of the Serenity Prayer was taking on new theological, moral, and political depth in the years 1934–36.

Though Heath was a place where he composed most of his major works, Pa never wrote out the lectures and sermons for which he was most admired. These were delivered extempore, with only a few words, plus the biblical text references, scribbled on the back of an envelope and hurriedly thrust into a breast pocket at the last Sunday morning moment, just before he ambled up the church or chapel aisle behind the choir and other clerics, singing the processional hymn with great gusto and completely off-key. "I like to preach," he acknowledged, "I'm a preacher." But in between the sermons, and especially during the summers, he also had to prepare for his classes at Union Seminary. It was not as if he was a trained university scholar: graduate-school instruction was a relatively new field for him to cultivate, and in the 1930s the academic work was excitingly rigorous at Union. He had to try to live up to the place.

The Union Seminary faculty then was, like the summer colony in Heath in this respect, a marvelously high-spirited group, noted for its vitality and liberalism in theological doctrine. It was famous for the virtuosity with which it taught students from many church traditions; this distinguished Union from other seminaries and divinity schools that trained pastors solely for one denomination—indeed, this was the purpose for which Union had been founded in 1836. (It was an unusual idea then, and it still is. Most pastors study under their singular denominational roof, which is why Baptist, Methodist, Lutheran, Presbyterian, and Episcopalian ministers, say, as well as Roman Catholic and Orthodox priests, learn almost as little about one another as they do about Islam or Buddhism. Union was different.) I remember well the remarkable scholars on the faculty during the years when my father taught there, for they were characters of real consequence: uniformly white and male, they came from strikingly diverse backgrounds and their personal styles were almost comically varied.

Paul Scherer, a Lutheran pastor who was professor of homiletics, verged on being flamboyantly dramatic, with his oh-so-silvery white hair brushed back from his forehead so handsomely! The eminent German émigré theologian Richard Kroner, who arrived during the war years, seemed on the other hand to be the model of academic austerity. Both were men of force and charm, as were the wildly contrasting Old Testament scholars James Muilenberg and the very French Samuel Terrien. All these gentlemen, and many more—including on occasion the Russian Orthodox Father George Florovsky and the great Japanese Buddhist D. T. Suzuki—regularly worked together, worshiped together, taught together, and even appeared together in hilarious theatrical presentations for the students. My childhood memories therefore include slightly loony evenings of drama not only in Heath but also in the otherwise dignified Edwardian academic precincts of Union Seminary. Tillich was an especially beguiling performer.

The Union students and faculty lived and worked together closely, for almost the entire institution was contained within a two-block quadrangle of pseudo-Gothic stone that had been built for the seminary in 1910. At the north end were the faculty apartments and at the south the offices and classrooms; on the long side facing Broadway were student dormitories and the library; on the other long side, to the west, were the big James

Chapel and the smaller Lampman Chapel, the Refectory, and a huge space called in a no-frills way the Social Hall, with an informal stage at one end where the theatricals were put on. Gardens and terraces, with brick walks and handsome shrubbery, filled the interior of the Quadrangle and linked the various parts of this self-contained world. We had our own doctor as well as our own churches, even our own electrical system (on direct, not alternating, current) and phone network. A secular-sacred, old-new kind of place, the Quadrangle.

The Union faculty taught their students with enormous learning, intelligence, and what appeared to be an implacable indifference to race, class, or gender—for the student body included men and (some) women, whites and (some) blacks, Americans and (some) foreigners. And they prepared them for all kinds of different "callings"—to pastoral work, scholarship, teaching, and a well-instructed Christian life in many settings. Students called the close-knit, rather conservative social cohesion of life in the Quadrangle "strangling fellowship," but the intellectual liberality was palpable.

Union Seminary found itself, geographically, in a congenial place, for the liberalism spreading across Morningside Heights marked most of its institutions. Columbia University, just to the south, was in some way the most liberal neighbor, but the least communicative one because the most secular. Still, my father had Columbia students in his classes, working on joint doctorates in philosophy and theology, taking courses at both Union and Columbia. And by 1940 its women's college, Barnard, saw fit to inaugurate a new Department of Religion, of which my mother was the first chairman. My parents had close pals on the Columbia faculty and my best buddies were Columbia faculty brats; our romps and explorations of the enormous campus ranged up and down Claremont Avenue, disregarding the grownups' boundaries.

One block to the west, with a spectacular view of the Hudson River below, a huge pseudo-Gothic church with an enormous bell tower loomed over the seminary: this was the famously "nondenominational" Riverside Church, built with Rockefeller money in 1930. Plenty of Union people had something to do with Riverside, for a host of reasons, not the least being that its pastor was on the Union faculty. The rambunctious, ebullient Harry Emerson Fosdick was considered the most popular preacher in America, and he was a very liberal one.

However conservative the Baptist John D. Rockefeller Jr. might have been, he was keen on Fosdick, and had admired him for years. Fosdick had caught Rockefeller's attention in 1922, when he had preached a sermon (from the pulpit of New York's First Presbyterian Church) in which he bewailed the fundamentalists' "apparent intention [of driving] out of the evangelical churches men and women of liberal opinions": this eloquent consideration of the need for charity in the churches had made him nationally famous overnight.

Like my grandfather, like my father and Bishop McConnell, Fosdick had been tangling with reactionary fundamentalists for decades, even before the Scopes trial in 1925 brought the quarrel to a head. Fosdick quoted my father's summary of the dispute then, which strikes me as being as apt today as it was eighty years ago: "That part of the church which maintained an effective contact with modern culture stood in danger of capitulating to all the characteristic prejudices of a 'scientific' and 'progressive' age; and that part of the church which was concerned with the evangelical heritage chose to protect it in the armor of a rigorous biblicism." Fosdick had intended his 1922 sermon to be inclusionary: he was pleading for an openhearted Presbyterian church in which conservative literalists could coexist with their more liberal brethren. He had prayed for what he called "a spirit of conciliation that would work out the problem within an inclusive fellowship."

But "if ever a sermon failed to achieve its object, mine did," he wrote in his autobiography. "It was a plea for good will, but what came of it was an explosion of ill will." The fundamentalists, led by the once noble William Jennings Bryan, a bigwig in the Presbyterian General Assembly, attacked him viciously. They hated him for his liberal theology but they got at him on procedural grounds, insisting that no doctrinally impure Baptist should be allowed to preside over a Presbyterian church. By 1923–24 a virtual war had been declared.

Fosdick managed to be feisty and reassuring in the same breath, warmhearted and levelheaded. But the outrage against his sermon unsettled him. He was dismayed by the "bitter intolerance" of the fundamentalists, and while he acknowledged that modern science held many mysteries that perhaps he didn't fully understand, "there is one thing I am sure of: courtesy and kindliness and tolerance and humility and fairness are right. Opinions may be mistaken; love never is." He could certainly recognize small-minded bigotry when he saw it, and he saw the power plays for what they were. Only partially masked by the sanctimony about literal biblical interpretation was a hard-eyed bid to gain political leverage and national power.

Fosdick quit First Presbyterian and went looking for a job, which wasn't easy, famous and beloved as he was. The Baptist fundamentalists hated him even more than the Presbyterians did: the pastor of Calvary Baptist Church in New York bellowed that "Dr. Fosdick is not only a Baptist bootlegger but . . . also a Presbyterian outlaw . . . a religious outlaw—he is the Jesse James of the theological world."

Fosdick wasn't the only person being hounded by the Presbyterian General Assembly in 1924. The Princetonian Henry Pitney Van Dusen, for example—who as a youth had had a conversion experience at a Billy Sunday revival meeting and who was to become a major Protestant statesman of the midcentury (and to succeed Henry Sloane Coffin as president of Union in 1950)—faced a challenge that year from the biblical literalist thought police just as he graduated from Union. A judicial commission of the General Assembly challenged his ordination because he had declined to affirm the literal truth of the Virgin Birth. He overcame this maneuver with the help of a notable brief in his support by an enlightened Presbyterian lawyer, perhaps the denomination's most famous twentieth-century layman—John Foster Dulles. (It's impossible for me to imagine Dulles as either young or liberal, but he was both in 1924.)

Things became even hotter for the Presbyterians in 1925, when national attention focused on the Scopes trial in Tennessee. Bryan in the courtroom there was as eloquent in defense of "creationism" as Fosdick was in deriding it from his New York pulpit. Fosdick continued to preach vigorously on behalf of the obvious truth that Christians not only could but should know about and believe in the basic tenets of modern science, from which after all the world much benefited. He was aghast at the way the fundamentalists used this dispute as a means to attract national attention. He knew that beneath all the shenanigans about monkeys, the underlying issue was a very old political one. The fundamentalists wanted to be in charge.

Having both Van Dusen and Fosdick on the faculty marked Union Seminary as an alleged hotbed of godless radicalism, even before you got to people like my father and Tillich. That the faculty wanted its students to study Hebrew and Greek so as to be able to read the Bible in its original tongues was considered another mark of dubious intentions. But Henry Sloane Coffin, an enlightened and farsighted church statesman (if a rather anti-Semitic and male chauvinist one), presided over this theological cauldron with cheerful openness, seasoning and stirring the contents to keep it at an even, savory simmer.

Despite or perhaps because of his notoriety, Fosdick was attractive to Rockefeller, who tried to persuade him to come to the Park Avenue Baptist Church, his own spiritual abode. Fosdick refused the offer. He didn't want to be in swank company on Park Avenue, didn't want, he said, to become "private chaplain to a small group of financially privileged people." He told Rockefeller, "You are too wealthy, and I do not want to be known as the pastor of the richest man in the country." But Rockefeller teased him—surely criticism on that score would be no sharper than the criticism Fosdick was already attracting on theological grounds?—and said he was willing to build a bigger and better church for Fosdick somewhere else, then. It was Fosdick's idea to have the new church be open to Christians of all traditions—his most important condition; to locate it in the heart of an impoverished part of New York City only blocks from Harlem; and to build it big, so that it could welcome the thousands of nearby Columbia students.

The year that Riverside Church opened was the year that Fosdick composed a wonderful hymn for its dedicatory service, which I and millions of Americans know from singing it to one of the most splendid hymn tunes there is, the great Welsh "Cwm Rhondda." It has Fosdick's characteristic buoyant modesty and simplicity, and of course it concerns exactly the same themes as those of the Serenity Prayer:

> God of grace and God of glory
> > On thy people pour thy power;
> Crown thine ancient Church's story;
> > Bring her bud to glorious flower.
> Grant us wisdom, grant us courage,
> > For the facing of this hour.
>
> Cure thy children's warring madness,
> > Bend our pride to thy control;
> Shame our wanton, selfish gladness,
> > Rich in things and poor in soul.
> Grant us wisdom, grant us courage,
> > Lest we miss thy kingdom's goal.

"That was more than a hymn to me when we sang it that day—it was a very urgent personal prayer," Fosdick wrote.

Riverside Church wasn't Union Seminary's only liberal ecclesiastical neighbor. Across the street in the other direction was the Jewish Theological Seminary, founded in 1886 by humanistic and enlightened rabbis from the Sephardic communities of New York and Philadelphia—rabbis who admired Giuseppe Mazzini and Abraham Lincoln, who were revered by Jew and Gentile alike. JTS trained Conservative young men for the rabbinate, and its general ethos included an appreciation of interfaith efforts.

Much later Pa developed a special friendship with one of the jewels in the crown of its postwar faculty, the great Polish (and Berlin-trained) Rabbi Abraham Joshua Heschel, who came to America in 1940 and to JTS in 1945.

Around the corner from both seminaries was a modest little Catholic parish, the Church of Corpus Christi, with an extraordinary priest in charge: Father George Barry Ford was renowned in the New York archdiocese for his radiant, joyous ministry to the poor, the voiceless, the needy, and the uncertain; and he was famous in the Columbia University community, which he had served as Catholic chaplain, for his open-minded charity to all students. He involved the lay congregation of Corpus Christi in the worship services; he handed out leaflets with the English version of the Latin mass for them (this was thirty years before the Vatican came around to abandoning Latin); he liberated the curriculum of the church school from its hidebound old narrowness, hired teachers trained in secular universities, and abolished grades; in an ecumenical gesture that was second nature to him he sent flowers to Riverside Church when a service there celebrated its tenth birthday in 1940; and he encouraged striking workers at Consolidated Edison to use his auditorium for their meetings. From today's perspective Ford's acts may seem safely and politically correct, but his independence then was judged impermissible. For each and every one of these moves, his superiors in the archdiocese gave him hell. Francis Cardinal Spellman, a most reactionary and unpleasant force in New York City public life, was enraged by Father Ford and worked to marginalize him and Corpus Christi. But the good man had a big fan club at Union.

THE UNION FACULTY included well-known authorities on prayer and liturgy, many of whom were themselves compilers or revisers of prayer books, hymnbooks, and "guides to worship." Among them—English, French, German, and American Protestants of almost every denomination—they seemed to know all the prayers that had ever been composed anywhere or perpetuated in any liturgical document, and they shared this scholarship generously with their students and colleagues. To use the thin, dry vocabulary of today's academy, they knew how to deploy many types of discourse: they could lecture or write monographs, of course, but they also knew how to preach and they knew how to pray. I mention this because people don't always recognize how detailed and comprehensive can be a priest's command of prayers, homilies, and liturgical practice. Working teacher-pastors, especially those trained in as liberal an institution as Union, know very well the difference between composing a brand-new prayer and ringing a change on an old one: the Union scholars did both all the time. They had mastered with real virtuosity this technical skill that all Protestant clergy must have (even Episcopalians, though of course they sail a course set by the Book of Common Prayer, one of the greatest books in the English language).

From September to May most of the Union community attended the Sunday morning services at the James Chapel unless they were at work elsewhere, which many of them were. The senior professors took turns in the pulpit and in leading these services, so we came to know their prayers well. (There were daily morning and afternoon services, too, in the Lampman chapel.) But we Niebuhrs were slightly disloyal to Union and varied our Sunday churchgoing: we went to the Union chapel often enough but also to services at St. Paul's Chapel at Columbia, paid an occasional visit to Riverside or to the rousing services at the East Harlem Protestant Parish (organized and run by Union students and faculty), and went quite frequently to the nearby Episcopal Cathedral of St. John the Divine. "We" in my childhood usually meant my mother and me, since my father was often out of town on weekends, preaching himself in Chicago or Philadelphia or Yale or Harvard or wherever, and my brother was in boarding school. During the boring bits of any of these services, I'd divert myself by exploring the hymnbooks and prayer books. Goodness me, what one could find out!

I liked the services at Columbia best because there was lots of singing, not just by the choir but by the college congregation—and not just the hymns but antiphonal chanting of psalms and anthems. Columbia's organist and choirmaster in the 1940s, Lowell Beveridge, was a gifted exponent of the best in Protestantism's musical liturgies, and like Father Ford, and like the pastors in East Harlem, he believed strongly—on theological and political grounds, not merely musical ones—that the men, women, and children who came to church should participate fully in the service. So he taught everyone in the congregation the beautiful Anglican canticles to be sung by priest *and* people, and he encouraged part-singing of the hymns. He so inspired the students in his choir that they couldn't contain their choral enthusiasms within the confines of a mere hour on Sunday morning: when we took our poodles for an after-service walk on Riverside Drive before Sunday lunch, we'd find the girls and men—their cassocks shed, with duffel coats and scarves to protect them from the winds coming off the icy Hudson River below—warbling in the park for the sheer joy of it.

It is impossible to sing hymns in a Protestant church without feeling the impressive shadows cast by the Feste Burg of the German Reformation. Not only did Martin Luther write some of the best ones, including the Mighty Fortress, but there are the dozens of chorales that Bach composed for St. Thomas's, the Lutheran church in Leipzig where he served as choirmaster; all these are and will always be essential to Protestant worship. You could feel the confident power of the Lutheran tradition in every chord of these prayers, lamentations, psalms, and celebrations. Still, I never felt at home at a Lutheran church service, even though I went to a few of them over the years, perhaps because I was polarized enough by my dual allegiance to the Book of Common Prayer and to the chaste simplicities of a New England Congregational service.

Subliminally, both these liturgies were coloring my sense of my own country and my mother's. What about this English Reformation that loomed so large in the prehistory of the American republic? I learned about it in a roundabout way from my New England summers, but then, in the winter, I amplified my paltry understanding with explorations of the Book of Common Prayer—and not just in its American version, which I got to know at St. John the Divine, but in the English edition that had been given me by my English godmother at my baptism. Here I was able to home in on the great Protestant debates.

It was easy enough to grasp that the Anglo-Catholic, or Episcopalian, prayers and services combined modern Protestant dogmas with forms and procedures derived from the Catholic mass, and I could see right away the difference from the plainer Prot setups I knew from my Heath experiences and from the Union prayer book. I could see the ominous difficulties, too. In my English edition of the Book of Common Prayer I would read about how it had all begun, in the reign of "Primo Elizabeth AE," with an "Act for the Uniformity of Common Prayer." Here was the language of an established church, loud and clear: "Where at the death of our late Sovereign Lord King Edward the Sixth, there remained one uniform Order of Common Service and Prayer, . . . Be it therefore Enacted by the Authority of this present Parliament, That the said Statute of Repeal . . . shall be void and of none effect, from and after the Feast of the Nativity of St. John Baptist next coming. . . ."

Enacted by the Authority of this present Parliament?! Statute of Repeal?! Void and of none effect after the Feast of what? Any red-blooded American could see right away that something was wrong here. A new law followed, five double-column pages setting forth the regulations concerning Christian worship in Elizabeth's kingdom. Knocking out of the contest all the heathen habits of Rome—"uncertain Stories, and Legends, with multitudes of Responds, Verses, vain Repetitions, Commemorations, and Synodals"—as well as the control-freak insistence on having the priests do their work in a language people didn't know, the writers of the Book of Common Prayer insisted on the liturgy in plain English: "St. Paul would have such language spoken to the people in the church, as they might understand, and have profit by hearing,"

Well, that was great. The idea, plainly enough, was *common* prayer, arranged as much for the people as for the priests—for the "holy common people of God," as the traditional phrase has it. Yet the Anglicans had filled their regulations with rich, juicy words and phrases like "assize," "impeach," "indict," "lawfully convict." Round, elegant sentences rumbled like thunder: "Archbishops, Bishops, and other Ordinaries . . . shall endeavour themselves to the uttermost of their knowledges, that the due and true execution hereof maybe had through their Diocese and Charges, as they will answer before God, for such evils and plagues wherewith Almighty God may justly punish his people for neglecting this good and wholesome law." The authoritarian weight of these menacing, mellifluous phrases was clear enough even to a ten- or eleven-year-old who didn't understand them. The Reformation in England had been achieved by force of armed violence and royal bloody-mindedness, and it showed in the syntax.

I was tremendously proud of the brave Brits who had dissented from or refused to conform to the Anglicans' heavy monarchical strictures. Our American ancestors! I claimed the *Mayflower* people as my political forebears. You could see at a glance what had stuck in their craw: those self-assured, worldly Anglican associations of church and royal power. How ironic, then, that the Puritans brought with them to America the very principles of an established church whose corrupted ways had alienated them in England. It was disgraceful to think that civil arrest and imprisonment threatened, let alone evils and plagues, if one did not obey the church in Salem as in Oxford, in Williamsburg as in Ely.

On the front pages of daily newspapers in my childhood there'd occasionally be photographs of Spanish Catholic cardinals and archbishops walking in procession with army generals and marshals fore and aft, sometimes with Generalissimo

Franco himself, and I could analogize. I had seen pictures of Germany's Lutheran and Roman Catholic bishops gratefully shaking hands with Hitler. Any twentieth-century person would know at least something about the punishments visited upon opponents of an established spiritual authority that marched arm in arm with the government. Thank goodness for the liberating clarity that our Founding Fathers had brought to this issue. I didn't yet know how murky the whole church-state thing still was. It amazed me to discover, as a college student, that in Massachusetts the Congregationalists had gone on being an established church with various legal and governmental powers until 1833.

As I rooted around in the succulent pages of the Book of Common Prayer, I would remember—and be grateful for—the contrastingly austere, plainspoken Scottish Psalter whose beautiful words filled the hymnbook in Heath, the dignified and modest sound of prayers in any Reformed service. There you heard real people's voices: not princes of the church, not know-it-all clergy, but ordinary people who cherished their independence and their freedom as well as their Christianity.

Still, my Protestant soul admired—and still admires—the sensible, elegant opening of a later Preface to this same English Book of Common Prayer, revised after the Restoration of the Crown in 1660, when a king was once again back on the throne after decades of civil war and yet more bloody disputation over these very issues had altered the landscape of England. What I liked was the way it addressed the perennial question, still contested in every Protestant church, of just how much conformity, and how much improvisation, there should be in a religious service: "It hath been the wisdom of the Church of England, ever since the first compiling of her Publick Liturgy, to keep the mean between the two extremes of too much stiffness in refusing, and of too much easiness in admitting any variation from it." Well, there you had it! A church should allow for variation and personal development, but one had to have a structure. For centuries the formulas had been fought over. Who was in charge of deciding? Who would keep the mean? This was a vital, real problem—not an abstruse historical one.

I had overheard plenty of stiff and easy arguments between my mother and father about the right way to worship: I got the general drift that one didn't want slavishly to follow rote formulas, on the one hand, as I was led to understand Catholics and all too many Jews and Muslims had to do, since that meant one had ceded to the priests the power and authority to determine the contours of one's faith. No Protestant would settle for this. On the other hand one couldn't favor unbridled self-expression, for that invariably led to self-indulgent sloppiness, pious banality, and triviality advancing under the banner of Personal Faith; that was mere entertainment. My mother was hilarious on the subject.

So, then, how far might people go in deciding for themselves how to worship? How much should you make up the prayers as you go along? How much should the congregation join in the action? What, indeed, was the purpose and point of a church service? of any religious service? And how did all this praying on Sunday in church key in with praying or not praying at home the rest of the time? What relation did worship have to being a worthy person?

My mother was dubious that pastors could come up with wise and goodly prayers of their own that addressed these spiritual problems week after week—as a matter of fact she found it theologically ludicrous to imagine that they should—and she believed there was much to recommend the Book of Common Prayer's solution: a properly-set-forth plan for every Sunday in the year that offered choices and alternatives, the whole setting your nose in the right direction for the workaday weeks ahead. And I must confess I found it hard to imagine that one could improve on the BCP's stupendous formulations, whose riches included prayers, supplications, and exhortations for virtually every moment of one's life. The collects, or daily prayers, were one-sentence masterpieces that seemed to strike right to the heart of the day. The one for the first Sunday after Epiphany is about prayer itself, in fact:

> O Lord we beseech thee mercifully to receive the prayers of thy people which call upon thee, and grant that they may both perceive and know what things they ought to do, and also may have grace and power faithfully to fulfill the same.

Many prayers imply, as this one does, that the praying is being done by a group of worshipers, and there's an entire school of Christian thought that says that's the only kind of prayer that makes any sense, i.e., the only kind that will be heard (or, in a more doctrinaire mode, the only kind that should be allowed). The BCP's Prayer of General Confession, intended as a most intense presentation of personal inadequacy and sin, which precedes and introduces Holy Communion, is cast in the first-person *plural*:

> We acknowledge and bewail our manifold sins and wickedness which we, from time to time, most grievously have committed by thought, word, and deed, against thy divine Majesty, provok-

ing most justly thy wrath and indignation against us. We do earnestly repent, and are heartily sorry for these our misdoings; the remembrance of them is grievous unto us; the burden of them is intolerable. Have mercy upon us, most merciful Father.

On the other hand, my Evangelical father, who wrote most of his prayers in this same plural mode, thought of prayer as in certain respects an individual matter—even when people prayed together in the essential activity of communal worship. The great liturgical model for singular prayers was the Psalms, whether mourning or rejoicing ones. "Save me, O God: for the waters are come in even unto my soul. I stick fast in the deep mire, where no ground is: I am come into deep waters, so that the floods run over me. I am weary of crying; my throat is dry." Still, there were plural ones, too, usually noisy: "Sing we merrily unto God our strength: make a cheerful noise unto the God of Jacob. Take the psalm, bring hither the tabret: the merry harp with the lute. Blow up the trumpet in the new moon."

Many Psalms emphasize this happy business of making a hullabaloo. But even more of them seem concerned that the noise isn't getting through, and again the individual voice cries out: "Hear my prayer, O Lord: and let my crying come unto thee. Hide not thy face from me in the time of my trouble; incline thine ear unto me when I call; O hear me, and that right soon." Or "Ponder my words, O Lord: consider my meditation. O hearken thou unto the voice of my calling, my King and my God: for unto thee will I make my prayer. My voice shalt thou hear betimes, O Lord: early in the morning will I direct my prayer unto thee, and will look up." (There's at least one sigh of relief, too: "I am well pleased: that the Lord hath heard the voice of my prayer; that he hath inclined his ear unto me: therefore will I call upon him as long as I live.")

What was this all about? Prayer was reliably familiar and at the same time mysteriously beyond reach. I don't recall getting any specific instruction about prayer from my father, and I learned his views only later, when I read his books. But I do remember a brisk reproach for an improper petition asking that an individual need—want?—be filled. We were on our way to Radio City Music Hall to see *Singin' in the Rain*, and had left late because of last-minute fussing by my mother—a bad habit I inherited and not one my father tolerated easily, since he was always early for everything. In the taxi going downtown we got stuck in the usual Manhattan traffic, and I was frantic with worry that we'd miss the beginning of the movie or maybe not even be let in. I was very keen on Gene Kelly. "O God, please let the light turn green," I wailed from the jump seat. The rebuke was gentle but instantaneous. That's not what prayer was for.

I got the point. Or rather, I suppose, I knew the minute I said it that I'd let the side down for a panicky adolescent moment there. If you acknowledged a contrite heart, worked for goodness, and hoped for salvation, then maybe you'd become the kind of person for whom the light turns green, but that's the most you could expect. To use prayer as a petition for specific improvements or alterations in one's life, or for gifts however spiritual, was to be a superstitious lazybones. Trusting in magical formulas that will fix the future was a natural mistake—part of the human psyche, a way of managing the unpredictability of our stories—but one shouldn't add to the silliness. Praying to saints and other intermediaries on behalf of this or that hoped-for improvement was, for this Protestant child, a childish, sometimes charming, and probably harmless pastime—I knew Catholics did it a lot, along with lighting candles and counting beads and other trivial pursuits—but it wasn't true prayer. That, by virtual definition, had to attend to the condition of one's own sinful soul. And as Catholics knew, it had to be engaged in habitually: one learns to pray by praying.

However much my father loved the Psalms—and he did—and however much he could acknowledge that the services in the Book of Common Prayer richly derived from them and from the Gospels, he nonetheless found the Episcopalian service too Anglo and too Catholic for his taste. Believing as he did that divine worship required of the pastor, as of the congregation, that one open up the soul to receive the inspiration that alone could bring forth true prayer, he was distrustful of having either party rely so dutifully on the formulas laid down by previous generations, no matter how great their ecclesiastical authority or gifted their prose style. A disciplined, deeply structured improvisation was the liturgical form he had been brought up in, and he found it spiritually more appropriate.

The writers of the Book of Common Prayer, centuries before, had acknowledged that their efforts to arrive at a just compromise on these matters could not be easily achieved. Indeed, a gentle allusion to England's Civil War indicated that brutal interruptions had canceled out their compromises: "by what undue means, for what mischievous purposes, the use of the Liturgy (though enjoined by the Laws of the Land . . .), came during the late unhappy confusions to be discontinued is too well known to the world, and we are not willing here to remember." This was a typically Anglican way to dismiss Cromwell and sweep his Puritan revolution under the rug—a vague, elegant wave of the hand to the "late unhappy confusions."

All this legalistic old-fashioned talk obscured the truth that my father, indeed any Nonconformist minister, could not forget: the Anglican prayers had been achieved at an unacceptably high price. The composers of the Book of Common Prayer had cut out certain familiar parts of the old Catholic mass, which was tricky but necessary, and arrived at new solutions: "There is no remedy but that of necessity there must be some Rules," they had written. But they had also kept themselves in the saddle of royal power. And they didn't make clear how many rules there would be. Nor did they specify who would lay them down, although again their language betrayed them; a presumption of their own continued ecclesiastical power colored every sentence.

The prelates knew that not everyone would agree with them: "Although we know it impossible (in such variety of apprehensions, humours and interests as are in the world) to please all, nor can expect that men of factious, peevish, and perverse spirits should be satisfied . . . , Yet we have good hope, that what is here presented . . . will be well accepted and approved by all sober, peaceable, and truly conscientious Sons of the Church of England." You couldn't be an American and believe this stuff. My father wrote in 1924, "Of course the Anglican services have their own appeal, but the technique which makes them possible is beyond us."

Any American schoolchild could once tell you that sober, peaceable, and truly conscientious men and women had fled this very Book of Common Prayer and all it stood for, and the revered founders of the Massachusetts Bay Colony hadn't been factious, peevish, or perverse. They believed the English Church had been traduced by its corrupt royalist leaders, and believed they could purify it in the New World. The Anglicans had claimed, "We think it convenient that every Country should use such Ceremonies as they shall think best. . . ." Very well then. Thank goodness that the Pilgrims had set sail for North America to found their New Jerusalems, their shining Cities set on a Hill.

Still, the Anglo-Catholic service and prayers had great power over my malleable soul, and I was in thrall to them. To hear that great seventeenth-century music, to learn in one's heart the immemorial phrases of those amazing collects and prayers, to feel the turn of the year through the dramatic progress of the ecclesiastical calendar—from the dark night of Advent to the joy of Christmas, from the wild thrills of Epiphany to the extraordinary weeks of the Passion, from Bethlehem to Jerusalem, from Gethsemane to the Cross, then to the astonishing moment when the women find the tomb empty and Easter is celebrated, from the mysterious conundrums of Ascension Day and Pentecost and then back again over the long summer and autumn weeks to the shadows of Advent—this was something rich, golden, and imperishable.

When I had a complete crisis of faith—later on, in my adolescence—it arose during an unbearably beautiful sung evensong service in Winchester Cathedral, for I realized I was worshiping the beauty of the service itself, and this was of course pagan blasphemy. I had become a hellish aesthete. Some months later I reported to my parents that I was obviously not a Christian anymore, if I ever had been. The very glories of the service I loved so had seduced and betrayed me into aesthetic idolatry. They were quite calm and reassuring, and didn't ask questions. Nor did they reproach me. Faith could not be forced. They left me alone—to find my way in the wilderness or to find my way home.

Curiously I can't remember much about the services at Union—except the wonderful candlelit Christmas Eve carol service—partly because I don't have its prayer book or hymn-book handy to remind me of them, and partly, I imagine, because the very requirement to be "nondenominational" drained the service of the juice and color that give life to more focused forms of worship. The same was true at Riverside, despite Fosdick's rousing sermons and the rather-too-glamorous sound of Virgil Fox's organ, the two features everyone always talked about. Fosdick had a superb understanding of a sermon's purpose—a pastor has "not merely to discuss repentance but persuade people to repent; not merely to debate the meaning and possibility of Christian faith, but to produce Christian faith in the lives of his listeners; . . . to create in his congregation the thing he is talking about"—but I'm not sure the Riverside services had this same power. You didn't hear much about the congregation's *worshiping*.

Still, I do recall that in our household all the different possible tones represented in the Union Seminary community, at Columbia, and at Riverside—Methodist, Baptist, French Calvinist, German Lutheran, Congregational, Presbyterian, and so on—were simultaneously respected and subjected to intense, often merry analysis. My Anglican mother was after all a formidable scholar of liturgy. And in my father's case? He didn't talk about his own practices in the chancel or pulpit, but it was clear to everyone who knew him that his prayers came not out of nowhere but out of a richly complex somewhere—of Heath, of Union, of austere German-American evangelicalism, of deeply studied biblical theology, of a closely considered style of daily worship.

> O Lord, hear our prayers not according to the poverty of our asking but according to the richness of your grace, so that our lives may conform to those desires which accord with your will.
>
> When our desires are amiss, may they be overruled by a power greater than ours, and by a mercy more powerful than our sin.

IT WASN'T ONLY my semiclandestine explorations of the Book of Common Prayer—during boring sermons or the endless long bits of dreary services—that gave me a bias of interest in English life, and it wasn't only that my mother's country was obviously the one to celebrate in the years right after the war, given its stupendous resistance in 1940–45 to the terror machine of the Third Reich. It was also that England had been the locus of much of my parents' prewar work, so I heard dramatic stories about their times there. And you could say the Serenity Prayer was virtually composed in England, though it didn't appear until that wartime summer Sunday in Heath.

In the summer of 1936 my parents sailed away to Southampton for several English months, proudly bringing their little son to show my mother's happy parents. In England they spent a great deal of time with another intriguing character in my Heath story, to me a character equal in significance to Bishop Scarlett in Missouri or Felix Frankfurter in Washington. The English lawyer and politician Stafford Cripps soon became a close friend, and the summer of 1936 was a notable season to be with him.

The political situation in England—in Europe overall—was appalling, and frightening to boot. The Conservative British government had more or less slept through the German occupation of the Rhineland that spring, with Hitler's invalidation of both the Versailles and Locarno Treaties. Now it was looking, not with disfavor, upon Franco's revolt against the Republic in Spain, which began in July. Mussolini's Italy, having finished its conquest of Ethiopia, started sending "volunteers" to help Franco's odious fascist insurgents and turned toward Hitler's Berlin—summertime developments through which the British government continued more or less to doze.

Cripps was one of the founders of a new organization called the Socialist League; the main problem with its politics, my father thought, was not so much its controversial favoring of a Popular Front with the Communists but that it was not very efficacious; still, Cripps's desire to move in strong opposition to Stanley Baldwin's do-nothing Conservative government was laudable. All year long the cabinet had been vacillating while the situation worsened. (Later in the year, Churchill observed, "The government cannot make up their mind, or they cannot get the Prime Minister to make up his mind. So they go on in strange paradox, decided only to be undecided, resolved to be irresolute, adamant for drift, solid for fluidity, all powerful to be impotent.")

When I was born a few years later, Cripps was to become my godfather, and he was a hero to me. Notwithstanding Churchill's famous put-down of a political foe whom he found self-righteous—"There, but for the grace of God, goes God himself"—I remember him as kindly, lively, approachable. Like a cleverer and more powerful Aunt Ethel, let's say, having easily disregarded the privileges of place, class, and personal safety in the interests of a larger social betterment, he had gotten right to work. His shrewd legal maneuvers in 1934 on behalf of the miners of Gresford, in north Wales, made for a story that I liked hearing my father tell. The miners and their families had suffered grievously in a terrible colliery disaster that had killed 266 men, and during the inquiry that followed the catastrophe, Cripps's pro bono work for the Miners' Federation culminated "in a sustained and devastating cross-examination of the colliery manager," as one historian has summarized it. The matchless skill of his legal work did more for mining safety in England than countless ignored regulations had done. *Of course* he and Frankfurter were friends. Here was a man who lived the injunction to change what should be changed.

Some of Cripps's biographers remark on the shifts and contradictions in his political trajectory, since it didn't conform to the conventional ruling-class English pattern of worldly, careerist ambition rising smoothly on an effortless curve during the insanely difficult years of the 1930s and 1940s. Well of course not. The issue of when a politician should or might change, and how, and over what issue, is subjected by political historians to very close scrutiny, but not the kind of moral and spiritual inquiry that students of the Serenity Prayer engage in. Seen from a different angle, however, Cripps was a remarkably consistent person—in the words of the diplomat Geoffrey Wilson, his (and our) dear friend, the "gay, passionate Christian crusader . . . who struck fire from all with whom he came in contact," and that is how I remember him.

Pa also preached all over the place in England that summer, although not in Anglican churches, since a pastor from a Nonconformist "chapel" sect was not permitted to participate in an Anglican church service. And he met with many Anglican and Nonconformist lay and church people to discuss the matters that concerned them all.

How could men and women of the church help to create polities that would attend to the often conflicting imperatives of economic health, social justice, and political strength, not to mention spiritual decency? And what would—what should— the church's role be in such a society? The debates raged and roiled through weekends at the Crippses' beautiful house, Goodfellows; at dinners with the noted editor and writer Kingsley Martin; in conferences at the BBC, colloquia in Birmingham and Edinburgh. Religion and the state: the balance between them was uncertain, as it still is, and murderously dangerous to adjust or challenge. This was not a new problem then and it isn't one now; it has torn continents, countries, and families apart for centuries. As my prayer books showed me, no one found it easy to agree on solutions.

Given that wars and threats of war were already destroying the equilibrium of Europe less than two decades after the nightmare of 1914–18, there was much work to be done on the ecumenical front, and the initial bond between Pa and Cripps concerned their shared interest in international church activities. They and other members of Life and Work, and of Faith and Order, stayed in close touch with their confreres in Germany, where the churches' distance from or affinity with the powers of the state was now a matter of extreme danger. The pastors of the Confessing Church were still trying to arrive at a modus operandi that would safeguard them from their Nazified colleagues and from Hitler's worst intentions—

an all but doomed enterprise—and they deserved international support. But the work was not easy in any country, be the government fair or foul.

The principal figure in Faith and Order was at this juncture William Temple, archbishop of York, who had become its chairman in 1929 after the death of its founder, Bishop Charles Brent. Temple was a larger-than-life figure, a quintessential upper-class Anglican big shot with an improbable, but profound, devotion to social justice and the welfare of working people. "The suffering caused by existing evils makes a claim upon our sympathy which the Christian heart and conscience cannot ignore," he wrote. And he pledged himself to attend to the "three main causes of widespread suffering—bad housing, malnutrition, and unemployment," the toleration of which he considered "a wanton and callous cruelty."

Since 1908 Temple had been a member, and for more than a decade president, of Oxford's Workers' Educational Association; in 1918 he'd become an active member of the Labour Party, though when he became Bishop of Manchester in 1921 he thought he should be officially "impartial" and gave up his Labour Party membership (to his friend Harry Tawney's disgust). Still, during the General Strike in 1926 he did in Manchester what Will Scarlett was doing in St. Louis and McConnell in Pittsburgh, mediating between the two sides and helping to bring about a settlement that both regarded as basically fair. As an ecumenist Temple also managed to create something called the Church of South India, a merger of Anglican, Congregationalist, Methodist, and Presbyterian churches in a single entity with provisions for safeguarding what each group thought essential—a mind-blowing innovation in the British

Empire. No wonder George Bernard Shaw called him "a realized impossibility." By 1936 he was semilegendary, and I find it both amazing and quite unsurprising that he and my father became such friends.

I'm also not surprised to learn that earlier in his life as a priest Temple had met with the same kind of difficulty that had plagued Pit Van Dusen. When he applied for ordination in 1906, the bishop of Oxford would not go through with it because Temple acknowledged that his belief in the literal truth of the Virgin Birth and the bodily resurrection of Jesus was shaky. (The then Archbishop of Canterbury, who must have been a skillful politician, decided after a careful examination that Temple's thought "was developing in a direction that would bring him to an orthodox position," and took a chance on ordaining him.) By 1913 Temple could write: "I believe in the Virgin Birth . . . it wonderfully holds before the imagination the truth of Our Lord's Deity and so I am glad that it is in the Creed. Similarly I believe in our Lord's Bodily Resurrection." "Wonderfully holds before the imagination"—what a gloriously imprecise phrase. Who is to pass judgment on this?

It has been said that when Temple met my father, he exclaimed as they shook hands, "At last, I have met the disturber of my peace." I have a nice picture of them together: Temple with his broad, wise face and impressive mien, wearing his lordly working uniform with its gaiters and swinging black coat over episcopal purple, my father taller and rangier, in Nonconformist mufti, with his bald head and eagle-y profile, his genial smile. But the austere Cripps feared that Temple was a compromised figure—how else could he have become an archbishop? This consummate insider knew well the inner politics of Lambeth Palace. Established churches were a dubious proposition, as any American could readily agree: connected as they were not only by custom but by law, right, and money to a national government, one had to say that on certain matters they were polluted at the source. Temple in fact did not disagree.

John Baillie, the superb New Testament scholar who had taught systematic theology at Union in 1929–34 (and come to know Bonhoeffer there), was now back in his native Scotland as moderator of *its* established Church of Scotland, and he reported on how the church-state issue was seen from a very different viewpoint. As chaplain to the royal family when it was in residence at Balmoral, he had the opportunity to discuss such matters with Queen Mary, who was, he told my parents, interested in and quite astute about church-state relations. The Queen was evidently distressed, even scandalized, to learn that during these Depression years Archbishop Temple was advocating the nationalization of England's banks. During a walk together in the Balmoral gardens the tricky subject arose.

"Do you agree, Dr. Baillie, with Archbishop Temple's views in politics?"

"I do, Ma'am."

"Do you think they are necessarily related to his Christian convictions?"

"Most of them, I should think, yes. There is a point at which political convictions do not necessarily follow from religious ones, but I do not know where the point is."

"Do you not think, Dr. Baillie," asked the Queen, drawing a line on the ground with her well-shod toe, "that there should be a line beyond which the Archbishop should not move or speak?"

Baillie observed that for different people the line might appear in different places.

The Queen, her toe still pointing at the invisible line, persisted: "*Wherever* we draw the line, should it not be that the Archbishop should not step over it?"

Now this was a very nice story, and my parents liked the Highland astringency in the way "John the Scot" told it, not to mention the wonderful ambiguity of that royal "we" in the Queen's last question. Who, indeed, should decide on what a churchman might or might not speak out? How did priests themselves answer this question? And what about their parishioners? In Nazi Germany the questions were already—and tragically—being answered.

My parents consolidated other friendships in England that summer of 1936 within this same ambit of progressive, internationalist, skeptical, hardworking activists. One of the most important was a figure even more remarkable than the benign Archbishop Temple. The great historian R. H. Tawney had been a friend of "Billy" Temple's since their schooldays at Harrow; they had known each other at Oxford and worked together in the Workers' Educational Association. Tawney's very name evokes to me bracing intelligence, intrepid morals, modest courage. My father had long admired Tawney's path-breaking book on *Religion and the Rise of Capitalism* (1926) and, even more, the profound critique he offered in his scathing study of *The Acquisitive Society* (1920). Now Pa had a chance to get to know this witty, kind gentleman in person, and felt enriched by the friendship. The war was to bring them together again in surprising circumstances.

Tawney is my idea of a really effective Christian, not least because he never talked about being one. During the 1920s and 1930s the celebrated socialist and "freethinker" Beatrice Webb kept trying to smoke out his spiritual commitments, which he refused to discuss; she made the typical secular mistake of thinking that these should be apparent in some recognizable, socially conventional way. "How far is Tawney a believer in the supernatural? . . . He profoundly dislikes and denounces the worldliness of the Anglican church and its toleration of capitalist exploitation." She completely missed the signals evident even in these denunciations. (Meanwhile he was astutely noticing that she believed in prayer—despite her announced agnosticism.)

And puzzlement continued beyond his death in 1962. The largely secular students of Tawney's landmark economic histories examine his socialism under a microscope, yet vague uncertainty reigns about his beliefs in the "Christian myth," as they call it. I don't see why. Tawney's books, his teaching, his social tone, his public activities, and his politics attest to his unwavering faith in the Christian message. And this was the case, as it was with Cripps, even though English politics in the 1930s left little space where a Christian social democrat could stand, let alone maneuver. They each may have fallen silent or backtracked or sidestepped in their public paths, but never in the fundamental direction of their spiritual beliefs.

Another friend was the pacifist Bishop George Bell of Chichester, who through Life and Work, of which he was a director, knew many of the Confessing Church pastors and was a friend of Bonhoeffer's; he had an acutely attentive, well-informed interest in events in Germany. Bell was a man of almost eerie vivacity and goodness.

My father was caught once in a dispute about political effectiveness and religious purity in which Bell figured: Pa had been saying, as he often did, that "saintliness" was an overrated quality, since people who knew a lot about life and understood the difficulty in its relative choices and relative values could not easily be as detached, as "pure," as saints were supposed to be. His friends disagreed, and boxed the compass, as my mother put it:

> "Well, is the Bishop of Chichester a saint?" And Reinhold said, "I would say so, definitely." "Is Archbishop Temple a saint?" Reinhold replied, "I admire him very much, but he isn't a saint. He's too shrewd, too intelligent, too relativistic." "Well," said one of the party, "then you are saying that only stupid people can be saints." Reinhold hastened to emphasize, "No, Bishop Bell is not stupid. There is a sublime simplicity in his goodness that puts him on the other side of cleverness."

The English summer was thick with political and religious discussion. Not only was Pa eager to talk to the bishops and the Faith and Order people, but there were significant debates with the great Kant scholar Norman Kemp Smith and, on a quite different level, John Strachey. Until that summer Strachey had been, like Tawney, what my father called "an unknown friend"—someone you didn't know but whose quality of mind you found congenial and whom you wished you did know. He had been elected to the House of Commons as a Labour member in 1929, but after he lost his seat with the formation of Ramsey MacDonald's National Government in 1931, he briefly joined the New Party, put together by Oswald Mosley. When the very next year Mosley went to Italy, met Mussolini, and returned to England filled with praise for him, Strachey left the New Party in a hurry and wrote a scathing little book on *The*

Menace of Fascism. By that summer of 1936 when Pa met him, he had finished another book called *Theory and Practice of Socialism.* Now he was becoming a Communist—a turn in the road on which Pa would hardly follow him (it lasted only a few years)—and he was planning to leave to fight in Spain with the Republicans. Strachey's mercurial political temperament was unreliable, but he was an intense, intensely intelligent new friend. "Fascism is war" was his famous slogan.

In Oxford the conversations soared, especially the learned, gossipy ones with Maurice Bowra, warden of New College and fabled as the wittiest scholar alive. My mother was happy to be back in the company of her admired teachers, and Pa was delighted to meet them, especially that formidable giant of biblical scholarship C. H. Dodd. Harold and Phyllis Dodd were treasured friends (my mother would have been his assistant in 1930 if she hadn't come to America). For their students the Dodd-Niebuhr axis was a theological one: the first commandment, Archbishop Temple suggested, should be "Thou shalt love the Lord thy Dodd and thy Niebuhr as thyself."*

Beyond the theological merriment, the immediate crises of democracy in Depression-weary Britain and America were the obvious central subjects of discussion amongst these teachers,

---

*Temple, my mother thought, had a pretty wit as well as respectable politics. After a Student Christian Movement conference in Swanwick, in Derbyshire, several years before, when my father had lectured on "The Inevitability of Sin"—his position being regarded as far too dark and pessimistic—Temple had composed this Augustinian limerick:

> At Swanwick, when Niebuhr had quit it,
> Said a young man, "At last, I have hit it!
> Since I cannot do right,
> I must find out tonight
> The best sin to commit—and commit it."

parliamentarians, writers, and activists. And Germany was never far from the thoughts of any of them. Indifferent to Hitler or complacent about him as the British government might be, these friends were all acutely attentive to—and well informed about—the increasing pressures of the Nazi menace, and every day's events in Spain were watched with anguished care. Bishop Bell was not the only one already involved in various plans and efforts to assist the resisters to Hitler's regime.

In a magazine article composed that summer, my father reported at second hand that the Nazi regime had still not "succeeded in quieting the religious opposition to its totalitarian claims," and he predicted that further conflict would come, since the Nazis were obviously determined "more than ever to subject the German youth to an anti-Christian education," which at least some church elements were determined to resist. The German government was doing what it could to destroy the fundaments of the German churches, and the situation was frighteningly bleak. He despaired of the "pessimistic and negative character of [Germany's] prevailing Lutheranism."

By that time 700 pastors in the Confessing Church had been imprisoned for opposing the regime's regulations against the church—a lot of pastors if you look at it one way, or nowhere near enough if you consider that Germany then had 17,000 pastors: it depends on your expectations of principled decency, your expectations of daily, ordinary heroism. A thousand or so Catholic priests were incarcerated, besides. And there was popular opposition to the Nazis: more than 42,000 people signed petitions for the release of the pacifist Carl von Ossietzky, who had been imprisoned in 1933 just before Hitler's accession to power and was still in a concentration camp. (The Nazis kept him there even though—or especially because?—he won the Nobel Peace Prize in 1936, which they demanded he refuse. He died in 1938, never having regained his freedom.)

My father wrote eagerly about the Confessing Church's impressive performance at a big church conference in July 1936, which the Nazis had hoped would impress foreign visitors to the Olympic Games, about to begin in Berlin. The Reich Christian pastors had a pallid reception while Confessing Church delegates attracted enormous, attentive audiences to whom they cited the large increases in attendance at their churches. So there was some hope. He was proud of the pastor Paul Humburg, who was calling on "Christians everywhere" to "resist the government's youth program"; the regime had denied Humburg the right to speak anywhere but in his pulpit (what might Queen Mary, I wonder, have said to that?), so he couldn't attend the conference, but his parishioners printed and circulated tens of thousands of copies of his sermon. Another of my father's prayers went like this:

> We pray to you this day mindful of the sorry confusion of our world. Look with mercy upon this generation of your children, so steeped in misery of their own contriving, so far strayed from your ways and so blinded by passions. We pray for the victims of tyranny, that they may resist oppression with courage and may preserve their integrity by a hope which defies the terror of the moment. We pray for wicked and cruel men, whose arrogance reveals to us what the sin of our own hearts is like when it has conceived and brought forth its final fruit. O God, who resists the proud and gives grace to the humble, bring down the mighty from their seats.
>
> We pray for ourselves who live in peace and quietness, that

we may not regard our good fortune as proof of our virtue, or rest content to have our ease at the price of others' sorrow and tribulation.

We pray for all who have some vision of your will, despite the confusions and betrayals of human sin, that they may humbly and resolutely plan for and fashion the foundations of a just peace between men, even while they seek to preserve what is fair and just among us against the threat of malignant power. Grant us grace to see what we can do, but also to know what are the limits of our powers, so that courage may feed on trust in you, who are able to rule and overrule the angry passions of men and make the wrath of men to praise you.

MY FATHER'S CHURCH POLITICS had been, up to this point, concerned principally with the condition of the Protestant churches in Europe and America. Of course he thought about the relationship those churches had with Roman Catholicism, of course he studied Roman Catholic theology, and of course he paid heed to the Vatican's political presence in the world. But when its policies toward the rising fascist dictatorships became an urgent issue in the mid-1930s, he began to write more extensively on it.

What, he asked in 1937, was the motive force behind "the intimate alliance between Catholicism and fascism"? He found the oft-cited answer that they shared a common enemy in godless Bolshevism inadequate, even hollow, certainly showing "a certain pathos." As if Mussolini and Hitler and Franco were the only alternative to Stalin?! No, surely there was also some affinity having to do with congruent authoritarian views. In any case, having a new pope, who Pa correctly predicted would be Cardinal Pacelli, would hardly make a difference, not only because

Pacelli had been such an important formative influence on Pius XI's policy earlier in the decade but because "the total situation is determined by forces on both sides too deeply rooted in history and too inexorable in their logic to permit the hope that a change in reigning popes will greatly affect the issue."

I don't think it's presumptuous to imagine that papal policy in the 1930s and 1940s was something my father prayed to have the serenity to accept; obviously one couldn't change it, though one could and did inveigh against it. His ardent comments on that subject have a cool analytical rigor that does not belie his appalled scorn—for the Vatican's praise of Mussolini's conquest of Ethiopia, for the Spanish cardinals' support of General Franco, and, later, for the servility of the French bishops who collaborated with Vichy. In one politicized situation after another one could discern the Vatican's support of its own hierarchy as against its congregants, as he put it, its devotion to its own power structure and its neglect of ordinary people. Always, always the big Catholic problem.

A good example of this in the 1930s was the Vatican's withdrawal of support for priests who were active in local political movements that expressed "the common man's discontent with the status quo"—understandable enough in the Depression years. You couldn't easily describe the political tendencies of these movements or generalize about them, Pa went on to say, but quite clearly they were "economically more liberal and politically more daring than anything ventured by the hierarchy," and many Catholics had joined them. While condemning these well-meant little groups, the Vatican simultaneously threw its support to Catholic Action chapters and other parish organizations that were kept directly under the bishops' thumbs. This typical policy of channeling and controlling the social energies of the laity bred resentment and stifled freedom.

It was a tragedy, he thought, if opposition to fascism in Catholic Europe might now be found more reliably among those who derived "moral self-respect" from Soviet communism and who appropriated the "moral prestige of Lenin's disinterestedness" than among true Christians. True, there were handfuls of brave Catholic priests who refused to kowtow to fascism, but only handfuls. The hierarchy gave little or no spiritual succor to the millions of Roman Catholics who faced harsh daily moral problems in their relations with Nazi or fascist authorities. The priests were not seeing this godless totalitarian nightmare for what it was. In America, Pa's cordial friendships and affectionate but fierce doctrinal disputes with Father John LaFarge and, later, with Father John Courtney Murray only deepened his distress. Here were two Jesuit thinkers of immense learning and great spiritual breadth (they were giants now remembered with awe, but then dismissed and frowned upon by the callow, reactionary power elite of the American Catholic Church), but even the Church's finest minds seemed tragically unwilling to alter their doomed acceptance of the Vatican's *raisons d'état*, and the ludicrous dogma of papal infallibility that hovered over the enterprise.

It is now known publicly that at about this time Father LaFarge was helping to compose an encyclical, drafted for Pope Pius XI but never promulgated either by him or by his successor, Pius XII, that denounced racism and condemned Nazi anti-Semitism. The non-release of this encyclical was a famous non-event with incalculable consequences. But it was not the only no-show in Catholic activities of the time.

Ecumenical activists at the Oxford Conference on Church, Community, and State, 1937, with Archbishop Temple, Visser 't Hooft, and my father in the front row

On a different but related front, the Catholics were absent.

All the efforts of the ecumenically minded Protestants who had been working so hard together since the end of the Great War culminated at a celebrated high point of the interwar years, the Oxford Conference on Church, Community, and State, held in July 1937. Four hundred delegates assembled for several weeks of plenary meetings in the Sheldonian Theatre—delegates from Asia along with Orthodox priests from Greece and Yugoslavia, bishops from all the established Protestant churches of northern Europe along with Methodists, Baptists, and Reformed pastors and important lay people. This was a summit meeting of world Protestantism, no doubt about it, but its political aims were hardly anti-Catholic and invitations had been extended to Roman Catholics as well. The idea was to welcome all serious Christians willing to discuss what they might do *together* to mitigate or thwart the impending wars. Three groups were absent: the German delegation, because the Nazis had withdrawn their passports at the last minute; American fundamentalists, who declined to participate; and the Roman Catholics.

So the Catholics had no influence over the conference's general themes, which were now largely set by the American Protestants. The first theme was inarguable: that the social disintegration apparent around the world—caused in large part by still unsolved problems left over from the Great War, hastened by the Depression, and amplified by growing industrialization and urbanization—was encouraging a resort to dictatorship. The absent groups could have gone along with that, though they might not have agreed that the loss of democratic freedom was regrettable. Some of them actually welcomed it.

The second theme was very Niebuhrian, though it surprised those who expected my father to be topical, political. In a major address early on in the conference, Pa proposed that the root problem of the time was not fascism or industrial strife or war but, simply, sin. Sin everywhere—in the "hypocritical pretensions of the rationalists" and their "implicit or covert self-glorification," which is "always the particular temptation of the victors"; and in the cynicism and "more explicit self-glorification" that mark "the sin of the vanquished." He continued:

> The civilization and culture in which we are called upon to preach the Christian gospel is . . . a devotee of a very old religion dressed in a new form. It is the old religion of self-glorification. This is a very old religion, because it involves the quintessence of human sin as defined by St. Paul . . . "they became vain in their imaginations, and their foolish heart was

darkened. Professing themselves to be wise, they became fools [and what an accurate description that is of the vainglory of our modern era!], and changed the glory of the uncorruptible God into an image made like to corruptible man, and to birds, and four-footed beasts, and creeping things" [Romans 1:21–23].

The conference's third theme was surely one on which a group of Christian priests, however diverse, could somehow agree. Indeed, it was a dish the Vatican could have digested easily if it had been prepared according to its own recipe, for it was that the church was the only institution that might be able to cure the world's ills. As Pa put it, "Christian faith must provide the foundations for the edifice of a social ethic and the minarets for its superstructure." I am intrigued by his architectural allusions here, but one can't imagine that Roman Catholics would have wanted to stay around to hear a Protestant Nonconformist sounding off on an insight they believed they owned. The questions remained: who would decide what this church was, who would compose it, and how would it relate to everything else?

The delegates at Oxford, despite their good intentions and all these rousing speeches, were having a hard time figuring out even how to pray together, let alone manage anything else. The regular services arranged for the delegates made the Anglican and Orthodox participants jittery: much too Protestant! But to have Holy Communion celebrated simultaneously in three different rites was embarrassingly at odds with the very purpose of the gathering. I suppose it might have been even more hilariously clumsy if the Germans, the American fundamentalists, and the RCs had been there, too. It went on like this for a fortnight, until the Anglicans pulled themselves together and actually invited all baptized and communicant delegates to a single communion service. Imagine! It hadn't happened before, except in moments of dire stress, such as in the trenches at Passchendaele.

The delegates' genuine efforts to discuss their differences amiably were praiseworthy, and having the whole conference crowned with this unprecedented instance of holy worship persuaded many of them that churchmen really might be able to help resolve international discord. The hopeful ones included John Foster Dulles, the Presbyterian lawyer from New York who had been devoting much of his time during the preceding decade to international church work. He contrasted his Oxford experience favorably with a rancorous League of Nations meeting he'd attended in Paris the week before.

Pa wasn't so sure. The churches' tenuous agreements would not necessarily avail them in the coming seasons, given that their pulpits were filled with what he called (following Jeremiah) false prophets, who promised false security. How could one tell the false prophets from the true? In a time of great insecurity and fear, this was a most urgent question, since "the most basic need of the human spirit is the need for security, and the most fundamental problem of religion is the problem of meeting this need."

And where in the world was there any kind of security? Certainly no European nation was affording its citizens any basic safety, and international mechanisms to enforce the peace had collapsed. The Mediterranean Sea had become a lake of war, with German, Italian, and Spanish patrols and warships skirmishing and threatening British and French ones. Mussolini consolidated his conquest of Ethiopia, and after this brutal aggression the League of Nations signed its own death knell when it decided not to reimpose sanctions (however ineffectual) against the aggressor. Italy began to glower hungrily at Libya. It was no better in Asia. Japanese forces, having conquered Manchuria, continued their hostile advance into northern China, where savage battles were accompanied by the merciless bombing of Chinese cities.

In a sermon preached at about this time and revised for publication in his book *Beyond Tragedy*, my father assessed the tragic conflicts that were still tearing at the heart of Europe. It was almost two decades since Germany had capitulated and withdrawn from French territory in November 1918, but the spiritual and political wounds were still raw:

> France's vindictive oppression of her German foe was prompted by genuine fears, lest she be destroyed if the foe should arise and regain his strength. But the spirit of vengeance against this injustice was the very force by which the foe arose; and now that he has arisen he seems to dream of gaining sufficient strength to become forever impregnable. The Germans speak with religious fervour of "an eternal Germany," but the policies by which they seek to gain this strength make the whole of Europe insecure. In this insecurity one may already discern the forces which will destroy German security before it is fairly established.

The churches' reassurances were not getting to the core of the danger, my father continued. Some false prophets, posing as worldly-wise realists, argued that the struggle for power in Europe was, as he put it, "an inevitable extension of the will to live and therefore morally permissible"—an interpretation that left everyone stranded and exposed in the fateful battles to come. Meanwhile other false prophets, who called themselves moralists, "believe that because such a struggle is obviously suicidal it should not be too difficult to dissuade men from it." How could one take this seriously? In the two decades since the end of Europe's last suicidal war, men and women had hardly weaned themselves from this strife.

Both types of false prophet were far off the mark. The defiant self-glorification of National Socialist Germany and the dangerous complacency of its foes created insecurity for everyone. Modern nations were filled with injustices, and citizens of both dictatorships and democracies had to recognize that, as my father put it, "sooner or later injustice will create the force of vengeance by which it is destroyed." When that happens the true prophet should be warning "that no nation can be strong enough to protect itself against all of its foes, particularly since its strength arouses new enemies against it."

Other false prophets imagined that global commerce had "discovered the law of mutuality by which social enmity is destroyed," and they glorified "the prudent internationalism of the trader." Dreaming that the globalization of Western business interests would ward off war, they were making the mistake of conflating democracy and bourgeois civilization with "something of the eternal and ultimate spirit of love." They were also forgetting that "a trading civilization is involved in more bitter international quarrels than any civilization of history." There was no guarantee that democracy, which "may be little more than the luxury of a stable civilization," could survive the inevitable social struggle that would break out when the comparative affluence and absolute power of an advanced nation were challenged.

It cast one into near-despair to consider the difficulties of preaching a Christian message in these circumstances:

> It is so easy to condemn flagrant pride and to condone a subtle form of it; to outlaw overt injustice and to sanction a covert form of it; to condone the security of power because its tentative necessity is recognized; or to accept injustice complacently as the price and inevitable consequence of power; or to encourage men to the illusory hope that they may build a world in which there is no power, pride, or injustice. How can all of these temptations be avoided? They cannot . . . wherefore we ought to speak humbly.

VI

In the anxious summers of 1938 and 1939, vacations in Heath had become partial ones, islands of recuperative rest in an ocean of ever intensifying, ever more urgent work. It was this way for everyone in my family's circle—or indeed for anyone with an eye to what was happening in the world. The danger of war in Europe was increasing, and in many ways the loss of security was all too clear. Yet, the war in Spain notwithstanding, even to get people to see that this was the case was not easy. The tempo of capitulation to the forces of war was accelerating.

To mention only events beginning in the spring of 1938 and only in Europe, Hitler's Germany, having reoccupied the Rhineland, proceeded to annex Austria in March and then dismember Czechoslovakia. Tensions rose between Italy and France, especially after the final defeat of the Republicans and Franco's fascist triumph in Spain in early 1939. The British government remained publicly conciliatory toward Hitler's regime if not privately rather enthusiastic about it—until, in 1939, Germany occupied the rump of Bohemia and Moravia, then annexed Memel: these moves alarmed even the imperturbable Neville Chamberlain, now prime minister. His government slowly abandoned the famous policy of appeasing Hitler, called for national

*Ex-Chancellor Heinrich Bruening and Niebuhr, outside the
Moorses' house in Brookline, January 1938*

conscription, and pledged to Poland that Anglo-French forces
would assist it in maintaining its independence.

In the United States, preoccupied with intense labor strife
and with itself, as usual, Congress took note of these European
developments only to distance itself from them: it had passed a
Neutrality Act in May 1937 that prohibited the export of arms
and munitions to any belligerents, and it stopped there. Though
FDR began more and more openly to indicate American support for the European democracies, especially after Germany
began to threaten Poland outright, the Congress ignored his
warning that the Neutrality Act was an indirect encouragement
to fascist warmongers, and the isolationist Republicans made
gains in the 1938 elections.

Family life proceeds while public life deteriorates, however—
as we all know. In the spring and summer of 1939, my family
went to England for a protracted stay. My mother was eager to
see her parents again, and to have them see her children—by

then Christopher was four, and I had arrived that very January. As for Pa, as usual he had various commitments on the ecumenical and scholarly fronts, as well as one giant theological assignment, which was to give the Gifford Lectures at the University of Edinburgh.

In London Pa met with his old student Dietrich Bonhoeffer, who was in anguish. He had just decided that he must leave Germany, where he had been working since 1935; he was ready to go "somewhere where service is really wanted," as he put it; the Nazis were cutting off funds to the pastors who opposed them and in other more sinister ways throttling their ministries; they were indeed extinguishing all hope of the free society to which he hoped to contribute. And war was approaching. So Pa helped to arrange a temporary appointment for Bonhoeffer in New York, teaching at Union Seminary for the summer term. President Coffin came through at crisis moments like this one.

Bonhoeffer's thinking had clearly evolved since 1935. From the beginning he had recognized that Hitler's well-armed, popularly supported, and frighteningly aggressive terror regime was endangering not just political opponents, or clergymen, or Jews, but the very life of civilization. Once he had imagined that somehow he could function as a priest and theologian in the National Socialist framework, but now he knew this was virtually impossible. Yet he was still uncertain as to what exactly he would do. His travels to and from Germany during the late 1930s were sanctioned ecumenical trips, but they gave the outward and visible sign of his inward and spiritual uncertainty, as he seesawed back and forth.

He went from Berlin to London twice in the spring of 1939; after seeing my father he returned to Berlin and thence to

America and to Union Seminary, where he got in touch with Paul Tillich, whom he greatly impressed. But by mid-June Bonhoeffer was in an agony of misgiving about having left his homeland, as Tillich could see. Four different job offers materialized for him in America, but they were dangerous to consider, since, as Bonhoeffer wrote, "I must not for the sake of loyalty to the Confessional church accept a post which on principle would make my return to Germany impossible." He spent time with Henry Sloane Coffin at his pretty house in Lakeville, Connecticut. ("I do not understand why I am here," he wrote in his diary, "Germany is missing.") He prayed and prayed. ("Prayers. I was almost overcome by the short prayer—the whole [Coffin] family knelt down—in which we thought of the German brothers.") He saw my Uncle Helmut. He returned to New York, and then, only a few weeks into his American sojourn, he decided he must go home.

Would he be required to sign up for compulsory military service, or should he somehow try to take "conscientious objector" status? Bonhoeffer had been deeply shaken when the head of the German section of the pacifist Fellowship of Reconciliation had been executed when he refused to be conscripted that year. Should he continue his pastoral work in Germany, which was harder and harder to accomplish, or— leaving aside the American option, which he had rejected— should he find some way of continuing it beyond German borders? His church did not help him in deciding any of this. As Pa reported to a friend, "The *Brüderrat* of the Confessing Church [its directorate, the Council of Brethren] would like to have him evade the issue." Evasion is what most churches were really good at, for most of the century. One might as well extend the indictment to all institutions of organized religion.

On his way back to Germany, Bonhoeffer tried to see my father again in London, but they missed each other. He returned to his destiny in Berlin. As his biographer says, "After 1939 the old priorities could be fulfilled only by exchanging them. To want to be only a Christian, a timeless disciple—that now became a costly privilege."

Bonhoeffer's life in wartime Germany perforce became grotesquely strange. On the one hand he did his best to continue his teaching and pastoral work, doing most of this clandestinely, for Gestapo agents were tailing him to watch for what they considered "subversive activities." The police prohibited him from making public speeches and obliged him to report to them regularly on his movements—impossible restrictions that he rightly found defamatory. On the other hand he accepted an offer to work for the Reich's Office of Military Counter-Intelligence (this, he and his fellow conspirators reasoned, gave him a good cover for his ecumenical travels), where he worked ostensibly as a confidential agent for Germany's war machine but in fact put his considerable resources at the disposal of the network of people working within the government to subvert Hitler's policies and, if possible, to supplant him. On the one hand he continued his work on pure theology and went on playing music with his siblings and cousins; on the other hand he gradually became involved in plans to end the Third Reich by killing Hitler.

To decide that this was necessary, let alone to decide to participate in such a plan, was not easy for a Christian pastor, to put it very mildly. Passive resistance to Hitler was the mode that many brave clergy had immediately adopted in 1933; and the

Confessing Church's open confrontation with the regime was the next step. But Bonhoeffer, learning about preparations for a coup against Hitler, not only became what lawyers would call an "informed accessory" to it but joined active planning for a post–Hitler government. This was a quite different order of resistance and political action from what the Barmen Declaration had set forth. Small wonder that Bonhoeffer's decision was preceded by many uncertainties. But nobody can come to easy judgments about this recognition of crisis. When *is* the moment to act? How *does* one decide that one's cherished, imperishable beliefs must be adjusted? Where *is* the line that separates what "cannot be changed" from what "must be changed"? And then one must not only discern the necessity for change but also have the courage to undertake it.

Bonhoeffer's clandestine work brought him closer to his remarkable brother-in-law the young lawyer Hans von Dohnanyi, who recruited him "at a relatively early point to the inner circle," as his biographer recounts, a small number of military-intelligence officers joined in an active conspiracy to kill Germany's head of state. This last stage in Bonhoeffer's political transformation was the most remarkable. He and his brother-in-law had long talks about the ethical and political consequences of their enterprise. One evening Dohnanyi asked Bonhoeffer "what he thought about the New Testament passage 'all who take the sword will perish by the sword' (Matthew 26:52). Bonhoeffer replied that this held true for their circle as well. They would have to accept that they were subject to that judgment."

The Nazis' preparation for their blitzkrieg in Poland, which began on September 1, 1939, did much to clarify and crystallize Bonhoeffer's mind. On his way back to Berlin in the spring, he had met in London with W. A. Visser 't Hooft, the remarkable Dutch ecumenical activist who was at the center of anti-fascist European church work. The two men found each other at Paddington Station and walked up and down the platform, talking about what should happen next. As Visser 't Hooft remembered it:

> He spoke in a way that was remarkably free from illusions, and sometimes almost clairvoyantly, about the coming war, which would start soon, probably in the summer. . . . Had not the time now come to refuse to serve a government that was heading straight for war and breaking all the commandments? . . . In the impenetrable world between "Munich" and "Warsaw," in which hardly anyone ventured to formulate the actual problems clearly, this questioning voice was a liberation.

DURING THAT SAME "impenetrable" season between the Munich conference and the Nazi conquest of Poland, the Niebuhrs were busy with both public and private English appointments. Somehow, in between all the meetings and conferences, there was time for family reunions, and, also, I was christened in a little church in Sussex in April: Stafford Cripps was my godfather; my American godmother was the pacifist Harry Fosdick's daughter Dorothy; there were two English godmothers, too. This quartet of godparents formed, for me, another unit of buoyant, hopeful, and ever resourceful friends.

One of my English godmothers had been my mother's favorite mentor at Oxford, Barbara Dwyer, then principal of St. Hugh's College; I later came to know her when I was a student myself. She was to confound my trite expectations of what an Oxford grandee would be like. She may have retired to a little

Stafford and Isobel Cripps at the Labour Party Conference, 1939

semidetached in Tunbridge Wells, where she fed me an ideally appointed tea, but the clichés stopped there. Miss Dwyer was pretty if wholly unfashionable, and not in the least fusty or donnish. She carried her considerable learning with a true lightness of being; there was radiant clarity in her outspoken, unconventional spirit, and the generosity of her beautiful manners seemed a quality of her soul, not her social upbringing. This formidable biblical scholar could hold her own with C. H. Dodd or Tawney or Bowra. No mean feat.

My second English godmother was the redoubtable Margaret Wedgwood-Benn, later Lady Stansgate—the daughter, wife, and mother of notable Liberal and Labour parliamentarians. Here was someone even more unlike the stereotype. My mother liked to speculate that this lifelong feminist was perhaps the shrewdest politician in her family, and she told me many stories about Lady

Stansgate's subtle political energies: I was to understand my great good luck in having such a fairy bestow a wish over my cradle. Indeed I did. As the years rolled forward I cherished my infrequent connections with her, and felt that she took care of me, from afar, for many decades. There were letters; little gifts; a godmotherly insistence that I stay with the Benns when first I came to England so as not to be adrift in London alone; renewed invitations; acute commentary on the day's headlines; delicious stories about her own youth; easy, apparently desultory conversation that delicately assuaged hurtful difficulties and then delicately soothed my confused adolescent heart. I may have seen more of Dorothy Fosdick, who became a pal—after all she was an American and often in New York, where I could enjoy her ebullient energy, her political savvy, her high-level Washington gossip, and her bright brown eyes. There's something wonderful about friends who are intermediate between one's own generation and one's parents' and who radiate their kindness equally in both directions, and Dorothy was like that. But Lady Stansgate was truly a god*mother.*

In 1939 Peggy Benn was as deeply committed a Zionist as my father was becoming, which is not to say that she was a "Christian Zionist," a type of mild bigot who thought the real solution to the Jewish Problem was to send all the Jews—especially East European Jews—to Palestine, and thus to avoid the question of what to do about them in the countries of which they plausibly or implausibly wanted to be normal citizens. (These Christian Zionists, who bear a distant doctrinal relation to today's right-wing Christian supporters of right-wing Israeli politicians, hid their natural anti-Semitism under a strident support for the most intransigent forms of Zionism.) For Peggy

Benn and my father, the question was how to bring about international support for some kind of organized "home" for Jews in Palestine that would also recognize and protect the Arab communities already found there. The issue was becoming more than urgent, since the unspeakable Nazi assault on German Jews was intensifying, while at the same time a British White Paper suspended further Jewish immigration to Palestine. These matters had the highest priority for her and other political activists and ecumenical clerics.

At the time of my baptism, my father was working hard on his Gifford Lectures, the first set of which he delivered in Edinburgh that spring; he was due to give the second set of ten in September, after he returned from a fortnight of lecturing in Sweden. In between he preached in London to a big meeting of the Student Christian Movement, and many of the young people remembered it with gratitude in the fierce seasons ahead. The text of Pa's sermon was taken from St. Paul, and it was well chosen: "We are troubled on every side, yet not distressed; we are perplexed, but not in despair; persecuted, but not forsaken; cast down, but not destroyed; . . . So then death worketh in us, but life in you . . . though our outward man perish, yet the inward man is renewed day by day."

Only a few weeks later, at the end of August, Hitler announced that he had concluded a nonaggression pact with Stalin, and this dangerous, shocking shift radically changed the war-peace valence, for among other things it allowed Germany even more directly to threaten Poland, which England and France had already pledged to help in such circumstances. Hitler drew up a list of impossible conditions to which he demanded Poland's immediate adherence. Military preparations accelerated on all fronts. Roosevelt appealed to the king of Italy, to Hitler, and to the president of Poland to negotiate rather than resort to arms—but in vain.

Pa never made it to Sweden that autumn. Forty-eight hours after the Wehrmacht invaded Poland with a force of 1.7 million men on September 1, the vicar of the little church in Sussex where my family was living brought a radio into the Sunday morning service so that everyone could hear Prime Minister Chamberlain announce that England was now at war with Germany. The next day came news that the Germans had torpedoed the S.S. *Athenia*, an English passenger liner; two days later still more vessels were sunk off the coast of Spain.

American citizens in England (in my family that meant my father, my brother, and me, since my mother had not yet taken out naturalization papers) were urged to leave the country right away, which meant by the next available American ship, the S.S. *George Washington*, due to depart from Southampton on September 12—American boats, at least, had some safety. But the U.S. embassy agreed with the University of Edinburgh that Pa should stay behind to complete his Scottish assignment, and in truth, much as he may have disliked being separated from his family at a time of such danger and uncertainty, he didn't mind being in a Britain at war. He wrote to Will Scarlett, with considerable sangfroid, that being long persuaded that "this thing had to be faced," he was "happy to be among a people who are facing it with grim determination and with a good deal of humility. . . . None of the pride and vainglory of 1914 is evident. A good deal has been learnt since then. . . . The air defenses are pretty good now, but the carnage may be bad nevertheless."

By the time Pa actually delivered his lectures in Edinburgh,

German planes were bombing the nearby bridge over the Firth of Forth, possibly trying to destroy the naval base there, too. Many of his text's most difficult passages—and they were not easy lectures to absorb—were presented to an audience who couldn't hear the words above the din of anti-aircraft artillery. Meanwhile my mother hastened to Southampton with her American children; the troop trains and army convoys on the roads reminded her of wartime moments from 1914–18, during her own childhood, which had been spent in this great port city, though "the enormous barrage balloons . . . were strange and new." The boat trip was a nightmare: the first-class decks were filled with Hollywood stars, assorted Kennedys sent home from the embassy to the Court of St. James, the Thomas Mann family; but only rudimentary services were available in the very overcrowded steerage sections. My mother once explained to me how she worked out a system for rinsing, washing, and (trickiest of all) drying my diapers in the woefully cramped public spaces where babies and their gear had to be tended to. I can't remember what the system was, only that it was ludicrously difficult.

When Pa got back to New York some months later, he plunged into catch-up work at Union and a host of other obligations. I'm not surprised to discover in reading about him—I never heard of this during my childhood—that he collapsed completely in March 1940 and was ordered to bed for a full fortnight to recover from "nervous exhaustion." That was his style: pounding ahead in top gear, in overdrive, even if there was very little gas left in the tank. Not easy for his wife, one has to note. When he was well again he worked on the revisions to the first set of Giffords, due to be published soon: that is to say, he finished what became the first volume of *The Nature and Destiny of Man* during the dark winter after Hitler and Stalin had carved up Poland. Soon Norway and Denmark were invaded, Holland and Belgium conquered, and then France defeated.

He found it almost impossible to work on his revisions to the second set of Gifford Lectures, for there was so much else to do and so many people to help—every week and month the war worsened. At least the U.S. government had moved off the dime. Though right after the invasion of Poland the United States had reaffirmed its neutrality in the European war, two months later Congress finally amended the Neutrality Act and repealed the embargo on arms; in May 1940 Roosevelt persuaded it to release funds to expand the army and navy, to authorize a program for building 50,000 airplanes a year, and then, several months later, and most impressively, to trade naval and air bases on British soil in the Western Hemisphere for the British use of fifty over-age American destroyers. Despite this essential and badly needed assistance to beleaguered Britain, many Americans believed passionately that their country should stay clear of the war, a position that FDR had to work around and that people like my father continued to argue against. The depth of hostility to interventionists like himself, especially among the pacifists, amazed Pa. "I wish some of these pacifists would hate Hitler more and me less," he remarked mournfully.*

---

*He kept one letter, from a theology professor in Chicago, as an example of the rhetoric used by his foes: the ripe flowering of its rage was especially effective. "My dear Sir, I have come to the point where I can no longer be silent at your shocking disregard for the fundamental decencies of your Christian ministry and professorship. I listened, last Thursday night, to your very feeble yet sinister sophistries about our never being perfect or ever being able to achieve our ideals in their perfection. . . . The sophistry, also, about there being things 'worse than war'; again, the 'moral value'

He and my mother were buoyed by a new friendship that blossomed in New York in the horrible winter and spring of 1941—with W. H. Auden, who had arrived to live in the United States in 1939. My mother could readily sympathize with his complicated Anglo-American dual loyalties (subject to predictable misinterpretation by English friends and New Yorkers), and they quickly developed a kind of sibling friendship, these two Oxford-educated children of provincial Anglican doctors. Auden became very close to my father, too, whose books he read, whose sermons he listened to carefully and critically, and whose spiritual advice he craved. Auden spent a lot of time *chez* Niebuhr, showed my mother his poems, and talked theology constantly. He sent affectionate notes beseeching her to get Pa to slow down: the Niebuhr social-action machine needed contemplative quiet to sustain the public work, he rightly thought. He proposed, wicked tease that he was, to lock "the Christian dynamo in your house" into a monastic cell for a suitable period of withdrawal from the world and nothing but a rosary to fidget with.

Naturally enough, after the attack on Pearl Harbor in December 1941 and America's entry into the war, things changed mightily. Auden cheered when Pa resumed his theological work more comprehensively and he could eventually complete the final revisions to the Gifford Lectures; the second

---

of war to this nation. (Hitlerism at its worst!) . . . To be sure, this propaganda has brought you national notoriety and large profits, owing to your rhetorical and literary ability. . . . It is apostasy, brazen and shameless. . . . You are a shocking spectacle to God, Jesus Christ and Humanity. Some of us, who are willing to be poor, unrenowned and unpopular, know the truth." The references to fictional "large profits" and to the writer's own "willingness to be poor" are dead-giveaway signals of the familiar fundamentalist mind-set, in which income and profits always figure. Misplaced, ancient class angers bubble up in the sanctimonious denunciations.

volume was published in 1943. The two volumes together were dedicated to his wife, "who helped," and his children, "who frequently interrupted me in the writing of these pages."

The Nature and Destiny of Man is considered my father's magnum opus, and so it is. This is not the place to discuss its enormous themes and its intricate, to me persuasive, analysis of so many of the most vexing issues in moral philosophy, in Christian ethics, in philosophical interpretation. But I am moved to see how strongly the tone that is now famous in the Serenity Prayer radiates throughout the two volumes; the work of true spiritual contrition, as well as the labor of true justice, never ceases. The second volume ends with a consideration of the quality that he was to place, just a year or so later, in the key position in his little prayer:

> Wisdom about our destiny is dependent upon a humble recognition of the limits of our knowledge and our power. Our most reliable understanding is the fruit of "grace," in which faith completes our ignorance without pretending to possess its certainties as knowledge, and in which contrition mitigates our pride without destroying our hope.

Meanwhile what were Pa's old foes in the American church doing? Most American pastors had the general attitude of indifference to world crisis that seems to be a chronic American habit. Even the Federal Council of Churches issued an appeal in early 1940 for the United States' continued neutralism (written by among others some of my father's students, he noted wryly). Espousal of the doctrine of absolute noninvolvement in the war against fascism, let us call it—I can't credit it with "pacifism"—was not limited to my father's old friends in the Fellowship of

Reconciliation, the honorable pacifist group that he had once chaired. McConnell, Scarlett, Pauck, and a few other prelates were as usual completely alive to the dangers, but mostly, people seemed asleep or distracted—or happy to insist on America's righteous indifference to the world's travails.

One can't credit the neutralism of these Americans in 1940–41 with "pacifism" for the simple reason that many of them weren't pacifist at all, and the ones who claimed to be were murky about the grounds on which they built their doctrine. What a strange, repulsive situation. The isolationist noise clanging in America's political air was making rational debate all but impossible. Clamorous denunciations of "foreign entanglement" came from many quarters but especially from the right, whose pigheaded spokesmen found harmonic comfort in the left's cautious pieties about the dangers of an imperialist war.

The brassiest in this band were the rich, influential, and bellicose supporters of America First, reactionary isolationists claiming Charles Lindbergh as their mascot—an American "hero" who admired Hitler, accepted a medal from Göring, and looked kindly on Mussolini. Some America Firsters were high-minded purists (quite a few of them from Yale) with a genuine concern about the international chaos that they believed was threatening America, but most of them did not mind lining up shoulder to shoulder with the tub-thumping, hypocritical, all-American thugs who favored their own local strongmen and fascists, native blackshirts who naturally also favored Hitler and Mussolini. These vehement political forces attracted millions of voters who would claim, piously, that they simply thought their country should steer clear of foreign wars. But the truth was that they either inclined to fascism themselves, turning their vessels gratefully on a tack that would let their sails fill with the authoritarian winds blowing around the globe, or were weak-minded people who couldn't and wouldn't recognize that the life-and-death struggles over democratic freedom in Europe concerned values at risk in their own country.

And now these isolationist forces, mostly on the right, were aligned with left-wing *socialists* and *pacifists,* and with the *Communists*, whose allegiance to the Soviet Union survived Russia's extraordinary *volte face* in the summer of 1939 and Stalin's pact with the Nazis. With this mixed bag of supposedly neutralist forces the Federal Council of Churches was now allying itself! It was not a situation in which any moral claim to the high ground could be sustained. In any case my father did not think that the pacifist Christian ground was high—or high enough.

THE GOSPELS SHOW Jesus preaching an uncompromising, absolute ethic to "love your enemy," "resist not evil," "be ye therefore perfect even as your father in heaven is perfect." These noble, difficult counsels of perfection have suggested to many that pacifism is the inevitable Christian position, even against such a dire and extreme threat as Hitler's. Pa certainly thought that devout Christian pacifists were to be supported when they expressed their "impulse to take the law of Christ seriously and not to allow political strategies, which the sinful character of man makes necessary, to become final norms," as he put it then. This ancient tradition was to be respected. A pacifism that "regarded the mystery of evil as beyond its power of solution," and that was content with rules for the conduct of life that disavowed the political task, was a "kind of pacifism which is not a heresy."

When Congress, at FDR's behest, passed the Selective Ser

vice Act in September 1940, requiring all men between twenty-one and thirty-six to register with the armed forces—the President had rightly judged that the country was genuinely at risk—some of Pa's students, including a few who were near and dear to him, went to jail for refusing to be drafted rather than have their principles violated on this score, and one's heart was with them. Such absolutist Christian pacifism, which the Quakers in many instances notably represented, was honorable. But it was also luxurious.

It was luxurious because it implicitly accepted that the larger society permitting the pacifists their views was in point of fact protecting them and enabling them to live out their convictions. The political responsibilities the pacifists took on were, they explained themselves, voluntary ones; their social contract did not bind them with overall ethical obligations to their fellow citizens. Quakers were famous for the speed and generosity of their voluntaristic charities, for example, as they still are; pacifism and the Quakers' modest, effective minority status as a "sect" (as Weber would have put it) went together. But did the pacifists acknowledge that their doctrine, which explicitly freed the individual from any overall responsibility for social justice, had as an unacknowledged premise that this responsibility would be borne by others?

Being only human, pacifists could also be as deluded about their own motives as they often were about their opponents'. And they sometimes mistakenly conflated their own principled refusal to bear arms with local, even selfish, desires to avoid conflict. Like their enemies, their ranks were filled with less than sincere, less than honorable adherents. This was and is a perennial problem, as it is with any political grouping. As Pa had written during another war, in 1918, "The crux of the whole question of pacifism is its sincerity." (At that juncture he was observing close up the hypocrisy of German Americans who claimed to have opposed the Great War and America's entry into it: their retroactive pacifism masked repressed shame at the humiliation of their fatherland's once mighty army, which they continued secretly to admire.)

In any event pacifism didn't have much to say, implicitly or explicitly, about situations in which the chance to live life charitably or nonviolently was entirely snuffed out. Myles Horton had tried to make this same point when he asked his pacifist friends in Tennessee to face the music. Sometimes the pacifist position was not only a luxury but unavailable. Pa thought that pacifists should acknowledge this and acknowledge that evil circumstances sometimes denied you the option of noninvolvement, even the option of noncooperation or nonviolent resistance—as Bonhoeffer and so many others were discovering in Germany, as Gandhi and the Congress Party already knew in India. They needed to see that when you found or put yourself in a position with any kind of public responsibility, you were bound to come into conflict or concert with nonpacifist forces. Then what were you supposed to do?

Europeans were learning in the most painful, debasing way that their eagerness to avoid conflict with Hitler had led or was leading to the destruction of all the standards of civilization that had allowed them their Christian or Jewish identities, or their pacifism, in the first place. Pacifism had contributed its own small quota of naïve misunderstanding to the Western democracies' failure to stand up to fascism in Italy and Spain as well as Germany. And now the National Socialists, together with those other fascist forces, were organizing victories that meant the virtual or actual annihilation of entire human communities. Then what was one's position supposed to be?

Indians who admired and followed Mohandas Gandhi had been learning with equal pain that his, and their, admirable determination to practice nonviolent resistance to the British governance of their country led inevitably to conflict and violence, the more so when Britain went to war. Gandhi himself knew this, and he knew that "it may be necessary at times to sacrifice a degree of moral purity for political effectiveness," as my father observed. Nonviolent resistance cannot be practiced in a vacuum, unrelated to the actual violence perpetrated by states, especially states at war. Nor can pacifism. Then what principles are you expected to honor?

With your Christian confidence in the law of love, did you now have to withdraw from the conflict, turn the other cheek? Were you to imagine that there was now no place in the world for idealism, no place for spiritual confidence in the value of human life? My father did not think so, any more than he had thought so during the atrocious carnage of the First World War. "Too often has righteousness been defeated in history because its champions refused to make compromises on methods in order to bring victory to their principles," Pa had written. He had made this argument in 1918, when he was a very young pastor, and when the issue was whether pacifists would engage in debates about the postwar international order.

To discuss, in wartime, what the structure of a postwar state should be is a risky, daring activity unless you are authorized to do it at the highest levels of government. In dictatorships this kind of talk was a capital crime, and in democracies it was often restricted or evaded. In 1918 the pacifists hadn't wanted to put their two cents in to such discussions, and Pa had thought they were wrong. One should not leave the field to "the enemies of a lasting peace," he had written then, and he deplored their unwillingness to engage. As anyone could see, powerful anti-democratic forces were abroad in every realm, contesting the renewed, even revolutionary commitments that so many people were pledging to genuine democracy, and if these forces were to prevail after hostilities ended, then "the war will have been lost no matter who wins it." This was not only to be pacifist but to be "futile" and "irresponsible," as he wrote in 1918. All this was still true in 1940. So he took up the issue again.

"The good news of the gospel is not the law that we ought to love one another," he wrote at about this time, throwing down the gauntlet. That law is of course a fundamental tenet of Christian belief, and central to the idea that a good Christian should not bear arms. Pacifists tended, especially in wartime, to stress the absolute commitment to this law of love. But that law is not the only instruction in Scripture. It can't ever be the whole story. He continued:

> The good news of the gospel is that there is a resource of divine mercy which is able to overcome a contradiction with our souls which we cannot ourselves overcome. This contradiction is that, though we know we ought to love our neighbor as ourself, there is a "law in our members which wars against the law that is in our mind" [Romans 7:23], so that, in fact, we love ourselves more than our neighbor.

In other words, the Gospels teach us not only to understand the law of love but also to acknowledge the experience of its negation, and to recognize that a mercy greater than any human one must overcome this contradiction. This, my father believed, was the Christian insight that could and should give strength and consolation in times of war.

Pa's view was that many Christian pacifists wouldn't take this paradox on board, although the Gospels insist on it, insist that we not only are born in sin but live and die in it, that "Man remains a tragic creature who needs the divine mercy as much at the end as at the beginning of his moral endeavors." He said and preached, over and over, "The New Testament does not . . . envisage a simple triumph of good over evil in history. It sees human history involved in the contradictions of sin to the end." And Christians like everyone else now had to face the contradictions of this terrible, looming war to the end.

If instead, as many Christians in 1940 were doing, you "reinterpreted the cross so that it is made to stand for the absurd idea that perfect love is guaranteed a simple victory over the world," then your efforts to grapple with the remorseless evil coursing through national and international public life were bound to be rather loonily off base. Pa offered a currently fashionable example: There were people, he said, who believed "that if Britain had only been fortunate enough to have produced 30 percent instead of 2 percent of conscientious objectors to military service, Hitler's heart would have been softened and he would not have dared to attack Poland." These were people who held "a faith which no historic reality justifies." They were not living in history, not living in real time.

Certainly Pa did not think that professed Christians should abandon the unattainable perfectionist injunctions of their faith, but, rather, he believed they must keep them all the more passionately in their hearts as they engaged in the real world. His concern was with the messy, often painful, and frequent compromises that history, and sin, force on responsible people who *do* live in history, who live in real time. And he had a natural skepticism about the kind of people who are armored with the certain conviction that they are in the company of pure in heart who will prevail in the end. How were they so sure? Plenty of ordinary folk could see what he saw, what Bonhoeffer and Tillich and others saw: that "even the most saintly life is involved in some measure of contradiction" to the law of love, that we are all, each one of us, enmeshed in history, enmeshed "in the contradictions of sin."

There was not a person on the globe who was not caught in intractable, unavoidable family, community, and even international difficulties. This is perhaps always the case—it is the case today—but some world-historical moments make it clearer than others, and 1940 was certainly one of those moments. Pa wanted people to see that it was the great strength of Christian thought that it offered a way of understanding the horrors of the time for everyone living in the nightmare, and especially for those who wanted to attach their faith to efforts "not only to avoid conflict, but to avoid violence in conflict." Acknowledging "the tragedy of human sin," as he put it, could be the first step in repentance and hope for redemption, even in the darkest night of despair, and an essential component in living fully in history, in coming to grips with the "complex facts of human experience."

But there was a kind of watered-down Christian pacifism that neglected these thorny instructions, and it was not only weak and flawed but also heretical, he thought. It had absorbed secular and moralistic illusions about human virtue—"the

Renaissance faith in the goodness of man" was Pa's shorthand term for these illusions—and had grafted them onto the "simple gospel of Jesus," calling the new tree a tree of goodness and love. This was not only heretical in scriptural terms—that is not what the Crucifixion is about—but heretical "when judged by the facts of human existence. There are no historical realities which remotely conform to it." It gave Christianity a bad name among tough-minded atheists, although that could be endured. Much worse, this sugarcoated pacifism, being so desperately inadequate to the evil obligations and difficult choices being forced on people everywhere, was bound to fall apart under stress, and it did. "No religious faith can maintain itself in defiance of the experience which it supposedly interprets. A religious faith which substitutes faith in man for faith in God cannot finally validate itself in experience."

Christian pacifists of the good-goody type were making the same mistake as mystics like Aldous Huxley or rationalists like Bertrand Russell. They all clung to essentially the same weak idea: that at the end of the day human history was not a tragedy but a story that would come out nicely so long as one trusted in people's virtue or rationality. "These rational or mystical views of man conform neither to the New Testament's view of human nature nor yet to the complex facts of human experience," Pa wrote. People who held such views could not have anything wise to say about the ethics of defending Britain against Nazi Germany, for example, or about opposing Hitler's regime within Germany and the occupied countries, or about Germany's treatment of Jews, or about Gandhi's challenge to the British in India. And indeed they didn't. What could they advise an infantryman in battle except that he was in the wrong line of work? "We might as well dispense with the Christian faith entirely if it is our conviction that we can act in history only if we are guiltless," he said.

No, on the contrary: religious faith is supposed to strengthen, not abandon, people suffering the extremities of horror. For Christians, Pa believed, their faith was not made irrelevant by war but became all the more necessary. The question was how to behave responsibly in an evil, morally ambiguous, and compromised world where things were getting immeasurably worse, and he thought that Christian doctrine helped to answer this question. The issue was how to act, and when. Yet many clergymen never even asked the question.

When Pa preached in college chapels, he frequently encountered, as the processional or recessional hymn, a rousing one written by the Harvard scholar-poet James Russell Lowell in 1845. (College chaplains probably imagined it was up his alley, since Niebuhr sermons often alluded to national and international problems.)

> Once to every man and nation
>> Comes the moment to decide
> In the strife of truth with falsehood,
>> For the good or evil side, . . .
> Then to side with truth is noble,
>> When we share her wretched crust
> Ere her cause bring fame and profit
>> And 'tis prosp'rous to be just;
> Then it is the brave man chooses,
>> While the coward stands aside
> Till the multitude make virtue
>> Of the faith they had denied.

Well, the hymn has a rollicking tune and is great fun to sing, but Pa thought the words were all wrong. There is never just one moment that comes when you have to decide, and it isn't necessarily the better choice just because the truth you've sided with is unrecognized, or hasn't yet achieved "fame and profit." Every day counts, and every day requires a person or a nation to act, to decide what to do. The 1930s had seen a cascade of unending crises, and the year 1940 was even more fateful. Crisis, as every good doctor or theologian knows, means not only the critical turning point where an illness turns toward either recovery or death, but "decision."

In the early months of the conflict, even though Great Britain was at war with Germany, its government did not seem to understand the nature of the crisis, and it continued its equivocal avoidance of decision. In A. J. P. Taylor's bracing words, it was a government "of National pretence . . . incapable of enlisting popular support. What was more, they did not want it." To mobilize the people was to mobilize energies that might threaten the social order, and the upper-crust types in Chamberlain's cabinet thought it wiser to tamp down any surge of popular feeling. "Better far that ordinary citizens should carry their gas masks, read official instructions, and proceed quietly with their affairs." As the winter wore on, as Denmark was occupied and Norway invaded in the spring, the war was costing Britain £5 million a day, but there was no clear understanding of where the nation was headed, nor of how the war could possibly be won. How would the military effort be paid for, and who would bear the brunt of the cost? What would be the social and economic consequences of this terrible circumstance?

The churches were not helping their flocks to understand the crisis, or the nature of the decisions to be taken. Britain was in a desperate bind, but, Pa noted impatiently, what could be expected from an Anglican establishment in which the Archbishop of Canterbury had praised the German takeover of Austria in 1938 for having been "achieved without bloodshed"? Such covert praise of Hitler's regime was the norm among all too many people in England's political classes, not just in the Duke of Windsor's circle or among the grandees who flocked to Lord and Lady Astor's Cliveden. They were walking "into war backwards, with their eyes tight shut," to quote Taylor again. Archbishop Temple and Bishop Bell were exceptions to the low-grade rule.

Of course, there were skeptics on the left who were now "full of self-righteousness about the sins of the British Empire which a good Christian must disavow," my father noted, but many of these pacifist equivocators were the selfsame characters who had been supporting the policies of Prime Minister Chamberlain in "appeasing" Herr Hitler. Clearly this wouldn't do, either. "Every empire is full of sin," my father wrote, and "not the least sin of the British empire is its playing the game of power politics so badly in recent years. . . . I do not find much virtue in the kind of moral sensitivity which gags at the sins of the British empire and leans over backward to appreciate the Nazis."

That outrageously unrepentant imperialist and anti-Nazi Winston Churchill would not have disagreed. After years of opposition to the feckless policies of his own political party, he had finally been brought into the cabinet as First Lord of the Admiralty right after the invasion of Poland; then, on May 8, 1940, thirty hours before Hitler began his full offensive on the

Western front, a House of Commons vote brought Chamberlain's government perilously close to its end, and by the close of the following day Churchill was prime minister.

The public spirit of Great Britain changed almost overnight. The ruling classes remained rife with equivocators, but among the people at large, whose spirit Churchill immediately mobilized, he produced, as Roy Jenkins has written, "a euphoria of irrational belief in ultimate victory. . . . The national mood . . . was not so much defiant as impregnable. The prospects were awful, but people pushed the consequences of defeat out of their collective mind."

Tawney, in an article composed for American readers, had a fine interpretation of this remarkable transformation in the public mood. The English people were no longer "fighting in obedience to the orders of our Government," he wrote. "Our Government is fighting in obedience to our orders. The country feels that at last it has got a Government to its mind." And Churchill knew this. "You ask," the prime minister said in a famous speech, "what is our policy? I will say: it is to wage war, by sea, land and air, with all our might and with all the strength that God can give us; to wage war against a monstrous tyranny, never surpassed in the dark, lamentable catalogue of human crime. That is our policy. You ask, what is our aim? I can answer in one word: it is victory."

This, surely, was a crisis moment in the history of Western democracy, a moment of real decision. It was there for any American to see. So consider the situation regarding the war against Germany in the summer of 1940 from the point of view, let's say, of an American pastor trained at Union Theological Seminary and attentive to what the Federal Council of

Churches had to say. It was now seven years after Hitler had destroyed democracy in Germany and five years since the Aryan decrees robbed Jews of German citizenship. It was seven years after Tillich and people like him had left Germany for America, six after the Nazis cracked down on the German churches and Karl Barth left Bonn to return to his native Switzerland, after Confessing pastors like thousands of other opponents of Hitler were sent to concentration camps. It had been two years since Hitler's troops marched into Austria and since the Nazi Party–sponsored atrocities of Kristallnacht, more than a year since Hitler's takeover of Bohemia and Moravia. Poland had been trampled; Norway, Denmark, France, and the Low Countries had fallen, the Battle of Britain was in full, desperate swing; and even in Congress, after years of isolationist inaction, the Neutrality Act had finally been amended. The Federal Council's appeal for neutralism at this juncture was not just an avoidance of decision but, my father observed simply, "completely divorced from all political realities."

Americans all too often forget, especially when they proudly boast of their country's vital contribution to the Allied victory over Hitler—the famous victory achieved by their "greatest generation"—that this eerie divorce from reality continued for a full two years and more after Hitler's invasion of Poland and England's declaration of war. During the very long months of 1940–41, as for many seasons before, America's generation of heroes displayed a hearty reluctance to be involved in the war that eventually made them so famous. Defeating fascism abroad was something they wanted other people to do for them, and they denied the threat of fascism at home.

In June 1940, my father noted, no surprise, that the morning mail was bringing "reports of disaster everywhere." Also in the post was a Socialist Party letter chiding him for deviating from its noninterventionist platform. He resigned from the party with this published comment:

> The Socialists have a dogma that this war is a clash of rival imperialisms. Of course they are right. So is a clash between myself and a gangster a conflict of rival egotisms, and there is a perspective from which not much difference may be perceived between these egotisms. But from another perspective there is an important difference. "There is not much difference between people," said a farmer to William James, "but what difference there is, is very important." That is a truth which the Socialists have not yet learned. They are right in insisting that the civilization which we are called upon to defend is full of capitalist and imperialist injustice, but it is still a civilization.

On the same day *The Nation* published a letter he wrote for a group he helped to put together called the American Friends of German Freedom. For some years Pa had been fund-raising for a network of labor and socialist opponents of fascism that operated within Germany and Austria and also in Prague, Lisbon, and Stockholm under the leadership of the ex-Communist political activist (and psychoanalyst) Karl Frank; Tillich had also helped out; and Stafford Cripps had been doing the same in England. When Frank arrived in New York in 1940, the supporters of his "Group for a New Beginning" reorganized themselves more formally as the American Friends of German Freedom, and my father, in his appeal for funds, wrote to explain that they wanted to support

> a group of almost forgotten men and women in the catastrophe

enveloping Europe . . . , the anti-fascist Germans who were fighting Hitler long before the armies went into the field. Driven from their own country, shunted about from one place of refuge to another, they have persisted in the courageous work of building the anti-Hitler underground movement. Some have been lost already . . . others are in danger of being . . . caught, and have no chance of survival; the firing squad or decapitation will be their fate. We owe it to these people who have sacrificed themselves to carry on the fight for freedom—most of them could have emigrated to safety, but have elected to continue their work—to exhaust every possibility to effect their rescue.

Recent writers sometimes refer sarcastically to this minute number of valiant people as the "much-vaunted German resistance," to use one much-vaunted writer's words. But this unpleasant sneer is alas also a slander: the resisters were never vaunted, not then and not since, indeed scarcely remembered and massively ignored, as Bishop Bell or Bill Pauck or Uncle Paulus could easily have attested. (The slanderers have perhaps not much lived experience of being in physical danger and don't seem to know what moral danger is. Their easy condemnations smell of the lamp.) Some of the resisters were church people, but of course many were not; there were good, bad, brave, less brave, atheist, *dévoué*, left-wing, right-wing resisters— they came in all stripes, but never in quantity.

Moreover, Hitler's regime had moved swiftly and remorselessly against them with a ferocity of which most Americans were unaware. In November 1941, in a book review of the sermons of the Berlin pastor Martin Niemöller—who had been one of the first to denounce the Third Reich from the pulpit— my father praised their "thrilling note of immediacy and urgency," but Niemöller (with whom he had grave differences of opinion on many key issues) was in a concentration camp on Hitler's orders and had been for years, even though a *Nazi* court had found him innocent of the trumped-up charges brought against him in 1937.

Some months before Pearl Harbor, and before America's entry into the war that had already taken so many lives, Pa finally resigned from *The Christian Century,* angrily fed up with its holier-than-thou neutralism and continuing anti-Semitism. The book reviews and commentary now came in other magazines, and he helped to start a little magazine of his own, much of which he wrote and edited himself, *Christianity and Crisis.* The reason for the name was clear enough.

My father's work on behalf of German refugees and German resisters brought him together, as did his teaching work, with his friend Paul Tillich, who had settled in to his classes at Union and to life in New York with admirable, stoic energy. He had every good reason to be personally devastated by the loss of his beloved world of German learning and scholarship, culture and art, law and landscape, and he had no easy time accustoming himself to the strange new accents of America, even to being an exile. But he had nonetheless embraced his fate, renounced the opportunity for bitterness, and plunged into a torrent of books, sermons and lectures, articles and radio addresses. And he did a great deal to help the thousands of German refugees newly arrived on American shores to help themselves—in practical, logistical ways, finding them jobs, places to live, ways to keep going. It cannot have been easy for Tillich to undertake this guidance of his fellow Germans in the painful but essential effort to reconstrue the fatherland as the enemy, to understand

and delineate the contours of exile, to imagine oneself no longer as German but as American. Once the United States was officially at war with Germany in December 1941, the issues may have clarified, but they were certainly not simplified. The German exiles were now not Germans anymore, but neither could they yet be Americans. They were enemy aliens.

THE WARTIME SUMMERS in Heath are not clear in my memory. What can ever be captured or retained of one's lost first years? Shreds of recollection about our apartment in Union, patches of memory about the summertime houses that preceded the Stone Cottage, tendrils and broken stems of flowering images from our family life. No memory of war or the threat of war, though; I can only summon up a vague infantile awareness of my family, including Mütterchen and Aunt Hulda, who became beloved fixtures of my postwar summers; they must already have been familiar and dear to me during the earlier years. My instinct is that the Stone Cottage was surely the locus of *peace*, or at least that the general tension and strain of wartime life was somewhat eased there during the holidays. But the war years themselves remain a darkly flavored, dissonant blur.

So it is with a sense of discovery and even amazement that I have reread the written records of what my parents were up to in 1940–45, their almost tempestuous nonstop activity relating to the war, since my shifting misty recollections have only to do with the inner family life. True, none of us was in immediate physical danger, though my father's frequent wartime trips to England were scarcely safe journeys, but the war changed the tone and altered the key in which one heard any of life's music, and I think I knew that, like everyone else. One prayer my father wrote at about this time, not so famous as the Serenity Prayer but clearly kin to it, addressed not only the community of Heath or of Union but all communities affected by "the sorrow of the world which works death and despair":

O God, the sovereign of nations and the judge of men, look with compassion upon this sad world so full of misery and sorrow. Enlighten our eyes that we may see the justice of your judgments. Increase our faith that we may discern the greatness of your mercy. Save us from the sorrow of the world which works death and despair. Fill us with the godly sorrow which works repentance, and the desire to do your will. Teach us how we may build a common life in which the nations of the world may find peace and justice. Show us what we ought to do. Show us also what are the limits of our powers and what we cannot do. So may our purpose to do your will be supported by our faith, for you are able to overrule our will and make the wrath of man to praise you. Recall us to our dignity as co-workers together with you. Remind us of our weakness that we may look to you who works in us both to will and to do your good pleasure and supplies what is needed beyond our powers.

I never heard my father speak this prayer, and I didn't learn about his wartime work until many years later, but its tone and intention are deep in my bones. If you have been born in wartime, the mode of tragic crisis is never unfamiliar. Decades may pass, but even a half century later the familiar groundswell of controlled terror and anguished contrition will swell up within you when some terrible event presses upon you the memory of chaotic carnage near or far.

"Show us what we ought to do." The presumption is that human reason and intelligence alone will not make the path clear. "Show us also what are the limits of our powers and what we cannot do." I have to think that this sentence was intended especially for Americans, whose vaunted assurance about their own force and righteousness was, Pa always thought, at best "morally precarious" and at worst sinful, illegitimate, and very destructive.

The underside of this American hubris, equally constant in American history, was the complacent indifference that could be just as dangerous as overweening power. A new friend of my father's grasped this right away when he came to America in self-induced exile in late 1940, after several decades of intellectual and literary work in Geneva and Paris. The celebrated Swiss humanist and anti-fascist Denis de Rougemont kept telling his American friends that "the real fifth column in our democracies is laziness of spirit." In January 1941 he spent an evening "*chez* Reinhold Niebuhr, one of the best minds in the country," and his recollections have a bracing European clarity about the political consequences of the moral sloth he was encountering everywhere:

> Theology professor, militant socialist, serious and sarcastic polemicist, [Niebuhr] is leading a campaign for America's intervention in the war. A virulent, dense little magazine which he's just founded, *Christianity and Crisis*, is trying to combat the inertia of the churches, which remain for the most part isolationist. The situation is not easy. If the churches oppose intervention, it is on grounds of conscientious objection, pacifism, anti-militarism, fear of the tyranny that all war risks fostering. Then it's also because in America nobody believes in evil any more. "It's too awful to be true," people say about what the refugees tell them. The result is collaboration with the grim supporters

of Hitler, Mussolini, Franco, and their "regime of the future." He who doesn't want to believe in the Devil works, fatally, for him.

My father's wartime essays addressed many domestic and foreign issues, but the core of them concerned the German enemy. Like how many of the German Americans who hated Hitler and were giving their lives in battle against him?, my father thought long and hard not only about the "unpolitical" Germans he so distrusted but about the anti-Nazi ones, whose hearts might well be torn, he thought, "when they contemplate the consequences of German defeat." That defeat did not seem likely, or certainly not imminent. Yet while "the most stout-hearted among them still find defeat preferable to victory and continued enslavement . . . it is idle to regard this choice as an easy one, or to deny the reality of the[ir] dilemma." The observation has his characteristic respect for the spiritual life of compromised and weakened opponents.

In Germany itself, the stunning development of June 22, 1941, with the Wehrmacht's invasion of Russia across a front that stretched 800 miles from the Baltic to the Black Sea—coming as it did on top of all the horrifying successes Hitler had enjoyed on the Western front in 1940—was even more tremendously unnerving than the Molotov-Ribbentrop pact had been in August 1939. Churchill, who was not surprised by the news, reacted instantaneously, promising on the very day of the invasion to "give whatever help we can to Russia and the Russian people. We shall appeal to all our friends and allies in every part of the world to take the same course and pursue it, as we shall, steadfastly to the end."

It is important to note that no immediate response to

Churchill's offer was forthcoming from the Soviet government. Stalin, we now know, vanished quite rapidly from the scene and disappeared, emerging from his noncommunicative seclusion only on July 3, and then merely to plead with Soviet citizens to understand that the old treaty with Ribbentrop had earned them a year and a half of peace and to acknowledge that the Wehrmacht had indeed advanced far into Soviet territory. The battle for "the freedom of our fatherland," he said, would now "become one with the war of the nations of Europe and America for their independence and democratic freedoms." A formal alliance between Great Britain and the Soviet Union was eventually scratched together by July 13 and signed by Molotov and Stafford Cripps, who had been in Moscow since June 1940 as special envoy and who like Churchill had anticipated Operation Barbarossa; the treaty guaranteed mutual help and promised that neither party would negotiate or conclude a separate peace with the enemy.

Stalin did not, in fact, officially reply to Churchill's June 22 statement for four weeks, and then only to plea—it was the first of many such requests—that the English open up a second front in the west (France) and/or in the north (Norway and Finland) to "draw off the weight of the German attack," in Cripps's words. Given that until June 21 the Soviet government had regarded Britain as the archenemy, "the bulwark of the world order Communism had set out to overthrow," as one historian has put it, Stalin switched with breathtaking speed into this peremptorily demanding mode, which lasted for the rest of the war. He betrayed an apparently willed incomprehension of the impossibility of beleaguered Britain's launching such a vast, complex amphibious offensive, when it was already stretched to the limit in the desperate effort to hold its own against Germany. Stalin was "thinking in terms of utter unreality," as Churchill put it. And of course he had not abandoned his deep suspicion of and hostility to the Western powers. Plenty of us imagine that the tense, ominous standoffs that marked what we now call the Cold War began only in 1945 or 1947, but one can see that the frosty strains and difficulties between the Soviet Union and the Western democracies weren't even new in July 1941.

Within Germany, Operation Barbarossa galvanized the clandestine opposition to Hitler into deciding they must act, and act very quickly, to remove him. Yet this became logistically more and more difficult to accomplish with each passing week. In September 1941, when Pa's good Dutch friend Visser 't Hooft managed another meeting with Bonhoeffer, this time in Switzerland, Bonhoeffer "opened the conversation by saying, 'So this is the beginning of the end.'" Visser 't Hooft was puzzled, because he knew that Bonhoeffer was a disciplined optimist, and this seemed unduly apocalyptic—did he mean that Germany was sure to be destroyed in the east, that the invasion of Russia spelled Hitler's doom? "He saw my startled expression and added: 'The old man will never get out of this.'" In short, Bonhoeffer did indeed grasp the full geopolitical catastrophe of Barbarossa, and his brief remark also indicated his active commitment to the conspiracy against "the old man." But for various complicated reasons the plot against Hitler did not much advance until the summer of 1942.

While the situation in Europe deteriorated with each passing, hellish week, summertime life in Heath proceeded apace. Americans were in the war but were also not in the war. At the big house in the forest with the shaded porch where we lived before the Stone Cottage, there were games, explorations in search of woodland treasure, romping with the terrier. (One afternoon the beast chewed up my arm and bit me badly on the lip—this I remember well enough. It necessitated a hospital trip to Greenfield, many miles away; my mother held me in her lap, with wadded cotton bandages pressed against my bleeding mouth, as we racketed down the mountain brook road to the Deerfield River Valley, Pa at the wheel of our 1939 Ford; the wound on my face was so nasty-looking that my father feared I might be disfigured and ruined, though eventually it left only a negligible scar. We got another terrier, our beloved Topsy, of whom more anon.)

My wonderful Aunt Hulda and Mütterchen came often to Heath, too; Uncle Helmut and his family soon found a holiday place in the nearby village of Rowe. Those glorious sun-filled days, with fragrant strawberry meadows and dappled forests, mist over the brooks, and sunsets blazing behind Mount Greylock! How amazing that the kindly adults around me—I think especially my grandmother—somehow preserved a happy routine of calm normality.

In the next few years Pa traveled twice to England—the roundabout transatlantic voyages took forever, given the deadly German activity against all Allied shipping—and once he was there, he went often with Archbishop Temple all over the industrial north, the two of them addressing huge crowds of workers and soldiers at programs under the rubric "Religion in Life." The gospel of freedom and spiritual commitment, whether for industrial democracy at home or for armed struggle abroad, was scarcely an easy one to get across in those deadly seasons. And the issues of conscience that every war act raised were deeply troubling to everyone, pacifists and warriors alike.

Once, my father found himself awkwardly poised between Archbishop Temple and Bishop Bell on such an issue. Bell had been outraged to hear that Temple had asserted that, in the present circumstance of world war, Christ could be thought of as a bomber pilot. Bell knew my father was no pacifist, but he suspected that even a pastor who supported the war against Hitler might find Temple's formulation unworthy. Temple should be corrected, he thought, and he begged Pa to do something about it. My father was startled to find himself in this predicament.

Here I was, a nondescript American Nonconformist, asked to mediate between an archbishop and a bishop! Fortunately I remembered a simple story. I told Bell that in my country, a pacifist clergyman [his friend Harry Fosdick of Riverside Church] had asked a colleague, "Can you imagine Christ wearing a military uniform?" His non-pacifist friend had replied, "No, I can't, but I can't imagine him being a preacher in your big church, either." I thought that was a good story, because it shows how both pacifists and non-pacifists use the figure of Christ, the symbol in Christian thought for sacrificial love, to address all the problems and norms of collective morality.

Bishop Bell was as stalwart a pacifist as ever, but by now he was also a vital link in the small network of English people who knew of the anti-Hitler conspiracies in Germany. He was eventually to be pulled, tangentially, into helping them—but not yet.

And by now the neighborly summer friendship with Uncle Felix became colored by a shared anxiety about the same issues that so troubled Peggy Benn: getting the United States government to increase the immigration of Jews to America, and to favor if not support outright the project of a Jewish home in

Palestine. In the summer of 1941, Uncle Felix and my father were visited in Heath by an old friend of Felix's and a new friend of my parents—the then thirty-one-year-old philosopher Isaiah Berlin. Zionism, not badminton, was the order of the day.

Berlin was in America awaiting word on taking up a position that the English diplomat Guy Burgess had organized for him at the British embassy in Moscow. Given that Berlin was hardly a conventional accredited Foreign Office type, to say the least, he wasn't certain whether the papers would go through, even though the Soviets had okayed them. Pa said he'd put in a good word for Isaiah when he next wrote to Stafford Cripps: Cripps's reply contained the useful tip that this was the first he'd heard of the plan and he didn't know if there was indeed a job for Isaiah to do in Russia. Berlin went on to the British embassy in Washington instead, where his range of social and political friendships became characteristically enormous. His dispatches about what was being said and done in the wartime capital, duly considered by Churchill's war cabinet, later became legendary.

Naturally, Uncle Felix and Isaiah and my parents had a million things to talk about, the collision courses on which Zionism and British policy were set being one, the strained relations between the dying Louis Brandeis and Chaim Weizmann being another. The now retired Justice Brandeis, with whom Frankfurter had served on the Supreme Court for only a few months but whom he had known for two decades, was perhaps the most important figure in the American Zionist movement; Weizmann, with whom Berlin had worked in England, was Zionism's leader there (and the future president of Israel). Brandeis and Weizmann had collaborated more or less effectively on behalf of the Zionist cause, but they did not now see eye to eye on what Jewish strategy should be—which was understandable, the divergences between American and British policies in the Middle East being what they were—and it was vital that there be no falling-out between these two.

The major theme concerned "what is to become of the Jews in the postwar world," as my father wrote a few months later, which "ought to engage all of us, not only because a suffering people has a claim upon our compassion, but because the very quality of our civilization is involved in the solution." All too often, the debate was being conducted at a hopelessly low level: a symposium on "Jews in the Gentile World" published around this time, for example, was exasperating in its silliness, my father thought, with "learned men" trying to illumine a "vexing problem" by "holding up the candle of the obvious to the daylight of common experience," talking pretentious nonsense, offering specious reasoning, idiotic psychobabble, or poor contrasts between Jewish and Christian ethics that slandered the first and misapplied the second. How relieved I am that my father did not live to see the new depths to which specious interpretations of Jewish and Christian "thought" have now fallen. The catastrophic difficulties facing Arab and Jew, Palestine and Israel, could, however, to some degree be anticipated. And within a few months the information about the fate of the Jews in Poland and elsewhere in Central Europe began to leak to the West.

The American milieu in which policy was discussed regarding local anti-Semitic prejudice, Nazi persecution of the Jews, and the Zionist ideal—issues that Hitler's evil had now inextricably linked—had become extremely complex. Hours of talk in Heath and New York were devoted to its intricate snarls. Everyone knew that many of the earlier efforts of farsighted

Catholics, Protestants, and Jews to encourage interfaith cooperation and to discourage anti-Catholic and anti-Jewish bigotry had been coming apart since the rise of Hitler. The National Conference of Christians and Jews, for example, after its promising beginnings, had been foundering because of Hitler's policies. Some of its factions claimed that the NCCJ should not take any public position on Nazi racial laws, that it should not have "for its object the importation into our American life of controversies engendered by the domestic policy of foreign nations," as one report put it. Well! When this attitude was linked with Reform Jewry's long-standing skepticism about Zionism, it induced a kind of do-nothing trance. Meanwhile other American Jews rancorously squabbled about whether and where to secure a haven for their persecuted cousins in Europe. Alas, these disputes allowed bigoted Christians to equivocate, saying cynically, sanctimoniously, that they could hardly go out on a limb for Jews, or for a Jewish national home in Palestine, when Jews themselves couldn't make up their minds what to do. So disputatious, those Jews!

Plenty of hypocritical Christians, and quite a few American Jews, had viewed the events of 1938–40—Kristallnacht, the riots in Jerusalem, the British White Paper, the sudden rush of desperate Jewish refugees fleeing the Wehrmacht as it advanced across Europe—as, somehow, deadly confirmation that Jews were rather tiresome and might well even have been fomenting some of the trouble from which they then suffered so grievously. It was rumored that Arthur Hays Sulzberger, publisher of *The New York Times,* had wondered whether it wouldn't be better simply not to mention Jews in the paper, in the hopes that the fuss would die down? But toward the end of 1941 the political situation was evolving: in New York the lucky combination of Governor Herbert Lehman and Mayor La Guardia encouraged a counterforce alliance of people ranging from Harold Ickes to Herbert Hoover to pressure Roosevelt to support the idea of a Jewish home in Palestine. (The British government, amazingly, tried covertly to stop them from organizing a fund-raising dinner in New York.) More and more Americans, including the leaders of the American Federation of Labor and Wendell Willkie, who had been the Republican presidential candidate against FDR in 1940, were beginning at least to see the point of this partial solution to an intractable, tragic problem.

At *The Nation*, the intrepid left-wing magazine that often published his articles, my father encountered some resistance to his views on this subject and reluctance to publish them. Uncle Felix urged him to persevere, thinking that "too many liberals are still enslaved by their romantic illusions and cannot face your clean, surgeon-like extradition of reality." He found the essays, which Pa showed him in manuscript, "as refreshing as is cooling spring water to a parched throat." When they finally did appear in early 1942, as "Jews After the War" and about the stake that all good democrats and Christians should consider they had in the future of Israel, FF wrote again, "I would give a cookie to see the letters you have had. I know nothing in print that faces the Jewish problem more trenchantly and candidly."

It was not such a huge compliment: silence on "the Jewish problem" was loudly audible in both England and America; and in occupied Europe, where the lives of millions of endangered Jews were being snuffed out, the matter could not be discussed at all. Archbishop Temple (as of 1942 supreme prelate of the

British church, having ascended to Canterbury) was a lone, noble voice supporting the World Jewish Congress in an otherwise pointless debate in the House of Lords. American church leaders and *The Christian Century* went on warning their flocks not to succumb to "Jewish propaganda" about alleged German misdeeds.

One interesting person in the tragic tumult was that intrepid activist Bishop McConnell. It's no surprise, given the record of his extraordinary public work for decades, that he kept his head during the long, slow months when it began to dawn on people that the news trickling in about Nazi actions in occupied Poland and Russia was not "Jewish propaganda" but the horrific truth. In December 1942 McConnell and my father attended a big public conference in New York where they insisted on the urgency of action, since, as McConnell put it then, "between five and six million Jews are now being subjected to a deliberate program of extermination." He was as forthright and truth-seeking as ever, and now his concern was one of the most terrible crimes history has ever recorded.

The Nazis' mass slaughter of Jews was a truth that had been pressed upon various arms of the Allied governments for some months—by Gerhart Riegner of the World Jewish Congress, by the intrepid resister Willem Visser 't Hooft, and by Rabbi Stephen Wise, who that autumn finally persuaded Sumner Welles, in the State Department, of the truth of the hellish reports filtering out of German-occupied Central Europe. It was almost unimaginably difficult to believe these bulletins—Felix Frankfurter couldn't, at first. Yet the really dangerous people were the people who Didn't Ever Want to Know, and they were prevailing. They had been prevailing for

Felix Frankfurter at the door of his house in Dell, 1944

years; their noxious influence still harms our understanding.

I remember well my parents' joint reminiscences, after the war, with Frankfurter and Berlin, of those terrible times, and their fierce, sometimes uproarious comments about those prevalent people. We all knew who the friends had been—but oh the guffaws and acerbic dismissals of the enemies: the appeasers, the reactionaries, the anti-Semitic Jews, the isolationists, the Nazi sympathizers, the bad Germans, the Germans who thought they were "good" but weren't! The speed and hilarity with which my mother and Isaiah would staff the imagined Establishment of a postinvasion Vichy England! would invent *Times* editorials about the importance of Keeping Order! would mimic the postures of famous Jews who were really "trembling amateur Gentiles," as Lewis Namier called them! My goodness, Uncle Felix had come to really loathe Walter Lippmann, and the *New York Times* columnist Arthur Krock wasn't even worth talking about. Who, among the notoriously pro-appeasement fellows of All Souls College, Oxford, would have been most obsequiously enthusiastic about the Germans had they occupied England? What had Cardinal Spellman in common with Charles Lindbergh? Oh the merciless drubbing of pious do-gooders who prayed for their own salvation and never risked their safety! Oh the mocking of Germans' weaknesses for the often phony depths of *Innerlichkeit*! My father, who did not hate easily, was discomfited by the merriment, but he would not have denied that many of these targets were contemptible. Moreover, like Uncle Felix and Isaiah, he had a good nose for the stench given off by that "unstable compound of materialist bombast, philistine rage and provincial sentimentality" which, as an English historian has said, is the vile but widely distributed source where one finds "the true intellectual roots of National Socialism."

R. H. Tawney had a good nose, too, and in 1942 he, like Berlin, was to be found at the British embassy in Washington. His assignment there was due to a clever Labour Party move: in Churchill's war cabinet, Deputy Prime Minister Clement Attlee had been scandalized to learn that Viscount Halifax, the appeasement Tory who had been Chamberlain's foreign secretary (the Holy Fox, he was called) and whom Churchill had wisely removed from the London scene in December 1940 by sending him to America as ambassador, was gallivanting around Virginia on long weekends of foxhunting with his upper-crust friends. There was a desperately dangerous world war going on, did he not know? Attlee observed to the prime minister that Britain might profit, given the circumstances, from having someone in the Washington embassy who had contacts in American labor and liberal circles; when asked who might fit the bill, he suggested Tawney.

Lord Halifax hadn't a clue who Tawney was or what to do with him, but plenty of Americans did. David Dubinsky, the activist leader of the International Ladies' Garment Workers Union, was one, and many American scholars who revered Tawney also quickly got in touch with the new Labour attaché. He gave talks at colleges and labor unions all over America, lectures at the University of Chicago, and, in Washington, a talk at the Union for Democratic Action, a fledgling enterprise of left-wing interventionists founded in 1941, of which my father was first chairman.

Pa described this precursor of Americans for Democratic Action as a center-left group of people "who believe that democratic civilization must defend itself against external peril, but must not allow this task of defense to beguile it from maintaining and extending social gains in the domestic economy." Here again one sees the effort to sustain the work, which my father, like Tawney and Temple, like Myles Horton and Felix Frankfurter, kept front and center: the work of maintaining—and furthering—social justice in the nations that might find themselves at war. (I note with a kind of scornful dismay that some writers call the anti-communism of the UDA an early sign of hard-line Cold War antagonism: this completely misses the point of the UDA's professed aims concerning industrial democracy and social justice in wartime America, aims that the American Communists did not and would not share.) One can see why Tawney would be the right sort of historian to address them.

Dubinsky, whose union was an important backer of the UDA, had the ILGWU donate clothes to the Tawneys, who had flown safely to America but had lost their personal possessions following by sea when German torpedoes sank the boat. Tawney was so touched by the gift that he proudly refused to have his ill-fitting suit altered and wore it throughout his American sojourn. Pa was not alone in thinking that "Harry Tawney is perhaps the most impressive man I've met."

THOUGH IN 1941–42 the Allies were very far from victory, it was not too soon to be thinking about the shape of the postwar world, to discuss what it might or should be like. Planning for future democratic structures, whether national or international, was a capital offense in Germany, and while that was hardly the case in the United States, it couldn't be a neutral activity, either. And to do it soberly, one had to have a view on whether the Germans could actually be redeemed, and if so how.

In April 1941, my father mused aloud, in a *Nation* article, about the historical roots of Nazism (then as now a safer subject than "The Future of the Jews") and about the curious truth that "for some strange reason" people seemed to "find satisfaction in regarding the present evil course of the Germans as the consequence of congenital defects." He correctly, in my view, saw that this "strange" habit was a simple clear inversion of Hitler's master-race theory, a temptingly easy "opportunity to discover that Germans are and always have been a race of sadists, monsters, and rebels against civilization." He called this Vansittartism, since the position was well expressed by Sir Robert Vansittart, the anti-appeasement British politician.

So that was not the right tack to take. Pa also rejected Emil Ludwig's theory of "good German culture and bad German civilization," because, he thought, it too easily separated thought and action, word and deed, which in real life were richly and inextricably connected. Still, it was true that "German culture has been as profound in measuring the ultimate problems of human existence as it has been perverse in dealing with the proximate problems of human society, particularly the problem of justice."

Equally, he rejected facile attributions of Nazi energies to Prussia, or to German romanticism, or to simple anti-Semitism. All these interpretations were inadequate because "they induce complacency about our own sometimes comparable, sometimes contrasting vices." These included, he thought, "moral sentimentality" and "senseless confidence in discarnate reason, emancipated from the vitalities of history.... No simple theory of German depravity squares with the complex facts of history," he concluded. "It is important to remember this, so that the hatreds of war will not lead us into a draconic peace." It is important to remember this for many reasons. Yet few people today, either Christian or Jew, of either the left or the right, would acknowledge that after all, "Hitler is a brother to all of us in so far as his movement explicitly avows certain evils which are implicit in the life of every nation." A half century later, the spiritual candor of this sentence has lost none of its shocking power.

Pa was alluding to a once famous essay by Thomas Mann on "My Brother Hitler." But he wondered about the overall effectiveness of Mann's 1942 book of radio addresses, *Listen, Germany*. Mann "frequently allows himself to taunt the German people for their political ineptness," which might be "justified, but that does not make it helpful to a people facing such desperate alternatives." Great as Mann was, his political rhetoric tended to be naïve: "sometimes he assures the Germans that 'if you are defeated the vindictiveness of the whole world will break loose against you.' Since Dr. Goebbels strikes the same note, one may question its value as propaganda against Nazism."

Thomas Mann was not the only anti-Hitler voice addressing the German people over the airwaves. From early 1942 until mid-1944, Paul Tillich went downtown from Union Seminary to the studios of the Voice of America—that is, to the Radio Program Bureau of the Office of War Information—and recorded more than a hundred little radio speeches that were beamed into Germany. These were the kind of radio talks that Stafford Cripps had earlier, and vainly, urged the British government to broadcast on the BBC—talks that would divide the German people from their hateful rulers.

Each of Tillich's amazing political mini-masterpieces shows his usual expansive moral power and deep faith. And they give testimony to his absolutely rock-solid understanding of another truth: that it is never too late, that faith and hope must persist even amid the catastrophe engulfing the fatherland, that there are spiritual possibilities still alive in the dark night of death. "My German friends!" he begins. You must take heart from the defeats and setbacks which (he deftly informs them) are facing Nazi forces in this or that battle theater. You can and must reaffirm the enduring strengths of what democratic and Christian beliefs you have, which the Nazis have wanted to eradicate.

It should be no surprise that in his very first radio speech Tillich addressed the transgression—his word—of anti-Semitism, and quickly implored the Germans to "realize this: the Jewish question is the question of our own existence or nonexistence as Christians and human beings. It is the question of our redemption or our judgment." He repeated this theme often, and beseeched his German listeners, including his fellow pastors, to wake up to this "crime that means blood guilt for generations for those who are doing it and for those who are tolerating it . . .

taking place with ever growing cruelty in Poland. . . . Hundreds of thousands of innocent people . . . are being hauled away to mass death by German hangmen . . . and you are standing by! . . . You want to continue to be spectators of that, German clergy, you who are praying for German victory?"

Even horribly confusing and morally complex junctures of the global conflict—the British crisis with the Congress Party in India in the spring of 1942 coming at the same time as Wehrmacht victories in Russia, for example—afforded Tillich opportunities to meditate on the message of hope that must be extracted from the carnage and deathly rubble of war. The National Socialists know all about tragedy, he tells his German listeners, for their creed "educates for tragic heroism, it educates for death." But that is all Nazism knows, whereas democracy, socialism, and Christianity "all have something that stands beyond tragedy, a hope . . . for the human race." Opposition to Hitler would in the end triumph "by means of hope, for the sake of itself and for the sake of the world."

Tillich continued his speeches as the war grew more and more hideous during 1942 and early 1943. It is sobering to remember just what was going on during that period. The punishing battles at Bataan and Corregidor accompanied the terrible news of the fall of Singapore in February and of Mandalay in May 1942. Colonel Doolittle sent his sixteen bombers over Tokyo in April. American destroyers in the north Atlantic were torpedoed. General Rommel recaptured Tobruk in June and swept against British forces closer and closer to Cairo, checked only at El Alamein. The Germans opened their offensive against Stalingrad in August. The Allies commenced their invasion of French North Africa in November and scuttled most of the

French fleet in Toulon, while the Germans took control of unoccupied France; before the end of the year Admiral Darlan was assassinated. The Red Army could not lift the terrible siege of Leningrad, which had begun in September 1941, until January 1943, and the brutal battle of Stalingrad continued all through the fall and early winter.

As the summer of 1942 came to an end, my parents prepared to leave Heath and return to New York. "I have kept a closer schedule than ever before and as a reult I am on my last chapter of Gifford lectures," Pa reported to his friend Lewis Mumford, the social critic and writer. "I expect to be finished by the middle of next week." He was hoping to see Mumford in the coming months so that they could continue their discussions about the world crisis. Mumford was of the opinion that Germans would have to be restrained punitively in any postwar arrangements, if peace and democracy were to flourish. "I am not sure that I agree with you about the German freedom business," Pa wrote. "To be sure we are losing the war at present and may lose it altogether. But that is a different problem. If we should win it your approach to the Germans seems to me too moralistic. I don't think nations can be quarantined or isolated until they are good. They have some elements of health, even when they are very sick. We do not know how much health there is in the German body politic. But whatever health there is can not be strengthened by purely repressive measures. For that matter our whole civilization is pretty sick, as now becomes more and more apparent. . . . Reconstruction will have to consider western civilization as a whole." Mumford would surely not have disagreed with this last point, but the sickening truth was that the task was dismally remote. "I confess that I am beginning to lose courage about the war. I don't see how or when it can be won," Pa continued. "I believe it can be won eventually but meanwhile it may take so long that the whole of our social fabric may be endangered."

Within Germany, the "opposition to Hitler" of which Tillich had spoken, and which Pa encouraged Mumford to remember, was in a desperate race against time as the international news worsened. By the autumn of 1942 Bonhoeffer was no longer "standing by" like the German clergy whom Tillich had implored to act, and he had moved to active participation in the plotting to remove Hitler. And by then Bishop Bell had his important subsidiary role to play. The plotters wanted the British government to know of the existence of opposition to Hitler within Germany, however invisible to the naked eye it necessarily had to be, for they hoped to obtain safeguards from the Allies were the Third Reich government to be overthrown. Bell was a message carrier.

But the larger politics of the war in Europe was against them, as even the sympathetic Cripps and the not unsympathetic American ambassador in London, John Winant, recognized. This was mostly because of the Russians: in the summer of 1942, with terrible battles scarring the Motherland and the Germans continuing a deadly summer offensive against the Red Army, the Soviet government continued to be aggrieved with their American and British allies for not opening the second front in western Europe that it persisted in demanding. Stalin's paranoid fear lest the western Allies make a separate peace with Germany had not lessened, even though the May 1942 agreement with Britain expressly forbade the latter to "enter into any negotia-tions either with the Hitler government or with any other German government that does not clearly renounce all aggressive intentions and not to conclude an armistice or peace treaty without mutual agreement."

Because of this and other constraints in the Allied situation, Whitehall was skittish about even acknowledging receipt of Bell's messages from the German resisters. Moreover, plenty of British diplomats and political leaders agreed with Vansittart that all Germans were depraved monsters anyway and these signals of opposition to the Nazis could not be trusted. Anthony Eden wrote, "I am satisfied that it would not be in the national interest for any reply whatever to be sent" to Bell's German petitioners.

Planning for the plot against Hitler nonetheless went ahead in Germany. Indeed, to have done nothing for so long weighed heavily on Bonhoeffer's conscience. It was not enough simply to pray for German defeat, as he did: "I am praying for the defeat of my nation. Only through defeat can it expiate the grievous wrong which it has done Europe and the world." He wrote to his confederates at about this time: "We have been silent witnesses of evil deeds; we have been drenched by many storms; we have learned the arts of equivocation and pretense; experience has made us suspicious of others and kept us from being truthful and open; intolerable conflicts have worn us down and even made us cynical. Are we still of any use?" It was not a rhetorical question. The utility of active opposition to Hitler, like the strength of Bonhoeffer's transformed convictions, was now to be fully tested. Bonhoeffer's conduct over the remaining few years of his short life answered his extraordinary question in an impressive, humbling affirmative.

In the House of Lords, Bishop Bell—addressing himself not

to the specifics of assassination plots, which of course could not even be hinted at—made repeated public efforts during 1942 and early 1943 to force the British government to recognize that were Hitler to fall, there would be "a vacuum in Europe. Unless the problem of how that vacuum can be rightly filled is squarely and immediately faced . . . , the victory of which we are certain will be turned to ashes." After Stalin gave a speech in November 1942 that for the first time made a sharp distinction between the German people and Hitler, it seemed possible to do the same in England, which Bell and others promptly did.

At Christmastide 1942, Bonhoeffer wrote a little essay, a copy of which he gave to his parents and to a few close friends. In it, he wrote:

> There remains for us only the very narrow way, often extremely difficult to find, of living every day as if it were our last, and yet living in faith and responsibility as though there were to be a great future. . . . It may be that the day of judgment zwill dawn tomorrow; and in that case, we shall gladly stop working for a better future. But not before. . . . The ultimate question for a responsible man to ask is not how he is to extricate himself heroically from the affair, but how the coming generation is to live.

One cannot improve on this, it seems to me.

Some days later the Red Army, which had counterattacked against the Wehrmacht at Stalingrad the previous September, began to prevail in this deadliest of the long-drawn-out, deadly engagements on the Eastern front; the German divisions that had been cut off at Stalingrad capitulated on February 2, 1943, and on February 23 Stalin was able to say, "There has begun a massive expulsion of the enemy from the

Soviet land." The tide of war was beginning to turn against Germany.

On March 10, in a debate in the House of Lords with Bishop Bell, a British government spokesman agreed "first that the Hitlerite State should be destroyed," which was easy enough to say, and, "secondly, that the whole German people is not, as Goebbels has been trying to persuade them, thereby doomed to destruction." So at long last there was hope for the opposition within Germany—or so one could imagine.

Three days after this, the most advanced of the plans against Hitler was put into motion, when a time bomb was planted on a plane carrying the Führer back to East Prussia from Smolensk, where he had been directing the action on the Eastern front. Bonhoeffer and his friends waited in Berlin for news that the plane had crashed, whereupon further moves would be made to carry out a coup d'état against the regime. But no such news came. (The ignition mechanism had failed. At least the conspirators were miraculously able to conceal evidence of their efforts.) Instead, Bonhoeffer received a new order from the Wehrmacht to report for military service; when it was rescinded, thanks to an intervention from an anti-Hitler major general, he plunged into still more intense planning for the form of church and state in a post-Nazi Germany. As it happened, new opportunities for doing away with Hitler quickly arose, but the next *attentat*, scheduled for March 21, failed as well.

Ten days later, Dietrich Bonhoeffer and his siblings gave a party in Berlin for their father's seventy-fifth birthday, a solemn and joyous occasion, with plenty of music. The party befitted the revered old gentleman, a well-known neurologist who directed the psychiatric clinic of Berlin's Charité hospital.

Incredibly, the event was festooned with a greeting from Hitler, whose office announced that "In the name of the German people I bestow on Professor Emeritus Bonhoeffer the Goethe Medal for art and science, instituted by President Hindenburg." Such were the ghastly paradoxes of Berlin wartime life.

A short week later Dietrich was arrested by the Gestapo, along with Hans von Dohnanyi, Dohnanyi's wife (Dietrich's sister), and two others. The charge was "subversion of the armed forces," but Bonhoeffer's subsequent Gestapo interrogations ranged over all his anti-Hitler activities. Thereafter his collaboration and cooperation with the plotters could be effected only by means of heavily censored letters and messages passed among the band of brothers whether imprisoned or free. But even in this gruesomely circumscribed setting, Bonhoeffer proved his extraordinary "use": his letters and writings radiated his deep and continuing struggle to relate his "faith" such as it was—and he acknowledged how frequently it faltered—to his works and life as the terrible circumstances had defined them.

Not everyone was so heroically positive as Bonhoeffer, who himself had many hours of torment and doubt. After four years of war, vindictiveness was darkening people's hearts everywhere—how could it have been otherwise?—though anger could not lessen the pain. In 1943 my father wrote an article in which he once again criticized "Vansittartism" for its crude, cruel view that all Germans were evil: this was "a rationalized form of vindictiveness which . . . leads to silly miscalculations of complex political factors."

And he marked as best he could—information about the resisters in Germany was hard to come by and dangerous to transmit—the sickening news that the Gestapo and SS had closed in on the once "very considerable democratic elements in Germany . . . which were the first to defy tyranny, some of whom tried in vain to persuade the democratic world of the peril which Hitlerism represented, and of the necessity to meet this threat with outside as well as inside resistance. The outside resistance did not materialize until after the internal resistance had been crushed." It was excruciating to witness the indifference of so many people to this tragedy, especially when they had been indifferent to the crisis *before* the war. How terrible the irony, Pa thought, that "some of the appeasers of yesterday are proponents today of the idea that there are no democrats in Germany."

This false idea was very popular by 1943–44, the more so as the tide of war turned against Germany and Japan, when Americans became as fierce and indifferent to nuance as any people will be whose men are winning hard-fought battles against an evil enemy, and they had no doubt the enemy was evil. In this mood, distinctions were not being maintained, and sinful anger could be seen in excess everywhere, with obvious policy effects. The next year saw the nightmare intensification of Allied bombings of German cities as well as military installations, and my father, like quite a few of his clergy friends, inveighed against this strategy of saturation bombing. As his countless editorials and commentary show, while he cautiously supported the Allied insistence on unconditional surrenders from both Japan and Germany, he was distressed by the shrieking public enthusiasm for this policy—on grounds obvious to any well-trained Niebuhrian, who understands that sin is in the heart of all of us, that pretensions to power and omnipotence delude even the saintliest dispositions.

In May 1943 Pa left Union for two months of insanely over-crowded work in England and sent my brother and me one of his typically inexpressive postcards: "Daddy is having a busy time in England and Scotland. Look these places up on the map. I will go to them: Edinburgh, Glasgow, Newcastle, Birmingham." His weeks were filled with meetings, public lectures, private conversations, conferences, endless debates with friends and colleagues—and of course the subject was always, What Comes Next? Wartime censors forbade reference to future events in private correspondence, so details of who said what to whom did not make it into his letters to my mother, but there's no mistaking the general drift:

Addressed the Congregational Assembly practically without preparation . . . (a) where Christian faith is irrelevant to problem of community; (b) its points of relevance. Insights: (1) the universal character of moral obligation. (2) recognition of the limits set by sin and creatureliness. (3) contrite recognition of the grace which overrules the pride of nations. (4) pity. . . .

Luncheon meeting of the Royal Inst. [of International Affairs] at Chatham House . . . very good discussion. Talked on (a) the necessity of organizing preponderant power (b) the difficulty of doing so, and (c) the danger of using it. Last question of a lively discussion: "Don't you think it is foolish to be concerned about the justice of our use of power? All the continental nations expect us [Britain] to keep order on the continent and they know that we will be just to them." I answered: "Madam, you may be good but not that good. No nation is in fact so good as to be above suspicion in its use of power." Had a good hand. . . .

Spent the day with Stafford and Isobel . . . Stafford is through with the LP [Labour Party]. Hopes for a complete new alignment. Happy in his job [as minister of aircraft production]. . . .

Meeting with Peace Aims group, Temple in the chair. Good discussion. Afterward a small crowd was asked to stay to talk with me on Jewish problem. Britain not inclined to do anything about Palestine. Some wish we [the United States] would come into the Middle East and carry some of that responsibility. Moslem problem too complicated for GB to deal with it alone, just as I thought. . . .

Dinner with the Soviet section of the MOI [Ministry of Information] prompted by my *Nation* article ["Russia and the West"]. Best discussion of any of my visit. Very illuminating. It crystallized many ideas about the B-A-R [British-American-Russian] triumvirate which must rule after the war. . . .

I can't help noticing, in the midst of all this political reportage, Pa's growing exasperation with the Anglican Church. His deepening friendships with Temple, with Bell, and with the radical Bishop Leslie Hunter of Sheffield, whom he visited in his gorgeous manse with a fabulous garden (a setting Pa found weirdly inappropriate for a bishop who favored the disestablishment of his church), did not moderate his dislike of Anglican pretensions and his discomfort with its doctrine. He was asked to participate in a supposedly ecumenical service at Westminster Abbey, but this did not turn out well, as he told my mother:

Am completely pessimistic about this reunion business. Your old church, despite its many great virtues, insists on an essentially Catholic interpretation of church and sacraments, and reunion will never come on that basis. . . . I am getting fed up with Anglicanism. Beyond the great personal kindness to me I resent the official pretension. No non-Anglican was allowed in the sanctuary. All sat with the congregation. What was meant as a "witness of the unity of Christians" turned into an Anglican show with a Norwegian pastor and me reading the lessons. This thing is not going to work. Resentment growing on every hand.

Wish I could visualize your life in Heath, particularly the quality of the new house! . . . My love to the children, and to Howard and Louise, and all the rest.

After talking with his London publisher and friend T. S. Eliot, at Faber and Faber, and after picking up an honorary degree at Oxford, he was home again in Heath in short order, for his first proper summer as owner of the Stone Cottage. Of the Oxford event, he reported to Ma, "The public orator made a most gracious concluding reference which ran something like this: 'Having had the temerity to marry a member of St. Hugh's College who took a First in Theology there is nothing for us to do but admit him into the Oxford family.' " He didn't tell her, but she learned later, that the orator's main point was that Niebuhr was someone who "held and cogently preached that the principles of Christ should not only be meditated on in the cloister but also direct the affairs of the workaday world."

Back in Heath Pa found his family in more or less good shape. I was recuperating from a tonsillectomy in late June, my brother, Christopher, was as usual full of beans, and my mother was as usual at her wit's end with us. Pa picked up where he'd left off in April, writing and preaching. But it was a dangerous, peculiar juncture, for the war had entered an ominously contradictory stage, and it was hard to focus one's thoughts. Allied forces invaded Sicily and bombed Naples, and then, miraculously, Mussolini was ousted. On the other hand, despite the stunning defeats inflicted on the Wehrmacht at Stalingrad, the

My brother and I at the pond in Heath, with the Robbinses' house in the background

Germans' renewed spring-summer offensive in Russia was having alarming success. The war had gone on for years, and it would not be over for years. Death and sorrow abounded, and there was as always an immense amount of work to do. The question was, at what level should that work be attempted? And what was its immediate goal?

Shortly after his return to Heath, my father received a letter from Stafford Cripps, with whom he had spent plenty of time during May and June. Cripps, back in London from Moscow since January 1942, had briefly served in the war cabinet as Lord Privy Seal and leader of the House of Commons, had spent invaluable months in India on the fabled, doomed "Cripps Mission" negotiating with Nehru and Gandhi, and was now minister of aircraft production, but he didn't write about any of that. He wrote more generally about his and my father's larger political aims; he was concerned, as always, with the nature and level of change that must be effected in order to make improvements:

My dear Reinhold,

... I am so certain that it is necessary for all of us to do our utmost between now and the end of the war in every way we can and in every class and section of society to stimulate the right ideas and the right approach. The people *are* I believe receptive—our trouble will be to crystallise our views and their views into that political form that will make them not merely pious aspirations but actions that will become part of human history. Somehow we must bridge that portentous gap between fine thoughts and actual policies which has been so wide and so difficult to bring closer. It was lovely seeing you. God bless you in your work.

Stafford

Bridging the gap between fine thoughts and actual policies was precisely what was so demanding; it required not only tremendous strength and resolve, but courage and wisdom. "Action that will become part of human history." This is yet another layer of meaning behind the little prayer my father wrote at just about this time for the Sunday service in Heath:

> God, give us grace to accept with serenity the things that cannot be changed, courage to change the things that should be changed, and the wisdom to distinguish the one from the other.

THE SUFFERING AND FATIGUE induced by war, like the energies and powers it unleashes, cannot possibly be overestimated, nor the grief-stricken horror of it. Somehow I hear these qualities, too, in the Serenity Prayer—safe and sound as the author's family may have been in the wonderful place where he wrote it. And as I reread the chapters of a book my father composed that same summer and fall of 1943, *The Children of Light and the*

Children of Darkness, with its eloquent denunciations of the malice and danger visited upon us by fascist and totalitarian "children of darkness"—even if they may be "in their generation wiser than the children of light" (Luke 16:8)—I am struck by the painful sorrow implicit in the book's formulations. True, it offers a spirited, confident defense of democracy as the best possible system of government, and that was very important to reaffirm in the chaos of the time; and it defends a robust engagement with the world no matter how shattered. But even its most famous aphorism has a dark tinge: "Man's capacity for justice makes democracy possible; but man's inclination to injustice makes democracy necessary."

A little later Pa wrote to Lewis Mumford to send what inadequate condolences he could when he heard the news that Mumford's cherished son had been killed in action in Europe: even here, while rejoicing in Geddes Mumford's fine and selfless life, he continued, "You say that we will have to be very good to be worthy of the goodness of such young men. To me the deepest tragedy of life is the certainty that we will not be . . . the world will obviously pass through some pretty terrible decades and perhaps a century before these sacrifices will bear fruit."

In 1944, the long awaited opening of the second front in the west began with the huge invasion of Normandy on June 6 of more than 1 million Allied soldiers. With that, and with the subsequent slow retreat of the Wehrmacht from France and the west, along with the breakthrough of the Soviet army and its remorseless advance from the east toward Berlin, my parents might have wanted to construe the European news as cheering. But there were terrible bulletins from Germany, including terrible news about the imprisoned Bonhoeffer and his confederates.

The situation for him and for all the others who had been arrested in 1943 became very much more dangerous during the early summer of 1944, when the most concerted, fully developed new assassination plan was set in motion. The objective was not only to kill Hitler but to have the bombing (for such it would be) initiate first a coup among the army leaders and then an uprising against Hitler's regime among the general population. The conspirators were almost frantically desperate: to some of them it seemed almost too late to bother to try to kill Hitler; others were rounded up and shot on unrelated charges; and still more were tormented by the spiritual truth that, as one of them put it, "There can be no blessing in tyrannicide." On July 20, 1944, the attempt was nonetheless made—and it failed. Enraged officers loyal to Hitler closed in on the six principal plotters, arrested them, and quickly shot them dead.

Bonhoeffer and the others who had been in prison since 1943, undergoing interrogation and in some cases torture, had successfully concealed from their military jailers the facts of the conspiracy, using what his biographer calls an "intricate web of camouflage," which held until after July 20. But thereafter it was all over: incriminating documents had been found that put Bonhoeffer and Dohnanyi and their jailed confederates at the mercy of their captors, and there was no one left on the outside who was working for the political transformation of Germany. They were entirely on their own, in solitary confinement and subjected to merciless interrogation. In February 1945 they were condemned to death and sent to Buchenwald.

One month later American forces crossed the Rhine; the German defense system was collapsing, as Russian troops simultaneously advanced in the east, already only miles from Berlin. On Easter day, April 1, the prisoners could hear the sound of American cannons, and of course they could hope that Allied forces might liberate them before the executions were carried out. Two days later, on April 3, they were transported from Buchenwald to the concentration camp at Flossenbürg. The transfer was chaotic, and the German high command seemed to be speeding up its plans.

On Easter Sunday, Klaus Bonhoeffer, Dietrich's brother, who had been arrested the previous October and had been tortured and tormented in the prison in Berlin where he was confined, sat down to write to his children; he also had been condemned to death in February, and he knew the end was near. Toward the end of his extraordinary missive, a letter wholly lacking in bitterness or despair, and only at the end, he addressed himself to the conditions under which he was facing death:

> The times of horror, of destruction, and of dying, in which you, dear children, are growing up, demonstrate the transitoriness of everything earthly, for all the glory of the human being is like the flower of the grass. . . . But here begins all the wisdom and piety that turns away from the transitory to the eternal. That is the blessing of this time. Do not only abandon yourself, then, to the pious sentiments that in the haste and confusion of this world burst forth from a feeling of emptiness . . . take for yourself possession of this world in which what matters most is what you have experienced and what you yourself have acquired in all honesty. . . . Farewell! God keep you!

On Sunday, April 8, at the request of another prisoner—it was Wasily Wasiliew Kokorin, Molotov's nephew ("a delightful young man although an atheist")—Klaus's brother Dietrich agreed to hold a service for the condemned men there; he read the lessons for that Sunday, and explained the text of the day: it came from the great chapter (53) of the prophet Isaiah, which Christians interpret as a prophecy of Jesus Christ but which can be understood generally as Isaiah's commentary on the Israelites' treatment of the received word of God. "Who has believed our report? And to whom is the arm of the Lord revealed?" it begins. "He shall grow up before him as a tender plant and as a root out of a dry ground. . . . He is despised and rejected of men; a man of sorrows and acquainted with grief: and we hid as it were our faces from him; he was despised, and we esteemed him not. Surely he hath borne our griefs and carried our sorrows." Bonhoeffer's text was the verse that followed: "But he was wounded for our transgressions, he was bruised for our iniquities: the chastisement of our peace was upon him; and with his wounds we are healed."

At dawn the next morning, Bonhoeffer and the others were hanged; the gravely ill Hans von Dohnanyi was killed the same day in the concentration camp at Sachsenhausen. On the night of April 22 an execution squad from the Reich Central Security Office took Dietrich Bonhoeffer's brother Klaus and a brother-in-law, Rüdiger Schleicher, who had been arrested with him the previous October, together with fourteen others in a Gestapo prison, and shot them the next morning.

By then the Allies were breaking the German lines in northern Italy. Mussolini was captured and shot by Italian anti-Fascist partisans, Russian forces began the shelling of Berlin, and Hitler committed suicide in his bunker. On May 8 a group of Wehrmacht officers signed the terms of Germany's unconditional surrender to the Western allies. The war in Europe was over. Not until many weeks later did the Dohnanyi and Bonhoeffer families learn of the fate of their men.

In July, Christine Bonhoeffer Dohnanyi—who had been released from prison some months before, who lost two of her brothers, her husband, uncles and cousins and other members of her large and devoted family—wrote to her son Klaus,

> About Father, I heard nothing factual. The last is that he was hauled away from a special bunker in Sachsenhausen, where he was brought on 6 April, and since 15–16 April there has been no further trace of him. So I have little hope that he is still alive. Papa himself firmly expected that the Gestapo would murder him. On 5 April, I saw him once again secretly. . . . He was very calm, asked that his greetings be conveyed to all of you, and was in good humor, as always. When we see each other, I'll tell you everything. You too will not have had many more hopes, and will reckon with everything. Be brave, my good child; your father was too. . . . May God help you in these terrible times to find the right path. All of you have good blood and a good heritage from your father in you, and you will be worthy of him. That is my comfort and my hope. . . . I embrace you.

IN AN ARTICLE for *The Nation* written in memoriam for his murdered friend, my father wrote a few weeks later,

> Bonhoeffer had remarkably clear religious insights and the purity of a completely dedicated soul. Considering how recently he had developed his political and social interests, his shrewdness in assessing political and military tendencies was also remarkable. . . . Not only his martyr's death but also his actions and precepts contain within them the hope of a revitalized Protestant faith in

Germany. It will be a faith ... that will have learned to overcome the one fateful error of German Protestantism, the complete dichotomy between faith and political life.

Bonhoeffer did indeed exemplify the hope for a revitalized Protestantism in Germany. More, he embodied a positive new vision of "how to be a Christian," as his biographer has written. But this was not recognized in his own country for quite some time. In the summer of 1945, while Pa was writing that memorial to Bonhoeffer, his own church in Berlin was making sure he was not even mentioned in a service held on the first anniversary of the July 20 plot. It had been different in London, where Bonhoeffer had worked and where hundreds of German émigrés had flocked to a memorial service for him conducted by Bishop Bell. Bishop Bell told the packed congregation of mourners that Bonhoeffer "represents both the resistance of the believing soul, in the name of God, to the assault of evil, and also the moral and political revolt of the human conscience against injustice and cruelty." Moroever, as Bell took pains to make clear, "It was this passion for justice that brought him, and so many others . . . into such close partnership with other resisters who, though outside the Church, shared the same humanitarian and liberal ideals." It took a very long time before the confused and conflicted Germans were willing to recognize the nobility of Bonhoeffer's life and death, to acknowledge its meaning.

It is an unedifying but unavoidable truth that many people, not only politically amoral and defensive Germans but triumphant Americans and British, found it difficult or frightening to think about those ideals that Bell celebrated and

Bonhoeffer had died for. Anguished hope and a determination to Make the World Safe for Democracy were not strong enough to prevail against the usual fear and inertia.

Fearful inertia also made it hard to think clearly about the plausible scenarios for a free and open postwar Europe. In some American quarters, for example, to imagine Germany participating in it was considered outrageous. Tillich's and my father's confident hope that Germany might eventually have an honorable, democratic government was not widely shared, even among the most sophisticated intellectuals or among German émigrés. In fact, it was often vehemently contested. And at the pinnacle of the American government, the most informed and responsible officials could not agree on what should be done with the remnants of the hated foe. Secretary of the Treasury Henry Morgenthau thought Germany should be reduced to a congeries of pastoral farm communities with no industrial or economic power. Secretary of War Henry Stimson and his principal deputy on German matters, John McCloy, disagreed, remembering that one of the root causes of the National Socialist catastrophe had been the vindictive clauses of the Versailles Treaty that had restricted and reduced Germany so punitively after the First World War.

The problems seeped down to every level of political affairs. Paul Tillich's valiant work for the Council for a Democratic Germany, a group that he initiated in New York in 1944, like my father's work for the American Friends of German Freedom, the Emergency Rescue Committee, and various other prewar antifascist groups, came under the surveillance of the United States government for being subversive. The FBI and other security agencies claimed, with lunatic, simplistic ignorance, that these organizations were motivated by a desire to see the triumph of the *Soviet Union* and of international communism. The American government had been therefore spying on both my father and Tillich for some time even before the war, and it went on spying after the war, well into the 1950s and 1960s.

I can see the fellows now, lurking around the card catalog at the seminary library, I remember the dismay and disgust with which "Reinie" and "Paulus" registered this surveillance—and then kept on at their work. They were not to be deterred. It was, of course, and is, a grotesque, even comical mistake. But why should one be surprised that ordinary, badly educated, ill-trained cops had this view? The FBI's error-filled assessment of this or that anti-fascist group was anyway only a pretext. The truth was that the U.S. government then, like governments everywhere and always, was suspicious about any energetic inquiry into or challenge to its most conservative elements. The beliefs that Niebuhr and Tillich had come to share in the 1920s—in spiritual rebirth after catastrophe, in the need for Christians everywhere to address the problems of political and spiritual reconstruction—were in the 1940s just as controversial as ever, and they were heartily disliked by the powers that be. They were bound to run into trouble.

Yet the spooks' mistake was a colossal one. Tillich and Niebuhr were living in a different world from anything the gumshoes could imagine. Bonhoeffer and his friends had risked their lives for their ideal of truth and freedom, in Germany as in other nations; Pa and Uncle Paulus, in their own way—granted, in relative safety, and of course not under such evil circumstances as Bonhoeffer and his friends had faced—had dedicated their wartime work to the same end, as had the millions

The Very Reverend John Baillie, then moderator of the Church of Scotland, at the Stone Cottage, having tea on the lawn with the Niebuhr family, summer 1945

of soldiers fighting in the Allied armies. Yet alas, the political harassment continued for decades, as we shall see.

CONCURRENTLY WITH the celebrations of the end of the war in Europe came the excruciating nightmare created by nuclear weapons. In the fall of 1945, Pa signed the Federal Council of Churches' denunciation of the bombing of Hiroshima and Nagasaki as morally indefensible, as a "sin against the law of God and against the people of Japan." When his friend James Conant, president of Harvard and, during the war, a director of the Manhattan Project at Los Alamos, chided him for not recognizing the strategic necessity of the new weapon, he acknowledged reluctantly that *perhaps* an argument could be made for its having been used: if these horrific acts had shortened the war and in fact saved lives, then *perhaps* one had to say one couldn't oppose the deployment of these utterly new means of mass destruction. But he didn't budge from his view that atomic weapons were profoundly sinful, as indeed all war was, and inarguably tragic beyond all reckoning.

As Conant himself knew all too well, every single person who had seen, heard, and watched the apocalyptic explosion at Alamogordo, let alone the events at Hiroshima and Nagasaki, understood that a nuclear device was not just another—bigger and scarier—weapon, but something of a completely different order, something indescribably other. A brigadier general remembered that when the device was set off at Alamogordo on July 16, the initial eerie silence and blinding light were followed by the detonation wave: a "strong, sustained, awesome roar which warned of doomsday and made us feel that we puny things were blasphemous to dare tamper with the forces heretofore reserved to the Almighty." "I am sure," wrote the eminent scientist George Kistiakowsky (later President Eisenhower's advisor), "that at the end of the world—the last millisecond of the earth's existence—the last men will see what we saw."

This was certainly not a mere quantitative improvement in America's strength, but a qualitative shift that would transform every known ethic of war and warfare, of peace and concord. The force of atomic explosions, and the unearthly evil of their poisonous aftereffects, had changed the very structure of the international order, whether in peace or at war, and this terrible new reality had to be faced.

So the primary question for him was not, I think, the endlessly contested one of whether or not the Allied use of the bombs against Japan had been justifiable. The whole war had been an incalculable, cruel catastrophe—how did one place Nagasaki on a scale that also had to encompass Treblinka, Stalingrad, Dresden, Auschwitz, Tokyo, and on and on? It wasn't in his nature to debate over *faits accomplis*. What really mattered was the stupendous question of how nuclear weapons would be handled in the future. From that summer in 1945, and in many animated, sometimes anguished discussions over the decades to come with some of the Los Alamos scientists, he struggled to formulate a sane and ethical doctrine that accepted the irrevocability of nuclear weapons and insisted, equally, on the absolute necessity to develop the political structures that could guarantee that they would never be used again.

One of my earliest specific memories of Heath in the 1940s is of the blue-and-gold magnificence of a late summer afternoon when we learned of the Japanese surrender and the final conclusion of hostilities. For decades I've pegged this memory to August 10, 1945, but now that I think about it, it must have been September 2, when the formal terms were signed and the war came to an end. At supper that evening in the Stone Cottage, while the sun was setting in a blaze of burnished orange and pink behind Mount Greylock, my father said the grace before the food was served, as he always did. (We didn't do much praying at home except for the regular graces before meals.) And then we stood around the table and sang the great hymn of thanksgiving that normally we sang at home only on Thanksgiving Day:

> We gather together to ask the Lord's blessing,
> He chastens and hastens his will to make known;

The wicked oppressing now cease from distressing:
Sing praises to his Name; he forgets not his own.

Beside us to guide us, our God with us joining,
Ordaining, maintaining his kingdom divine;
So from the beginning the fight we were winning;
Thou, Lord, was at our side: all glory be thine!

We all do extol thee, thou leader triumphant
And pray that thou still our defender wilt be
Let thy congregation escape tribulation:
Thy Name be ever praised! O Lord, make us free!

I learned later that this beautiful Dutch hymn had been composed to celebrate the liberation of the Netherlands from Spanish oppression in 1579, but even before I knew that, I felt it suited our American Protestant hearts, and it felt right to sing on that frightening evening. We might be celebrating the end of the war, but the unspeakable horrors of the last years, and of the two atomic explosions over Japan just the previous month, had completely changed the world. "We pray that thou still our defender will be." I remember the dark roiling purple and cinder gray of the clouds around the sunset even more than the blaze of dusky light.

VII

By those who do not fight in them or live through them, wars are remembered as having straight-edged finishes—the day the unconditional surrender is signed, the day the enemy concedes defeat, the moment the capitulation is acknowledged. "The strife is o'er, the battle won," as the Easter hymn puts it. Parades and cemetery services commemorate these definitive moments of triumph and tragedy for the ensuing decades; students are taught the famous dates; prayers are reiterated, hopes renewed on the anniversaries. But wars never end so cleanly, and they begin in darkness. This was surely true of the global conflagration that consumed so many millions of lives on hundreds of fields, across hundreds of fronts between 1939 and 1945.

We all remember the bright clarity of King Henry's summons to his men, on St. Crispin's Day, just before the Battle of Agincourt, but that's because Shakespeare made sure to turn this prelude to battle into a Key Moment. Yet Shakespeare understood the opposite truth, too: the cessation of conflict in his play is signaled by poignant marks of fatigue and uncertainty. When the French herald approaches the exhausted English warrior-king toward the end of the battle, asking leave to "wander o'er this bloody field / To book our dead, and then to bury them," Henry replies, "I tell thee truly, herald / I know not if the day be ours or no." (This scene, like others depicting cruel paradox and confusion in the circumstances of England's victory in its aggressive war, was omitted from Laurence Olivier's celebrated wartime film of *Henry V.*) All over the world in 1945, hundreds of millions of men and women could have expressed the same sentiment: the Allies had defeated Germany, then Japan, and the nations associated with them, but the incalculable, gruesome carnage suffered by every belligerent nation did not make it clear whose day it was. Wars begin in incoherence and chaos, and they end in incoherence and chaos. Prayers are one of the necessary expressions of our response to these dirty, ugly truths, our hope to redeem them.

It is therefore not such a strange irony that the Serenity Prayer first became known, beyond the handful of people who had heard it in Heath, to soldiers. It had been composed in wartime, so we should not be surprised. Still, this early chapter in its life was an accidental one—another unexpected pattern in the fabric of life in Heath. And it had to do with our neighbor Dean Robbins.

Uncle Howard was a mysterious figure to me in my wartime childhood. He was often not in Heath for one reason or another, but I remember him well enough from my brief encounters. And in my mind's eye I see him still, his brown-jacketed silhouette plunging down the hill from his house and toward the woods where he'd made those beautiful ponds. The light from the sun over Mount Greylock is behind him, shimmering over the long meadow grass and through the maples. He didn't talk to me much, which was just as well, since he intimidated me, but I liked watching him as he went out into the world of deer and rabbits, of ferns and mountain brooks that I think of as his natural home. I didn't know anything about his multifaceted church work; I didn't know he was what the Germans call a "major animal" in the Federal Council of Churches; I knew him only as a melancholic gentleman with a passion for wooded country.

At some point during late 1943 or early 1944, this good man suggested to Pa that the little prayer about grace, courage, and wisdom, which he remembered from the summer church service, might be appropriate for inclusion in material that he was helping the Federal Council of Churches prepare for army chaplains in the field. Ministering to soldiers was an essential task. So my father gave Dean Robbins a copy of the prayer, and in 1944 it was indeed included in the *Book of Prayers and Services for the Armed Forces, Prepared by the Commission on Worship of the FCCC and the Christian Commission for Camp and Defense Communities*. This was its first publication in any form and in any language, and it's because of this little booklet that eventually it became famous. I have been told that the booklet was translated into German, presumably for use in an occupied Germany, but I've never seen a copy of this. A short while later Alcoholics Anonymous, then a fledgling small organization scarcely a decade old, with my father's permission, also started to use the prayer in their regular meetings.

I don't know when or how AA simplified the text—perhaps from the very beginning. Their version frames the prayer in the first-person singular and simplifies the opening. It omits the spiritually correct but difficult idea of praying for *grace to accept with serenity that which we cannot change,* and focuses instead on the simpler notion of obtaining *serenity to accept what cannot be changed*. My father let this happen and didn't fuss when the wordings were altered, though he minded it. There are, after all, several large differences between the two formulations.

Another change is more serious. In the second clause, *courage to change what should be changed* becomes, in the AA rendering, simply *courage to change what can be changed*. Goodness me, just because something can be changed doesn't mean that it must be! More important, this way of putting it reduces the scope of the imperative. It speaks merely of what we think we might manage to alter at a given moment, *to change what we can change*. But there are circumstances that *should be changed* yet may seem beyond our powers to alter, and these are the circumstances under which the prayer is most needed. The shift in the text reduces a difficult, strong idea to a banal, weak one, and I suspect that this dumbing down of the prayer has contributed to its enormous popularity.

I don't have any idea where the additional clauses of the prayer came from that AA adds to the tripartite original—their message and their tone are not in any way Niebuhrian. But since my father never copyrighted his prayer—it was inconceivable to him to construe prayers as a source of revenue—he could not control its misquotation, misattribution, or embellishment. I can't begin to count how many nice people joshingly and good-heartedly advise me that he made a big mistake here: it's an all-American virtuous idea, I suppose, that if you've done something valuable you ought to make money on it, and knee-slapping laughter breaks out if you failed to make a buck when you could have. Unquestioned worship of the golden calf is the norm.

Not that other people haven't made money from the Serenity Prayer. There was an immediate postwar fashion for pairing it with Dürer's drawing of praying hands—this was deemed aptly Germanic and suitably pious. Examples cropped up on bookends, tea towels, pieces of etched stained glass to hang in library windows. Former students or distant admirers sent these trophies to my father—they meant to be kind—and he shook his head in wonderment. My more caustically anti-pious, though very devout, mother, who considered that one's taste in certain matters signified one's spiritual condition, would raise an expressive eyebrow and mutter about vulgarity of the soul. (She was very good on this subject, as was my father in a different way. Well can I remember their reactions when, at the Thursday evening receptions they held during term time for their students,★ an eager-to-please young clergyman-to-be, wearing banal piety on his sleeve, might introduce an opinion with the phrase "Speaking as a Christian, I would say . . ." Talk about vulgarity! True and good people never spoke like that. My mother's huge blue eyes would open wide, and her ready smile would become icy. My father would rub his nose and look embarrassed, interrupt the poor boob with a distracting question.)

Many of my parents' best friends, who instinctively understood all this, were amused by the irony of having the austere Niebuhr associated with feel-good Hallmark sentimentalities (the greeting-card company also asked to use the prayer). Most

★The students composed a song about those "at homes," sung to the tune of "When the Roll Is Called up Yonder, I'll be There." Here is the first verse:

> When it's eight o'clock on Thursday night
>   And books become a bore;
> Then we'll leave our desks and climb the golden stair,
> We will gather at the master's feet
>   A-sitting on the floor,
> When the beer is served at Reinie's
>   We'll be there . . .

Suggested Activity Before Worship

Read today's psalm, Psalm 51, from the pew Bible on page 520 of the Old Testament. Then read the following list of the traditional twelve steps of Alcoholics Anonymous. Next to each step write the verses of the psalm that parallel that step.

The Twelve Steps

1. We admitted we were powerless over our sin—that our lives had become unmanageable.
2. We came to believe that a Power greater than ourselves could restore us to sanity.
3. We made a decision to turn our will and our lives over to the care of God as we understood Him.
4. We made a searching and fearless moral inventory of ourselves.
5. We admitted to God, to ourselves, and to another human being the exact nature of our wrongs.
6. We were entirely ready to have God remove all these defects of character.
7. We humbly asked God to remove our shortcomings.
8. We made a list of all persons we had harmed and became willing to make amends to them.
9. We made direct amends to such people wherever possible, except when to do so would injure them or others.
10. We continued to take a personal inventory and, when we were wrong, promptly admitted it.
11. We sought through prayer and meditation to improve our conscious contact with God, praying only for knowledge of His will for us and the power to carry that out.
12. Having had a spiritual awakening as a result of these steps, we tried to carry this message to others and to practice these principles in all our affairs.

SERVICE OF BAPTISM
AND RECEPTION OF NEW MEMBERS

PRESENTATION
Friends: In presenting yourselves for baptism or membership in the church, you announce your faith in Jesus Christ, and show that you want to know him and serve him as his chosen disciple. I ask you, therefore, to reject sin, to profess your faith in Christ Jesus, and to confess the faith of the church, the faith in which we baptize.

Trusting in the gracious mercy of God, do you turn from the ways of sin and renounce evil and its power in the world?

I do.

Do you turn to Jesus Christ and accept him as your Lord and Savior, trusting in his grace and love?

I do.

Do you intend to be Christ's faithful disciple, obeying his word, showing his love and participating actively in the worship and mission of Christ's church?

I do.

CONFESSION OF FAITH: THE APOSTLES' CREED
I believe in God the Father Almighty, Maker of heaven and earth; And in Jesus Christ His only Son our Lord; who was conceived by the Holy Ghost, born of the Virgin Mary, suffered under Pontius Pilate, was crucified, dead, and buried; He descended into hell; the third day He rose again from the dead; He ascended into heaven, and sitteth on the right hand of God the Father Almighty; from thence He shall come to judge the quick and the dead.

I believe in the Holy Ghost; the holy catholic church; the communion of saints; the forgiveness of sins; the resurrection of the body; and the life everlasting. Amen.

COMMITMENT OF THE CONGREGATION
Our Lord Jesus Christ ordered us to teach those who are baptized. Do you, the people of the church, promise to tell these new disciples the good news of the gospel, to help them know all that Christ commands, and, by your fellowship, to strengthen their family ties with the household of God?

We do.

PRAYER

BAPTISM

DECLARATION OF BAPTISM

GIVING OF SCRIPTURE VERSE

The *Instrumental Praise Ensemble* begins rehearsals for Easter Services on Sunday, March 14, from 11:45 a.m. to 12:30 p.m. in the Chapel. Rehearsals continue Sundays, March 21 and April 4. Instrumentalists with at least two full years experience who are interested in joining for the first time should contact Bruce Preuninger (624-4757) for more information.

INSTRUMENTAL MUSIC MINISTRY

Attention All Women...

We will be Assembling the Necessity Bags for Mission Avenue Outreach on Tuesday, March 2, 7:00 p.m., at the Women's Coordinating Team meeting. Any extra hands would be appreciated! For more information, please contact Sandy Jones (448-1592).

Introducing Another Session Member ...

> ➢ <u>**Mike Dugger**</u>, a second year elder, is chair of the Finance and Administration Committee. Today he is serving as the Lay Assistant for the 10:30 a.m. worship.

Nick Preuninger's Whitworth Senior Theatre project is <u>March 7</u>, not March 6 as stated in Whitworth's last issue <u>of Mind and Heart</u>. He and his partner, Sarah Larson, are directing <u>Louder than Words</u> at 7 p.m. in Cowles Auditorium's Stage II at Whitworth. This is an interactive theatre event using techniques developed by Brazilian theatre artist Augusto Boal, who has used theatre to spur political and social change throughout the world.

of these friends were secular Jews or agnostic ex-Catholics or cheerfully irreverent "Prots," by which I mean that my family's world was populated by people largely free of that self-congratulatory piety which is phony religion's basic fragrance. The friends would send along ghastly samples of Serenity Prayer kitsch they'd encountered, for they knew the response would be disbelieving laughter, and they wanted to cheer Pa up when he was in his melancholic phase. Painted trays or crocheted hymn-book covers, say.

These artifacts keep turning up. I met someone recently who swore she'd seen the prayer painted on the side of a Swiss chalet (with the false German attribution), and only the other day I came across bookplates inscribed with its words. My friend Arthur M. Schlesinger Jr. keeps me up-to-date: not long ago he sent me a mail-order catalog offering a "Serenity Afghan" with the prayer's words knit in "forever" on its "100% cotton." AA encourages its appearance on coffee mugs, naturally enough; I wonder whether it's on ashtrays?

After half a century, there are plenty of riffs done on the prayer, and some of them are ghastly, others quite cheery. I like a goofy one that turned up in the *Calvin and Hobbes* comic strip. Calvin says to Hobbes, "Know what I pray for?" Hobbes: "What?" Calvin: "The strength to change what I can, the inability to accept what I can't, and the incapacity to tell the difference." Hobbes: "You should lead an interesting life." Calvin: "Oh, I already do!"

Another friend of mine discovered in a local bookshop a tiny "folding screen book" entitled *The Serenity Prayer*. It has eight panels of pretty pictures to go with a simplified version of the text, like a child's picture book: the "wisdom" panel has a nice photo of a waterfall, and "to know the difference" features a bird in flight. I suppose it looks spiritual? Does the bird know the difference? Is it flying away from the waterfall? This little booklet costs eight dollars. But of course making aerosol spray cans of spiritual whipped cream out of public-domain "virtue" is a well-respected custom in the American marketplace, as, for example, the right-wing ideologue William Bennett and his ghastly best-seller *The Book of Virtues* demonstrated: it was compiled from snippets of freely available good-hearted literature composed by dead authors with whom Mr. Bennett did not have to share royalties.

DURING THE HARSH postwar winter of 1945–46 my father heard directly from his German cousins for the first time in many years; the German Niebuhrs were asking him for food and help. It was one of Europe's coldest, rawest winters in memory, though 1947 was to be even worse. He told them—he rarely spoke of this, for he hardly enjoyed, though he did not evade, this task—that he would not attend to their requests until he had first done everything he could for the victims of the regime they had welcomed and supported. The larger public truth was not to be avoided, however awkward the family strain. Dozens of letters were pouring in every week from friends and acquaintances in dire need of immediate succor; the cousinly letters had to wait at the bottom of the pile.

In our apartment in New York, there was a constant stream— not of guests, exactly, but of "displaced persons," as aid agencies called them, European friends who would stay with us until they settled in homes of their own. Not only our guest room but the otherwise unused maids' rooms behind the kitchen housed a never-ending succession of Europeans in transit: relatives and friends of my parents' European colleagues, former students, concentration camp survivors, people whose families had been torn apart by the war. The tumultuous dislocation and trauma that mark *postwar* seasons should never be underestimated—a point worth making in *prewar* seasons.

The Heath summers in the little Stone Cottage continued as oases of private calm, though, and my grandmother made them exciting for me. The Robbins forests were magical terrain, and I peopled them with Algonquins and their squaws—Deerfield was only eighteen miles away, after all, and the massacre had happened only recently, at least in my dreams—with Pooh and Piglet, with all the Kipling beasts of India and of Sussex that I learned about in the books my English mother gave me. Mütterchen taught me how to collect princess pine to garnish the church decorations, how to make sun prints of ferns, find lady's slippers in the hidden sunlit glens, sew clothes for my dolls, and distinguish among mushrooms.

How lucky I was to have been able to roam around those glorious woods! The Robbins land ran south of our house for miles of spruce, pine, oak, birch, maple—well-managed, healthy woodlands. From the meadow pond, the first of the three that Uncle Howard had built, the brook spilled into a little waterfall and then trickled down to the second, bigger pond at the bottom of the Robbinses' garden, with its beautiful fringe of evening primroses and blue flag irises; after that one could follow the water course as it meandered into the woods. This was not easy to do, but there were big rewards—mushrooms, Indian pipes, ground pine, ferns, granite outcroppings, bogs, and little trout hollows. The third pond, deep in the forest, stony green-black under the huge pines, intimidated me, but I always hoped to see deer there. If you kept going long enough, you emerged into high meadows and pastures on an abandoned road where lilacs and roses growing lustily in the pretty wilderness were signs of earlier domestic precincts. You came, eventually, to a windswept hilltop that featured the South Heath Cemetery and one of Heath's world-class sky-filled mountain views.

When my parents were away, which was often, I would bicycle along a different road to this same high point, thence down a further road to the Landstroms' farm, where I would stay with the family until my parents returned. It was a familiar and beloved place for me. Indeed, one of my very earliest memories of anything at all is of standing just below the lawn in front of the Landstroms' house, with its connected dairy shed and barn, and watching horses pull the hayricks across the swelling yellow field to the east; beyond were the further dark-green fields and woods that separated the Landstroms' land from Aunt Ethel's. This must have been during the war years, when gasoline was rationed and the horses were being used in the age-old way; they were retired in 1946. Later, when I spent quite a lot of time at the Landstrom farm, I was allowed to visit the retirees in their field, and Mr. Landstrom even let me ride one of them; they are my ur-horses.

When I was with the Landstroms I'd try to help with the chores—haying or putting up vegetables—but I probably just got in the way. I liked best helping Mr. Landstrom to feed and milk the cows in the late afternoon, after hours of shelling beans or baking biscuits or chasing after lost heifers; he treated me, as he treated everyone, with generous courtesy, and he taught me whatever he thought I needed to know as I trailed after him up and down the stanchions with the milking equipment, up and down the aisle between the cows with the feed scoop; into the hay barn above, where I would dive from the highest hay-filled sections down fifteen or twenty feet to the lower ones, though he thought this foolish; into the stone-lined separator room, with its amazing dairy fragrance of very, very fresh cream; around the corner to the pigpens. Restless powerful animals, pigs: they made me nervous. Much more fun to swing on the swing hanging from the enormous sugar maple tree on the Landstroms' front lawn, or to learn cross-stitching or jam making from Mrs. Landstrom, whom I adored, or to play with their benign gray German shepherd, Smokey, or, at home, with our terrier, Topsy; she had puppies in the last year of the war—we named the greedy one Goering and the long-legged one Halifax.

Back at the Stone Cottage, life went on. The beloved Topsy eventually went to her reward, and I can't remember what happened to Goering and Halifax or their siblings. Aunt Hulda and I would go for long woodland walks, arrange picnics on the Dell road, adventures on the abandoned Oxbow trail after an afternoon of blueberrying on Burnt Hill (named for some now forgotten Indian blaze two centuries before); and I drew pictures of Jesus at Galilee in my Sunday school coloring books before the Sunday services, where Pa preached now and again. I knew where Galilee was: I had heard talk about it.

My simplistic childhood memories are one thing; what my father was up to during these years was quite another. In the fall of 1946, after an idyllic Heath summer, my father returned to Germany for the first time in sixteen years—a trip, and therefore an absence from home, of which I have no active memory. But I know now that as a member of a U.S. Government Commission to Investigate the Occupied Territories, he could see for himself what the world of the defeated enemy looked like up close. He met with university chaplains, with Social Democratic politicians and even some conservative Christian Democrats, with pastors and teachers all over the place, including the questionably accommodating Bishop Otto Dibelius (not one of his favorites). He talked with theologians and poets at a conference at Bad Boll (where his father's favorites, the earliest Christian Socialists in Germany, the two Blumhardts, had founded a retreat). And he went to Berlin, the tragic destruction of which appalled him: "The inner city is a city of the dead . . . people walk about in a daze," he wrote to my mother. The "whole nation writhes in agony," as he put it. There he managed to see Dietrich Bonhoeffer's parents; my English aunt Barbara, who knew them, too, met with these stoic and resigned old people during that same fall and winter.

In the midst of the wreckage many brave, sensible men and women, including clergy, were courageously picking up their broken lives and facing the future after twelve years of spiritual desolation and political horror, after more than five years of hideous war. But, Pa reported ruefully, all too often the German pastors seemed oblivious, somehow, of the landscape of death and social dismemberment, physical torment, spiritual chaos, and moral confusion around them. They acted as if none of that was real, as if the terrible past and present might be overlooked while the spiritual future was preserved in some holy elsewhere. At one Sunday morning service, "The sermon was the purest other-worldly version of Christianity I have ever heard, understandable in the present circumstances but nevertheless pathetic. This is surely a place of the dead, and the kind of Lutheranism I heard this morning was pretty pure escape."

My father on shipboard with fellow commission members,
en route to Germany in 1946

Those comments were in letters to my mother. To me (by now I was seven) he wrote more plainly, but even in the short, blunt postcard sentences I see the moral instruction. A typically terse note came from Stuttgart: "I wrote Christopher a letter but have not written you. But you haven't written either. . . . The children here are all hungry. They do not have enough to eat. Almost all the buildings were destroyed by bombs. We must pray for these children and help them."

In that same year, a professor at the University of Kiel named Theodor Wilhelm received a copy of the Serenity Prayer, in English, from some Canadian friends who sent it to him "as a first sign of postwar reconciliation," he wrote later; they called it an "old little prayer." Wilhelm—evidently unaware that it had already appeared in Germany thanks to the U.S. army—then incorporated the prayer in a book of his own which he wrote under the pseudonym Friedrich Oetinger; it was published in 1951. I can only guess why Wilhelm chose not to use his own name, but if he was going to have a *nom de plume*, it was easy enough for him to pick one: his mother's forebears included Swabian Pietists, so the known historical figure of F. C. Oetinger, an eighteenth-century Pietist theologian, was a pleasant option for him. However, Wilhelm's book, which is about political pedagogy (what a subject for Germans!), not about the Word of the Lord, had nothing to do with that trivial and obsolete thinker, and vice versa.

I am ignorant of the history of the reception of the Wilhelm-Oetinger book, but I find it peculiarly repellent that German readers quickly attributed the prayer, buried in a book that was manifestly the work of a pseudonymous modern writer, to the *earlier* Oetinger. This happened very rapidly. How did the double mistake come about? Whatever the answer, one thing seems clear: Germans wanted the Serenity Prayer to be German. (German Protestants, anyway: Catholics everywhere believe it was written by St. Francis of Assisi.) The curious dynamic by which we all revise our memories of our own history, adjust our sense of the present to a comfortable accommodation with an endurable past, had very peculiar manifestations in Germany. So a reassertion of German spiritual purity, and evasive silence about what had gone on in 1933–45, allowed my father's little prayer to become a German one.

Wilhelm himself remained more or less mum while the mistaken attribution he had perpetrated took on a life of its own. He and his wife "came to enjoy" the oddity of the mysterious prayer having an Oetinger lineage, he wrote. How charming. So far as I know they corrected the record only once: when they learned it was cited as Oetinger's prayer at the Bundeswehr's cadet academy in Koblenz, they pointed out the error to an officer in charge. "His response was as sensible as it was useful," Wilhelm reported later: "to leave the text intact but remove the name Oetinger. I hope it was done." Well, that's one way of looking at it.

Wilhelm and other Germans who were intrigued to solve the mystery of the prayer's authorship were not theologians or church historians; his account of their efforts shows how little they knew about the traditions of prayer. Yet Wilhelm knew enough to know, or belatedly came to learn, that it was quite implausible to ascribe the Serenity Prayer to a Swabian Pietist. After all, he eventually acknowledged, Oetinger had been

a preacher to the birds and in the woods, and his books are full of mystical sentimentalities. Anyone with even a little knowledge of Swabian pietists, of their special mixture of sectarianism, mystical eccentricity, and apocalyptic frenzy, must know that such a sober reflection [as in the prayer], such a pragmatically argued distinction between the possible and the unchangeable, even more the challenge of active social change, could never grow in the soil of Swabian conventionality. But the prayer, cloaked with this pietistic godliness, made its way in the Federal Republic and became a favorite ending for solemn talks, notably by Klaus von Bismarck. It became the motto of the Bundeswehr's academy, and General Speidel began using it to characterize the spirit of Germany's new military leadership. In Koblenz the false attribution is carved in stone and surrounded by flags.

Wilhelm never answered the question of how or when he finally learned that yes, indeed, the author was Reinhold Niebuhr, but he seemed to resist the idea. In an essay published in 1976, doing his lame best to account for the prayer's postwar history in Germany, he got most of the facts wrong and then suggested, sleazily, that Niebuhr, "even if he is not the composer of the text, is the one who introduced it to the wider American public." Mercifully this condescending smear is only a minor footnote to history, but it is hard to erase. While several German-language Lutheran hymnbooks and prayer books properly attribute the Serenity Prayer, the Oetinger attribution remains in wide circulation, and many Germans go on enjoying the notion that the prayer is surely German. Goodness, how easily they armor themselves with the weird, awful presumption that in the Profound Spirituality ball game they must surely have been the first to score a goal.

Even the plaque installed at the Bundeswehr academy to explain the provenance of the now *un*attributed Serenity Prayer is oddly misleading, with the same sanctimonious German slant. (Its text was written, I believe, by the ever helpful Wilhelm.) Though it acknowledges that Oetinger is not the author, his irrelevant birth and death dates are cited (as are those of Epictetus, because his teachings "lead toward" the Serenity Prayer's formulation). No information is given as to where or when Reinhold Niebuhr composed it, and naturally enough no reference is made to its first publication in 1944 in a U.S. Army booklet. The prayer's modern popularity *in English* is merely, and grotesquely, ascribed to "its being used in the German-American theologian Reinhold Niebuhr's sermons." (Even calling Pa a German American in this context seems inappropriate.)

In all, the notion is somehow sustained that the prayer was originally German.

My distaste for this misappropriation of a beautiful Heath prayer is stronger than my father would have approved of, I imagine. But I can't help it, perhaps because it makes me so sad: the slippery evasions of this sorry story are in such striking contrast to the Serenity Prayer itself and to the honorable way it found its public everywhere else. In our own family, however, it developed into a burden, but not until much later.

THE TEMPO OF THE Serenity Prayer story in the first decade after the war accelerated, given its new fame. And as my father and his colleagues and friends were drawn into more and more public work, their story also broadened out and became more intricate, with subplots and asides.

For my father, the teaching at Union was still and always the main thing, and he found it an especially great privilege to work with the remarkable students who flocked to the seminary in 1946–50. They were among the very best students he ever had. Many were men who had seen combat in Europe or the Pacific, who had lived in hell and endured the absolute rock-bottom worst in randomly cruel, hopeless experience—and now they wanted to understand what it had meant in both the ultimate and the proximate senses, and to make something valuable of the remainder of their days. They knew better than most that America's spiritual and public landscape was damaged by the war's huge psychological traumas and by ancient political and social inadequacies. They had not only new but old concerns, and they weren't sure they knew how to accept with serenity what cannot be changed or courageously to make necessary changes.

How would wealth and power be distributed in (and among) the postwar democracies? What would be the social organization that would allow the right relations among free and independent citizens to evolve? How might the United States deploy its now enormous power for the good of its own people and for the strengthening of a safe world community, as it evolved away from the old imperialisms and faced the new ones? How should a Christian, or any religious person, think about these issues in the context of an ever more secular republic? How did one offer spiritual security and freedom in these new times? These were among the many old questions to which fresh answers were needed.

Later generations tend unwittingly to presume that 1945 was *eine Stunde null*, as the German phrase puts it, a zero hour when everything began anew with a new set of imperatives: that overnight Great Britain and Western Europe set off on the road to recovery with the help of generous American aid; that the brave Russian ally became the dangerous foe—either because American policy forced the Soviet Union into hostility or because Stalin himself enacted unacceptably aggressive policies or both; that the New Deal's social benefits were consolidated and extended thanks to the heady upward swing of postwar prosperity; that Joseph McCarthy and his cronies were ugly new distortions of the Cold War political landscape who came along unexpectedly; and so on. Pa sometimes turns up in this cliché-ridden, erroneous story as a Cold War theorist, a former radical turned anti-Communist, a once lively critic turned in-house establishmentarian gadfly.

But it wasn't like that at all, as his students knew well. The situation was both more ironic, more tragic, and more pathetic— to use the terms he used at the time. And the real problem was that too many people, in both the church and American public life, kept on giving the same old answers to the old questions, answers that had failed before and during the war and would fail again. Would they succeed in carrying the day? The future was extremely unclear, and the outcome unknown.

Pathos, tragedy, and irony are found in all human cultures, but Pa was focusing on the ways in which they manifested themselves in the postwar United States. The present tense was his natural habitat. And it was the ironies in American history that seized his imagination most strongly, the dangerous paradoxes he saw at almost every turn in the path by which this young, idealistic, generous, headstrong, and inexperienced nation had risen to global eminence, this nation that boasted of its religious commitments yet took secular materialism to new heights, this nation that was so grossly self-confident yet had such an unstable and insecure sense of itself.

The ironic moral dilemmas were especially sharp in consideration of American nuclear power and the temptations to brandish it: atomic bombs had helped America help the Allies to win a just war, so this encouraged pundits to assess the weapons benignly, and to praise themselves for being part of a triumphant culture. Yet many of the scientists who had done the work to make these weapons possible were now locked in a struggle to contain their use and to restrict the development of even larger, thermonuclear "superbombs," which hawkish proponents insisted might be necessary to ensure America's complete impregnability. My father wrote, "We might remember the prophetic warnings to the nations of old, that nations which become proud because they were divine instruments must in turn stand under the divine judgment and be destroyed. . . .

If ever a nation needed to be reminded of the perils of vainglory, we are that nation, in the pride of our power and our victory."

In the spring of 1947, Pa had a sabbatical leave from the seminary and spent the term in Europe; he was to return in the summer of 1948, for the First General Assembly in Amsterdam of the World Council of Churches—the final fruit of all the prewar and wartime ecumenical efforts; again in the fall of 1949, when he was a delegate to UNESCO's Fourth Conference in Paris; and for the last time in 1951. As an American abroad in those early postwar years, he had useful opportunities to observe the often clumsy, often inspired ways in which the United States was engaging with the world.

The international context meant a great deal to him, and the ecumenical meetings gave him the chance not only to bring himself up-to-date on European developments but to debate and reconsider the different formulations offered by Calvinist, Lutheran, liberal, and orthodox Christian forms as he knew them in both America and Europe. He had several bracing encounters with Karl Barth, "a very charming man but also very honest, and we had some very searching discussions," Pa wrote in a letter to my mother. For a long afternoon in Geneva in the spring of 1947, they ranged over "the whole question of the relation of faith to philosophy on the one hand and to ethics and politics on the other. I found it most stimulating and helpful. I told him I was too much of a preacher not to look for points of contact between the truth of the Gospel and the despair of the world." Barth was amazed that Pa was a preacher—he hadn't thought of this as part of his makeup, it turned out. Oh yes, my father acknowledged, and my wife accuses me of preaching on religion "to its intellectual despisers," like Schleiermacher. "This pleased him very much, and he repeated, 'Did she say that, really?' "

Pa also noticed Barth's immersion—I use the word mischievously—in a number of sectarian disputes, "having thrown the church in an uproar here by his criticism of infant baptism. Now he is on the Congregational tack, insisting that the real church is only in the simple community of faith in the congregation, and that theologians, bishops, secretaries [only] imagine they are the church. I went after him on these issues pretty hard," he reported, though Pa granted that Barth was absolutely right to emphasize "that faith, hope, and love in the life of believers are the real substance of the church and that all else is superstructure." This was not an emphasis that American church leaders were likely to recommend.

In Amsterdam in 1948, the summit meeting of the diverse church groups joining in the World Council was a huge gathering, even larger than the prewar Oxford Conference, lasting for a fortnight—like a kind of ecclesiastical Olympic Games, with subevents and contests and intricate international negotiations over terms and conditions. Constant "difficulties of language and theology" thwarted progress, Pa told my mother, but the ecumenical spirit was strong and positive.

Unpleasant wrangles about the advisability of, let alone the scriptural authority allowing for, women in the priesthood did not go well, however; Peggy Benn arrived from London to report that the Anglicans, at their preceding Lambeth Conference, had been completely obtuse and recalcitrant on the subject. Angus Dun agreed; you couldn't even "raise the issue significantly" with them, he said, which boded ill for further negotiation in Amsterdam. As usual, the politics of the thing turned not on the merits of the argument favoring women priests but on matters of power and control. Pa reported to his feminist wife: "Everyone thinks the [Lambeth Conference] section on women in the church is indefensible. Dictated altogether by fear of losing caste with Eastern Orthodoxy. Angus did say that the conference gave him the impression of a lot of old men clutching at familiar things in a world of perdition." (It was a pity England didn't have a Bishop Scarlett: in 1946 he had finally prevailed upon the American Episcopalians to relax their position on the marriage of divorced persons, for example, and he was a master at inducing positive change among groups that feared it, even anxious, status-proud old bishops.)

After weeks of talk in Amsterdam, "little has jelled except the decision to come into being," my father had to acknowledge at the end. "One realizes how inadequate we all are," and "much of the experience is frustrating rather than creative." But still, there were gains. One of the regular evening church services at the conference Pa found worth commenting on: it was conducted jointly by Bishop Bell of Chichester, the German Lutheran Bishop Hans Lilje of Hannover, a Dutch Reformed professor, and Father George Florovsky, the Russian Orthodox theologian whom Pa came to know at Union. "I realize that the only time the church is really sufferable is when it is at prayer," Pa wrote. That evening devotion was "really the true church."

The political junkets were equally interesting for Pa, in their different ways. (And they were notably more luxurious than the ecumenical ones. He was horrified by the pretentiousness of the opulent quarters where UNESCO put its delegates, just as he had been by the proconsular grandeur of the palatial German settings where the government had put him in 1946.) History had bestowed on the United States huge political responsibilities, and its legacy empowered it to strive to fulfill them justly, he thought. But he wasn't confident that the nation would rise to the occasion: the propensity to pride and self-congratulation was so strong! American wealth, power, and success had created extraordinary pressures of expectation, and the country now had to conduct itself in a trustworthy, accountable way in a host of volatile, strange new situations. Especially after the victories of 1945, Americans should not, could not, shirk the task. In any event, as Pa put it, "Life has no meaning except in terms of responsibility."

At about this time he wrote a prayer for "all who have authority in the world, for the leaders of our nation and for those who bear office in all the nations." It has what I think of as his characteristic tone of paradox, vigor, benevolence, and what Isaiah Berlin interestingly called his "moral charm." He prayed that these leaders "may seek the peaceable fruits of justice . . . that they may know the limits of human wisdom in the perplexities of this day . . . that they may learn the wisdom of restraint and the justice of charity." I would like to hear this prayer often.

There was one political leader who I am confident would have been grateful for the prayer, and Pa was lucky enough to see him during those European trips. It was grand to witness the wise, expert way in which Stafford Cripps, first as chairman of the Board of Trade and then as chancellor of the exchequer in Clement Attlee's Labour government, deployed his political skills to restore the economy and, hence, the social energy of an exhausted and depleted Britain. This was courage to change at a very very high level.

In the years 1947–50 Cripps was presiding over a vast, revolutionary restructuring in the economic planning of a modern democracy, and this was neither technically easy nor politically safe: yet the perceived fairness and principled intelligence with which he accomplished the Labour government's quasi-socialist, quasi-Keynesian budgets of those stringent years were understood and appreciated by British voters. "You feel with Cripps that almost nothing is politically impossible," wrote Hugh Gaitskell. "He sails on simply concerned with what is the best solution from every other point of view and ignoring all the rocks which lie ahead." He became, as Roy Jenkins put it, "the very embodiment of responsible government and self-disciplined patriotism." When Cripps came to America in 1948 and again in 1949, it was a pleasure to learn more from him about how he had gone about accomplishing—to use his own formulation—"actions that will become part of human history," that would "bridge that portentous gap between fine thoughts and actual policies which has been so wide and so difficult to bring closer."

At home in America, the political situation was much less promising. I have no actual memory of the dreadful 1946 election, when Republicans took control of the Congress and did as much as they could to thwart and distort what became President Truman's Fair Deal program, the plans to continue and extend the benefits of the New Deal to new generations of veterans and other Americans. My conscious political education began with the 1948 campaign, when we'd listen to Truman's whistle-stop speeches on the radio, and mirthfully enjoy his ribbing of our local New York Republican, Governor Thomas Dewey, with his waxed mustache and his waxy mind. That was also the year that Pa joined others in founding UDA's successor, Americans for Democratic Action, a liberal action group that kept up pressure on the Democratic Party to include in its platform planks that committed the party to support legislation in favor of civil rights, fair employment practices, and responsible internationalism. He and his allies in the ginger group—the irrepressible young mayor of Minneapolis, Hubert Humphrey; Walter Reuther, head of the United Automobile Workers; Senator Paul Douglas of Illinois; Arthur M. Schlesinger Jr., and Kenneth Galbraith—actually did make a difference to the politics of the time: the ADA contradicts the tired and tiring notion that liberals are by nature ineffective.

I remember more vividly the disgraceful 1950 election, when the scowly young congressman from reactionary Orange County, California, Richard Nixon, viciously attacked my heroine, the beautiful and principled Representative Helen Gahagan Douglas—a strong supporter of President Truman, who had introduced anti-lynching bills in the Congress to provide more federal civil-rights protection and who had served as a delegate to the first sessions of the fledgling United Nations, which many Republicans opposed. Nixon accused her, with a complete disregard for the truth, of being a Communist sympathizer.

These were the first, and among the most memorable, of more than a half century's worth of dishonest, slanderous Republican election campaigns I have consciously suffered through. The party seems to have an insatiable appetite for exploiting the worst in the political climate in order to gain power, and in 1950 that meant suggesting—as Republicans went on suggesting thereafter, whenever it helped them gain office—that anyone with an interest in better race relations or in American participation in international peacekeeping must be a supporter of the evil Bolshevik empire. I hadn't yet heard of Joseph McCarthy, but that came soon enough.

I certainly had heard of the House Un-American Activities Committee, and I knew about "the Attorney General's list." Every time Pa got put on a commission at the State Department or for UNESCO or the like he'd have to get a security check, and then there'd be trouble because of the committees and leagues and councils that he'd joined during the 1930s, all those outfits that had concerned themselves with anti-fascist protest, the furtherance of industrial democracy, and aid to refugees. These groups were now appearing on a list kept by the Attorney General of "subversive organizations" membership in which was considered prima facie evidence that one's loyalty to the United States was questionable.

This was a disgusting effect of the Loyalty Review Board system that the Truman administration had installed, partly in a futile effort to defuse right-wing Republican attacks on it for being "soft on communism." What a sad, sad consequence: Americans had fought for four years in an all-out war to save Democracy and Freedom, and now mere membership in groups that worked for change and improvement was said to suggest you weren't a decent citizen.

Now in quite a few of those prewar outfits Pa had indeed had run-ins with American Communists; often enough they wanted to control these groups, and when they succeeded in grabbing the helm of one, the course would shift to whatever line the Comintern was laying down that year—in which case Pa and like-minded social democrats, having already wasted collaborative time in trying to keep the thing afloat for its initial purpose, would give up and quit, maybe start another group on their own. This was predictable sectarian life on the left in the interwar years, and a very important reason that many left-wing people became anti-Communist. But its familiar dynamic was unknown to the Justice Department or the FBI.

The postwar experiences were therefore doubly and unpleasantly ironic: the groups had not been truly subversive in the first place—Pa had considered many of them irrelevant and futile, actually—and he could hardly agree with the FBI's assessment; but now hundreds of Communists and anti-Communists alike were subjected to state-sponsored harassment. The Loyalty Board assault on civil liberties was bad in itself, and even if federal employees to whom it applied got themselves cleared with the Loyalty Board, they, along with thousands of people in the private sector, faced the added danger of being hauled up before the Congress—by the House Un-American Activities Committee or, in the Senate, by the slovenly, black-jowled Joseph McCarthy. Every child of a left-wing family has memories of the fear, uncertainty, and threats of those years, and I certainly have mine.

There were good reasons, therefore, to be skeptical about the cheerful, flag-waving simplicity of the usual triumphal American belief in the sturdiness of American democracy. Oh, the pride of victors! A democracy needed more hard work than it was being accorded. Pa wrote:

> Democracy has a more compelling justification and requires a more realistic vindication than is given it by the liberal culture with which it has been associated in modern history. The excessively optimistic estimates of human nature and history with which the democratic credo is linked are a source of peril to democratic society, for our contemporary experience refutes this optimism and there is danger that it will seem to refute the democratic ideal as well. Modern democracy requires a more realistic philosophical and religious basis.

To establish that basis, and to insist on the realism of it, was the central purpose of much of my father's work.

Realism, in the Niebuhr vocabulary, meant being aware of inevitable human failing, whether in domestic national affairs or in foreign policy. Nations, like all communities, like any church or political gathering, cannot presume an absolute claim on truth, rectitude, virtue, force, or power. Democratic debate of the sort to which Pa had given so much of his life—discussion, dispute, inquiry—was an essential component in the formulation of policies and plans, he believed, for democracy's leaders must always take account of the contingent human errors that will inevitably alter what we do. Open, tolerant, engaged respect for the differences among us is essential. There is no freedom without it. Repudiation of "deviations" was a Communist habit that Pa had decried, and the strident right wing had its own version of this authoritarian mind-set. The net result was a loss of democratic freedom when the state itself, with its unmatched mechanisms of coercion, repressed civil liberty.

Of course, in an open society where one may speak democratic truths to power, power may not listen. I don't mean just governmental power, but social and church power, too. Large sectors of society *prefer* restricted debate, and opt for closed minds. Pa had learned that in Detroit in the 1920s, it was true in 1950, and it is even more true today. It was certainly the case with the leaders of American churches.

I am regularly amazed when I read in this or that magazine that my father, like his friend Paul Tillich, was a "major leader" of postwar American Protestantism. If only! American Protestant churches mostly paid the two of them no heed. A small minority of intrepid souls may have enjoyed having my father vent his feisty views on the need for racial equality, for a committed curriculum of social justice, for a radical reorganization of industrial democracy, just as they liked having the exotic Tillich explore for them the boundaries and outer spaces of theology's encounter with art and culture, psychoanalysis and music. But most of them simply didn't want to listen. Ministers all over America might have been pounding the lecterns and delivering fire-and-brimstone sermons, but their social conformism was pretty complete. Little changed in their privileged lives. They pussyfooted around feel-good mega-preachers like Norman Vincent Peale or Billy Graham—who like so many of their successors never risked their tremendous personal popularity by broaching a difficult spiritual subject, and rarely lifted a finger to help a social cause. They checked up on their pension funds and ignored their parishioners' lives. It's easy enough to assert today, as I do, that Tillich and Niebuhr, or Dun and Temple, or Horton and McConnell were vital presences in the modern life of the Gospel. But they weren't acknowledged as such by most American parsons, and I doubt that they would be today. Freedom and democracy, meanwhile, were being traduced or betrayed.

In the case of the Niebuhr family, spirits were buoyed nonetheless by the friendships of unstoppable and stalwart pals both within and outside the church—like Felix Frankfurter and Bishop Scarlett; like the intrepid John Bennett, my father's closest political and theological ally on the Union faculty; like Pa's political friends. We kept in touch with Jim Dombrowski's and Myles Horton's challenging work in the South. Firebombings, lawsuits, physical intimidation, and harassment were the lot of everyone working for the civil rights of blacks there. Jim Loeb delivered regular reports on ADA developments. Alan Paton, a new friend, arrived from South Africa (after having endured a disgraceful detention by the Immigration and Naturalization Service, which had initially questioned his credentials and forbade his entry into "God's own Country," as my mother called it angrily at such moments); a single afternoon with him was enough to give one spirit for many a season. C. C. Burlingham, edging into his nineties, stayed on top of developments in Washington and New York and intervened once to help with a Loyalty Board problem. And Wystan Auden sent on his new poems. Here is the ending of the last one in *Nones*, a book he dedicated to my parents:

> For the present stalks abroad
> Like the past and its wronged again
> Whimper and are ignored,
> And the truth cannot be hid;
> Somebody chose their pain,
> What needn't have happened did.
>
> Occurring this very night
> By no established rule,
> Some event may already have hurled
> Its first little No at the right
> Of the laws we accept to school
> Our post-diluvian world:
>
> But the stars burn on overhead,
> Unconscious of final ends,
> As I walk home to bed,
> Asking what judgment waits
> My person, all my friends,
> And these United States.

ANOTHER POEM IN *Nones*, "Music Is International," delivered as the Phi Beta Kappa poem at the Columbia University commencement in 1947, contains this passage:

> Deserving nothing, the sensible soul
> > Will rejoice at the sudden mansion
> Of any joy; besides, there is a chance
> > We may some day need very much to
> Remember when we were happy—

Auden's beautiful lines would have been quite opaque to me at the age of eight, when I probably first heard them. At that stage of my life I wasn't a sensible soul, and I insensibly presumed that the happy worlds of Heath and the Quadrangle in New York were more or less permanent. I knew there were real problems, private and public, inner and outer, but the gaiety and energy of my family and their friends seemed to be based on eternal truths that do not tarnish or fade. And since almost everyone I knew was working so hard to make things better, the world would surely improve in the future, would it not?

My presumption was naïve, but still, I can't help feeling that the wonderful happy tone was in some way imperishable, that the efforts made, however clumsy or inadequate or even futile, to encourage people in the direction of decency and humility and charity, should not be consigned to the historical dustbin. "We may some day need very much to remember when we were happy." Without such memories, I doubt one can reach for serenity, courage, or wisdom.

Ludicrous as it may seem, some of the happiness in my family's difficult postwar years can be represented in the unlikely, odd pleasure we took in getting a new dog. Sometime in the late 1940s, after the demise of Topsy the terrier, my mother set her heart on getting a poodle—a large standard one, like those you see in Belle Epoque posters for Paris circuses. A more unlikely animal for my father you couldn't have imagined, but he went along with the idea and came to enjoy the beasts. And I see now that the postwar poodle can symbolize a new era for my family, for soon we joined a network of ardent poodle enthusiasts who were, naturally, left-liberal.

Though Ma started out looking for a poodle we could afford in Boston, our poodle friends were mostly New Yorkers. First and foremost were June and Jonathan Bingham, who were virtually *over*connected in the liberal power elite of what was then a very liberal city. Jonathan was a son of the lamentably reactionary Senator Hiram Bingham of Connecticut but mercifully of a very different political stripe; he was to become an excellent New York congressman and in the 1950s was working for Averell Harriman, former (and future) diplomat who in 1955 became governor of New York. June Bingham, a splendid person in her own right, was a great-niece of the legendary Senator Herbert Lehman, who had been FDR's lieutenant governor and then governor of New York himself in 1932–42—*the* great political figure in the liberal New York world. The Binghams and my father became friends at an early meeting in Chicago of the Americans for Democratic Action in 1948. Informal and lively lunches at their sunny Riverdale house after Sunday sermonizing were always fun: with poodles underfoot, of course, we reveled in the usual mad mix of gossip and opinion about New Yorkers both Jewish and Christian, about the Democratic Party, about theologians worthy and unworthy.

I suppose it's fair to say that the ADA people were, for Pa, not only welcome political-action allies but a welcome relief from the sometimes inane, always piously cautious, and frequently self-congratulatory churchmen among whom he might otherwise have had to spend his time. Even at the seminary one had to guard against the constant threat of sanctimony, whereas the ADA people were exuberant, skeptical, and energetically committed, after all, to *democratic action*.

The ADA friends were legion, as were our ADA loyalties. In the presence of Joseph Rauh, Hubert Humphrey, Jim Loeb, Walter Reuther, Ken Galbraith, and other feisty luminaries of that organization, it was impossible to be pompous. For me the ADA was like an extended family of outspoken, *engagé* cousins, and their presence either physical or political kept us from being mired in provincial New York, or pious seminary, backwaters. Lyndon Johnson depicted the ADA group, to the Southern reactionaries he had to court in the Senate, as bomb-throwing radicals, but he knew as he spoke that that was sheer nonsense.

The poodle network also featured *Time* magazine's drama critic Louis Kronenberger and his wife, Emmie, vividly stylish, skeptical, good-hearted people who seemed to know everyone interesting in political and artistic New York; Louis took me to Broadway premieres when Emmie had had her fill of them. And the superb scholar Arnold Wolfers, Yale professor of international affairs, and his wife, Doris, were another family with fine politics and dogs.

I didn't know this at the time, but Arnold Wolfers—a Swiss émigré, as was his wife—had studied with Paul Tillich in the *kairos* circle of religious socialists in Berlin in the 1920s. I knew only that Pa had a high regard for Wolfers's acute and nuanced historical analysis of problems in international relations, and that they collaborated often, in the classroom and at the Council on Foreign Relations, in which they were both active after the war. When the Wolferses came down from New Haven to visit us in New York, they sometimes brought their gorgeous black poodle, superbly trained by the impeccable Mrs. Wolfers. While our visitors went across the street to visit the Tillichs, the dog would sit close by the front door of our apartment, patient but alert, waiting for the moment of exuberant release when his master and mistress returned. The Wolferses both canine and human had refined, elegant profiles, and I admired their glowing European panache. They were wonderful company.

My mother confessed to me—she didn't mention this until many years after my father's death in 1971—that she had had to navigate her way through a rather Republican conversation with the Boston gentleman whose wife ran the kennel whence our first poodle came; tea on Beacon Hill was the essential first step in establishing her bona fides as a person worthy of owning a Puttencove Kennels dog. She had never dared tell my father that Mr. Putnam had inquired as to "the race of your servants, Mrs. Niebuhr?" The question would have scandalized Pa, as indeed any of our friends or any Heath resident, and put the kibosh on her getting the dog.

My mother was appalled, of course, but she wanted the poodle, so she answered cannily, taking into account both a Bostonian's antipathy to the social chaos of New York and the actual truth that we had no servants—only a smattering of part-time help, and none in the summer. These New York helpers were effective parts of our family for decades, but she didn't think a proper Bostonian would appreciate the ramshackle arrangements. They included a formidable Jamaican cleaning woman who, being a devout High-Church Anglican, disapproved of my father's liberal church politics and muttered snootily about his absurd ideas as she polished the floors, about which she was fanatical. Occasionally two seminary maids (in those days educational institutions provided maid service in the dormitories, which seems unimaginable now) helped us out with laundry and with extra holiday preparations; one Irish and the other Portuguese—both good Catholics, which I mention only because they were so warmly devoted to the welfare of the Protestant pastors-to-be in their charge, and because they so enjoyed the theological ribbings they took, and gave. And a series of lively Japanese students at the Juilliard School of Music, across the street, did household chores and baby-sitting in return for the use of the maids' rooms behind the kitchen. Could a dog object to these friends? "Oh, you know how it is in New York, Mr. Putnam," said my mother. "A little bit of everything."

So the first poodle came from Massachusetts, a rambunctious, charming addition to the family. During our New York winters she was a perfect urban pet: well-behaved and vivacious, a friendly presence in my mother's Barnard classes. She or her successors kept company with my father and his new friend Abraham Heschel, of the Jewish Theological Seminary, on their Riverside Drive walks. During the Heath summers she reverted to rural antiquity and behaved like a working hunting animal— except when she got out of hand. There was one unfortunate August when Christopher and I had no ducks to show at the Heath fair because Vicky ate them: she had taken advantage of a drought, which gave easy access over caked mud to the little

My mother teaching at Barnard College, 1956

puddle left in the center of the pond below our house, and killed the ducklings. A ruff of white feathers around her muzzle and a water retriever's blaze of accomplishment about her mien belied her phony, poodly innocence. We were furious with her, but she was eventually forgiven, as dogs are. And she was forgiven later that summer when she disappeared for two days, out a-roving in the Berkshire hills, even though impatient Pa had to postpone our departure for New York while we bit our nails and anxiously awaited her return.

That was one of the last happy summers in Heath. But even before everything changed for us, as it did in 1952, shadows were darkening the landscape, and my parents were not the sort of people who sheltered me from the bigger crises. In any case life did not allow one to block out the difficulties.

One morning at the Stone Cottage, Auntie Lou came over to talk with my parents while I was out on the terrace reading more Albert Payson Terhune. There was a hushed and whispered plan, and soon we were climbing into the car, still the same old 1939 Ford, and driving off to see someone to whom she had lent a cottage in the woods some miles away. She had cottages and cabins all over the place, it seemed. It was important for this friend and my father to talk, evidently, and also important that

we tell no one of the man's presence in the countryside or of our
seeing him.

The gentleman in the cabin
hidden in pinewoods was pleasant, tense, rather gray: he was the
then famous William Remington,
a New Deal economist who was
one of Senator McCarthy's first
innocent victims. He had been
accused of being a Communist
spy—by the dreadful Elizabeth
Bentley, whose appallingly unreliable reports to the FBI gave her a

*W. H. Auden listening to a
student's question*

renowned career on the right wing but who had no instinct for
truth—and he had sued for libel; the case had been settled out
of court, and he had been cleared by the Loyalty Board. Then,
however, having also denied the charge before the House Un-
American Activities Committee, he was twice indicted for per-
jury by a grand jury that seemed bent on determining him to
be a traitor: the foreman was coauthor of Bentley's autobiography. The grand jury's unprincipled, belligerent conduct shocked
the noble Judge Learned Hand when he read the transcripts,
and on the Second Circuit Court of Appeals he twice voted to
reverse the convictions, the second time unsuccessfully; the
Supreme Court then refused to review the case.

We must have made this trip for my father to see Remington during the period when his lawyers were still working on
his appeals. Perhaps it was all hush-hush because of FF's prox-
imity. Soon the doomed Remington was sent to jail, and only a

few months later he was murdered there by an anti-Communist fanatic who believed he was helping to save the American Republic. Even in tranquil, hardworking Heath, I was learning that—the victories of the recent war notwithstanding—the United States was still itself a battleground. "Always the enemy is the foe at home."

IN THE WINTER of 1952, my father suffered the first of a series of strokes that less than twenty years later were to take his life. After an unpleasant spring while his condition stabilized in New York, the family repaired to Heath for the summer. But Heath was not a good place for him to be so sick or for my mother to take care of him, with the Stone Cottage being so small and the remote, spread-out village being so far from medical aid. He suffered further mini-strokes, or "episodes"—a word I came to hate—during July and August.

Over the next year, Pa regained his strength and could resume lecturing and preaching, though he never again rode circuit as he once had and never again traveled, and though he was in almost constant pain. We returned to the Stone Cottage in 1953, but my parents were beginning to think about what they would do when retirement from Union and Barnard came. Pa was then sixty-one years old. The family reassessed its Heath arrangements. I didn't listen to the discussions, for I hated the very idea of losing Heath. When my parents learned of a large yet affordable house, comfortably and safely situated in the well-established valley town of Stockbridge, Massachusetts—only a few miles from excellent doctors and a good hospital—they sold the Stone Cottage. In 1955 we left Heath and headed south.

Stockbridge was only fifty miles away if one were a crow, but

I saw that it was in a completely different world. I tried to get a grip on the global change, which seemed monstrous to me. I made much of the difference between feisty, up-country Franklin County, now lost to me, and the well-populated, well-organized, spacious lower slopes of Berkshire County, in which Stockbridge was but one of many beautiful historic towns along the Housatonic River. Melville and Hawthorne had climbed the hills here, Emerson had come visiting, the Boston Symphony Orchestra spent its summers at nearby Tanglewood, Ruth St. Denis danced at Jacob's Pillow, the beauteous and well-stocked Atheneum in next-door Lenox was a jewel of a library, bankers and big shots from Boston and New York captured some of the most splendid houses, the famous nearby dairy farm was owned by someone whom we all addressed reverentially as the Colonel. All this grand stuff. Edith Wharton's estate, the "Sedgwick pie" in the Stockbridge Cemetery, antique stores, riding stables. My heart was breaking. Where were the real farmers? Berkshire County wasn't true country, I complained to my mother, as I gazed out over the verdant meadows and well-tended lawns, with the well-paved roads winding speedily from town to town. It was more like exurbia for the power elite. I came to enjoy Berkshire County eventually, after my parents retired from New York and went to live in Stockbridge full-time, but Heath was never displaced in my heart.

My father's illness marked only the first of the changes we lived through in 1952. Everything seemed to be shifting and precarious. My father was morose, my mother preoccupied, myself consumed in adolescent rage. Even Heath had become problematical. And then, after a nasty and degrading election campaign during the summer and fall, lightened only by the civilized wit and intelligence of Illinois' governor, Adlai Stevenson, there were the Republicans. The consequences of Dwight Eisenhower's election that autumn did much, I believe, to intensify the long depression that Pa suffered after his strokes. The genuine political despair he felt about the prospects of the Republican administration was very real.

I remember going for a walk with him the morning after the election. He had allowed me to play hooky because the family had stayed up until the wee hours listening to the devastating statistics slowly mount up against Stevenson, and I had had no sleep. We took the poodle for the usual walk on Riverside Drive, and he said to me sadly, "You poor girl, you've never lived under a Republican administration. You don't know how terrible this is going to be." There were all the unresolved problems about race relations, on which Republicans were evasive and noncommittal. There was Joe McCarthy, whom Eisenhower and all too many other so-called moderate Republicans did little or nothing to curb, and the mounting hysteria about left-wing treachery. There was the Korean War. There was concern that the business community, as usual ranked solidly behind the party that did its bidding, would inject its one-sided aims into the international-affairs agenda. (Looking for a silver lining, Pa hoped that Wall Street and Main Street might just possibly become more responsible about foreign affairs with Eisenhower in the White House; he thought that businessmen and financiers tended to be especially irrational and obtuse when left out of power and to their own devices. But I myself don't believe they necessarily improve when in public office.)

And there was the ominous cloud of anxiety created by the lack of a clear policy on nuclear weapons, and by the possibil-

My father in 1952, the day before his stroke

ity they might be used. The forthcoming Dulles-Eisenhower policy of "massive retaliation," which promised just that to any purported threat against our or our allies' freedoms—a short-lived policy that is mercifully mostly forgotten by now—formed the backdrop for my father's continued meditations on the problems of forming a just and durable peace in a nuclear age. This seemed to be an almost impossible task.

It is implicit in virtually everything Pa wrote on the subject that there's little point in having a foreign policy, or an arms policy, unless, as a nation, you know who you are, what sort of nation you are or imagine yourself to be. I don't mean in the narrow sense of an instrumentally calculated "national interest" but in the larger spiritual and cultural sense. Pa's constant gripe was that American political leaders imagined a diminished America and presented it falsely, that they themselves were stupider, prouder, more self-righteous, more moralistic, more vainglorious than the American people on whose behalf they spoke.

The victorious politicians who had disregarded so many of America's intractable economic and political problems during the 1952 campaign were betraying the American people who cared to have those problems addressed, Pa thought. And we did not expect that their foreign policy could be anything but bankrupt, given their paucity of courage and resourcefulness on the domestic front. It's a Republican thing, we thought in our family, to separate international issues from domestic priorities, to sever the vital links that should bind the two. By which my father meant that for much of the twentieth century the Republican Party had been indifferent to true democracy.

And then there was the Dulles factor—the pious, dishonest, and manipulative tone which that self-righteous Presbyterian was going to bring to the State Department, and which would surely change everything for the worse. John Foster Dulles lamentably personified his denomination, I believed, and I wanted my Presbyterian friends to explain him away. They could be proud of the high-minded Woodrow Wilson, with his genuine, quite Presbyterian impulse to insist on the virtue of democracy and self-determination for all people, but Dulles was another matter.

Pa knew him of yore, since Dulles had been active in the ecumenical movement, and they had crossed paths. A member of the famous New York law firm of Sullivan and Cromwell, he easily mixed in the Washington–New York worlds of politics and money. (He was no good on the hustings, however, and Governor Lehman had trounced him in the election to fill out the remaining term of Senator Robert F. Wagner after his resignation in 1949.) Dulles had campaigned hard for the Republicans throughout the summer and fall of 1952, attacking the very policies to which he and they had given bipartisan support when they'd been enacted—in the Marshall Plan, in the North Atlantic Treaty, in Korea. He couldn't wait to be Secretary of State—as his predecessor, the superb Dean Acheson, knew.

Dulles seemed to exemplify everything my father taught me to be wary of in a publicly proclaimed Christian: sanctimonious display of religious commitment, proud rigidity about so-called principles and easy accommodation to their breach if that assisted the pursuit of power, intolerance, and disdain for social justice masquerading as high-minded public service. These were weaknesses presented as strengths, and they have become more and more prevalent in American public life. When a respected colleague of my father's edited a book entitled *The Spiritual Legacy of John Foster Dulles*, Uncle Felix could not contain his magnificent scorn. "I must believe that people who thus invoke 'God' or 'Christ' or 'spiritual heritage' have not the remotest realization of their blasphemy," he spluttered in a letter to Pa, who did not disagree.

FF was calmer when he replied to a written comment of my father's about the "pettifoggery" and the "fantastic stupidity" of American foreign policy in the Dulles-Eisenhower years. He had to remind him to be serene. "For the first time in many decades," Pa had confessed, "I feel seriously concerned about the future of this great country, because the two men who seem to be guiding its destiny seem both to be stupid. The one is amiable and the other not, but the stupidity is equal."

Dearest Ursula

. . . These are days, aren't they, when one's capacity for serenity, for rational judgment on our rulers, is severely put to the test. When Reinie speaks of stupidity, remind him that "*Gegen die Dummheit kämpfen selbst die Götter vergebens*" [Against stupidity even the gods fight in vain]. And when stupidity is mixed with self-righteousness we have devil's bread.

Affectionately, Felix

The devil's bread was indeed cast widely upon the waters. Eisenhower, his affable grin safely intact, condoned the poisons of McCarthyite slander, and the high-minded Dulles allowed the destructive senator his run of the State Department. The resulting demoralization all but destroyed the Foreign Service. And we knew what we thought of Vice President Nixon: we'd had our eye on him ever since 1950. On important domestic fronts, even the most unobjectionable and conscientious efforts made on behalf of poor, disenfranchised, and working Americans were subjected to defamatory, malicious misinterpretation.

The Methodist Federation of Social Service, for example, got its knuckles rapped: Bishop McConnell had made his efforts on behalf of the striking steelworkers in 1919 in the context of what was more than a century's worth of Methodist community service, but now McCarthy and his allies attacked the enterprise as a Communist one. "The Federation and its beneficial works were almost destroyed, but it has recovered and continues the visions of the founders," an official history mournfully recounted after Senator McCarthy had sunk beneath the horizon.

The situation in the South was even more sinister. At the Highlander School, Myles Horton and his colleagues had decided to address the issues of segregation more openly than they had at first, when they'd focused closely on workers' rights.

Even before the *Brown v. Board of Education* 1954 Supreme Court decision, Highlander had become a place for blacks and whites to work together in planning and practicing civil-rights actions. School-oriented programs helped people gain enough literacy skills to pass the voter registration tests that were being used all over the South to keep blacks from voting, while blacks and whites together trained in the essential skills of nonviolent protest.

Some Southern governors, including Tennessee's, were determined to stop Highlander; its interracial classes were intolerable for them. Naturally they accused Highlander of being a nest of Communists. The inevitable hearing before HUAC was staged. Various court cases were brought over the years, and eventually the segregationists got their way: a fine example of sunny Eisenhower-era activity. By 1961 Highlander's charter was revoked, the property sold at auction, and the school closed. Myles said at the time, "You can padlock the buildings, but you can't padlock the ideas," yet the efforts to lock up integration continued well into the 1960s. Highlander, phoenixlike, eventually rose again. Billboards appeared all over the South showing a picture of Martin Luther King Jr. at the old school with a banner caption charging "Communist Training School."

In New York, my father's new friend Rabbi Heschel had an especially vivid appreciation of the lunacy of this charge. Until my parents moved away from New York the two men developed a regular ritual of having walks together, up and down Riverside Drive, and they talked and talked. Martin Luther King Jr. was to become one of their principal subjects.

Students of my father's work have sometimes tartly observed that the huge amount of time and attention Pa gave in the 1920s and 1930s to issues of social justice, race equality, and the churches' commitment to both were perhaps not matched by equal involvement in later decades. But if one looks at what Heschel was doing in the 1950s and tumultuous 1960s, the decades when my now-disabled father came to know him, one can see Pa's commitments sharply limned in their late-blooming friendship.

In 1951, Pa had favorably reviewed a book of Heschel's, *Man Is Not Alone*, and when they came to be friends—my father fifteen years older, ill and weakened after the first of his strokes, the younger Heschel on the brink of his American fame—they were each in their own way distanced from the compromised, corrupted intellectual and spiritual traditions of Germany that had nourished them both, and they were both at odds with their respective American establishments. They needed each other. Pa's vivacious, cheering secular friends seemed to understand him well enough, but they were oblivious of his theology; only a few of his theological colleagues saw things his way; and despite a lifetime's devotion to the Hebrew Bible and a lifetime habit of philo-Semitism, he had few associations, let alone friends, among America's rabbis. After three hectic, overcrowded decades he was confined by bad health to his home, and Republicans were running the country. I think he was lonely, spiritually speaking.

For both Heschel and my father, the old pastoral problem, the old prophetic problem, the old issue of living the true religious life, the issue of true piety, was newly urgent in these post-Auschwitz, post-nuclear seasons. Pa continued to be appalled by the superficiality and self-contented pride of America's churches and synagogues. (He wrote to Frankfurter that even at the seminary of which he was such a loyal faculty member, "piety has been reduced to triviality here, and indeed in the whole church. You can imagine my state of mind after having devoted all these decades to the religious enterprise.") Heschel was someone he could talk to about all this.

Heschel was the great interpreter of the Hebrew Prophets, and Pa had always emphasized that it was the Prophets' vision of God's transcendent righteousness that gives us a standard and the dynamic for ethical action. So it is no surprise that he and Heschel hit it off from the start: there was much for them to share and explore together. "Prophecy is a sham unless it is experienced as a word of God swooping down on man and converting him into a prophet," Heschel had once written, and my mother observed, "I think others would agree with me that the word of God indeed swooped down on these two friends."

"The demand as understood in biblical religion is to be alert, and to be open to what is happening," Heschel wrote once. This quality of great prophetic religion is also the quality of true friendship. As my mother pointed out to me, Loren Eiseley got the Niebuhr-Heschel point when he wrote that the habit of prayer can be equated with the habit of listening. Listening deeply, experiencing awe, praying, and nourishing friendship are related activities. Again Heschel: "Awe enables us to sense in small things the beginnings of infinite significance, to sense the ultimate in the common and simple." So off went the prophetic new friends on their walks, alone but for our poodles.

The dogs were discreet, as dogs wonderfully are, so we can't know for sure exactly what the two men talked about. Still, to me, it is inconceivable that they did not discuss their favorite texts in Second Isaiah, Amos, and Jeremiah, that they did not exchange views on the controversial new books by the Jewish philosopher Martin Buber. Unthinkable that, Christian and Jew as they were, they did not explore the meaning of ecumenism. Or of prayer. Unimaginable that Germany never came up. Or that Zionism, Israel, J. Edgar Hoover, Cardinal Spellman were never mentioned. But the Heschel and Niebuhr families knew that in the conversations race relations were central.

My father could no longer travel, but Heschel did regularly, to speak at universities, in synagogues, and to social-action groups, and he would report back on his meetings around the country, bringing that humming, busy world to Riverside Drive, sharing his reactions. And my father gave Heschel everything he would have taken along himself if he had been on those trips, the data and the insights he had gained over forty years of active clerical-political work in the Middle West and the South. A splendid alchemy of interchange and mutual reinforcement was going on.

One person who recognized and appreciated the alchemical magic of the Heschel-Niebuhr elective affinities was Martin Luther King Jr. As a student, King had been influenced by Pa's interpretations of the prophetic tradition and his analyses of the way that Christian commitment must lead to a life of skeptical travail with the powers that be. So when King and Heschel met in Chicago in 1963 at an ecumenical conference, it is perhaps no surprise what happened. As Taylor Branch's fine biography of King puts it,

They raised strikingly similar cries. "May the problem of race in America soon make hearts burn," said King, "so that prophets will rise up and cry out as Amos did, 'let justice roll down like waters and righteousness like a mighty stream.' " Heschel quoted the same passage from Amos, which he had used in his book to illustrate the emotive force in the prophetic conception of justice. And they both quoted Reinhold Niebuhr. When King declared that the durable sins of race stressed "the need for prophecy," he meant prophecy as described by Heschel as the voice that God has lent to the silent agony, through prophets able and willing to draw upon themselves the excess poison in the world. Their communion on this rich subject was a pleasant surprise to both men, who vowed to see more of each other.

But, Branch concluded, "after generous applause, the Chicago delegates reacted cautiously to the summons for prophetic wisdom. . . . *Time* magazine ridiculed the meeting and said the theologians had proved themselves unable to offer much wisdom." So much for *Time*. Whatever *was* offered at that meeting, by proxy and in person, was transmuted into the imperishable wisdom that King was soon to show the nation in Birmingham, in his great speech on the Washington Mall, and at Selma and Montgomery.

There was good reason, then, to keep the age-old agenda of social justice and civil rights, and that of getting the churches and synagogues to support both, front and center. Heschel and my father did not abandon it—on the contrary—even after King's murder. By then Pa was living in Stockbridge, and he and Heschel would write to each other. Exigencies of old age and frailty, which they had faced together on their walks, now kept them geographically apart but spiritually ever closer.

Pa also nourished his essential friendship with regular letters to—and from—the ebullient Will Scarlett, who had left St. Louis for retirement in Maine. In one, my father commented on

the fatuity of what passed for religious commentary, the subject
that so bothered him and Heschel; it never ceased to amaze him
how trivial people could be. Uncle Will reported that the clerical temper in Maine was no improvement. "What you say
about the triviality and irrelevance of the Episcopal meeting
worries me," Pa wrote in reply to one bulletin, "because it rein-
forces my fears that the terrors of the day have tempted the
church to flee into these cellars of irrelevance." Pa cared to
know how Uncle Will was assessing the Niebuhrian skepticism:
"Your opinion is more cherished than that of any friend." But
Scarlett could only concur with him.

It wasn't easy for either of them to watch as the new generation retrenched and even reversed many of the advances they
had fought for. Uncle Will wrote sadly about the new perspectives that retirement forced on him, and Pa commiserated: "You
say you are no longer at home in the PE church. I don't blame
you." He told Uncle Will of an article he'd read entitled "Which
Church Shall I Join?" "The point of the article was that every
church had so many vices that you could not belong to it unless
you became accustomed to its vices from youth. Sad but true."
I wonder what their students and colleagues might have made
of this bleak assessment.

Not all churchmen were hiding in the basement, though. Jim
Dombrowski was arrested in 1965 in Louisiana, where his leadership of the Southern Christian Education Fund was called
criminal and subversive. My father and Jim had had political dis-
agreements over the years, but Pa never lost his admiration for
Jim's fearless insistence on living the committed Christian life,
and on devising courageous strategies for necessary change.
Soon his lawyers developed a bold new tactic: they countersued

in federal court to challenge the prosecution for its "chilling effect" on Dombrowski's civil rights; on appeal the Supreme Court finally struck down Louisiana's anti-sedition statute as unconstitutional. Those Southern anti-sedition laws had been on the books for far too long. The victory validated the soon celebrated legal technique used to advance the cause of social justice, and it infuriated the segregationists. I think of Jim Dombrowski every time I hear an angry Southern politician talk about the cold repressive hand of federal law clamping down on his beloved region. (Unfortunately, in 1971 Chief Justice Warren Burger's Supreme Court undermined the use of this safeguard against abusive state prosecutions, and required federal courts to abstain from blocking state actions, even when civil rights were at stake. We must pray for the courage to change what must be changed again and again and again.)

Courage and serenity were in short supply in America's interventions in global affairs, which continued on their errant and unpredictable course even after Dulles's departure from the State Department. The cruel folly of America's war in Southeast Asia, the "awfull mess in Viet Nam," as my father called it in one misspelled letter, and the "arrogance of power" displayed by America's leaders in that conflict were dismaying. He was predictably disgusted by the disconnect between the foreign adventure and America's own domestic needs: "So thousands of our boys die" and the country spends "billions for the war," even though it was obvious that "even an affluent nation" cannot engage in such folly and at the same time "treat our worsening urban and ghetto problems with force." Citizens had to concern themselves with the manner in which Washington's plans and policies respected or betrayed the welfare and safety of American citizens, with the approaches it made to peers, friends, and strangers in the ever shrinking world. That was as true in Democratic as in Republican administrations.

AS THE SERENITY PRAYER became more and more famous during the 1960s, my father was deluged with requests for the exact wording and with demands that he verify his authorship of it. (This was during the period when, in Germany, Theodor Wilhelm and his wife were "enjoying" the anomaly of the Oetinger mistake he had created.) It was easy enough to verify the wording and the authorship, since no prayer like it had been traced or found in any language before Dean Robbins had it published in 1944. But Pa found the whole discussion awkward: prayers weren't something to make claims on. Moreover, although it was incontrovertible that he had written this one, he was not about to insist that he was the first to have thought of its instructions.

The daily letter box full of inquiries was a tiresome new feature, even as the prayer itself became an inspiring liberation for so many thousands of people all over the world. My father answered these letters, but his heart wasn't in it. For many years he could not conquer the dark clouds of melancholia that swept over him as a consequence of the strokes that had put him "on the sidelines," as he described it. "My present state of anxiety defied the petition of this prayer," he wrote in the late 1960s. In such a frame of mind he often felt like throwing in the towel, letting people ascribe the authorship to whomever they wanted.

Which is what many people did. Sometimes the invented ascriptions, like the Oetinger one, were conflated with the true one. Many wildly inaccurate AA "histories" of the prayer evolved (and now proliferate on the World Wide Web) in some of which the Oetinger story somehow crept in—I hate to think how. The international mistakes multiply. Countless booklets and plaques and Websites tell us that Pa gave the prayer to AA in 1939; or that he himself said it came from Oetinger; or that he wrote it in 1932 (a mistake that may derive from a typographical error in June Bingham's otherwise fairly accurate biography of my father, which gave 1934 instead of 1943 as the date of composition), and so forth. *Bartlett's Quotations* says it was written in 1934. These errors exist alongside other more bizarre ones and alongside the truth, which surfaces only occasionally.

I was moved to learn from a friend working in Johannesburg in the 1970s that he had seen the Serenity Prayer, often with Dürer's praying hands, on the kitchen or living-room wall of many black South African homes. Now if ever there were circumstances that required great courage to change and great serenity to endure, they were certainly those in which South Africa's blacks lived in the apartheid years. This was a spiritual crisis to which my father had devoted much prayer and thought, having been alerted early on to the struggle against the hideous postwar regime there by many of the same English clerical friends who had helped German resisters to Hitler. (It is no coincidence that the same people would be, only three short years after VE-Day, active in Johannesburg as they had been active in trying to support the German resistance.) And my father often mused over, and preached on, the ironic tragedy of the Dutch Reformed Church's evil perversions of the Gospel in an African setting.

In our family, Nelson Mandela was a stupendous hero: I

remember that my mother cut out of *The Observer* (our subscription to this English newspaper being a gift from its publisher, David Astor, yet another fellow soldier on the liberal, anti-fascist front) its reprint of Mandela's closing statement to the court that convicted and sentenced him to prison on Robben Island in 1963. She sent it on to me so I'd be sure to read this precious document. And one cannot forget the sublimely serene message Mandela sent from his solitary confinement after many long years: "I abound in hope," he said implacably. "Our cause is just, and the people will be free."

This principled, rock-solid understanding of faith, hope, and charity even in the darkest night of despair is not, I fear, what a simple enjoyment of the Serenity Prayer's superficial charm can aspire to. All too often, the Serenity Prayer has been construed as a way to say something clever about life's difficulties, rather than as a true petition for grace and wisdom in an impossible world, though I think most AA members understand it rightly. Perhaps it's that for many people praying is a kind of reassuring, pleasant activity which in itself they find soothing. The contrition and renunciation that one must experience to arrive at real hope or reassurance aren't part of the scheme. Praying *as* reassurance is what they're after, as if the act of recitation itself will do the trick. Praying *for* reassurance and strength is another matter entirely.

Some months before his death in June 1971, when he was bedridden and failing, my father received a letter from a Lutheran editor telling him that in Germany the prayer was attributed to F. C. Oetinger and asking what he thought of this. This was the first time the name Oetinger appeared in the

Niebuhr household, and I don't know whether he ever actually saw the inquiry. By that point my mother was dealing with most of his correspondence on his behalf, and this was just another routine letter answered by a secretarial assistant. Then, after his death, when my mother inherited the chore of answering the letters—she would repeat the standard reply that no, the Serenity Prayer was not copyrighted and could be used for free—she began to hear again about the persistent Oetinger rumor.

Years passed before anyone could explain to her where it originated. Wilhelm's explanatory article wasn't composed until 1976 and not drawn to my mother's attention until 1984, when the Reverend Professor Reinhard Neubauer—who knew my father's work, who was irritated by the misattribution, and who *had* traced the Oetinger story to its origin—explained it to puzzled Niebuhr scholars at a conference in London devoted to Pa's work. We found it both appalling and hilarious. My mother was never so forgiving or perhaps understanding of Germans as my father had been (very English, in this respect), and her amused scorn for Wilhelm's weirdly dishonest account left much unsaid. The German subplot of the Serenity Prayer story was truly bizarre.

Imagine the prayer now at the army academy in Koblenz, carved in wood (not stone, as Wilhelm had said) and inscribed in gilded paint, surrounded by proud black, red, and gold banners, at the place where—at the end of an incredible century in which German armies went into battle in two horrific world wars—German officers must, in a wholly different frame of mind, train young German soldiers in a wholly different world:

> Gib mir die Gelassenheit Dinge hinzunehmen, die ich nicht ändern kann. Gib mir den Mut, Dinge zu ändern, die ich ändern kann; und gib mir die Weisheit, das eine vom andern zu unterscheiden.★

My father was a connoisseur of irony in history, but this poignant oddity would surpass even his expectations. What a startling place for the prayer to end up, given his family background and his life work, given that he spent his best years in what he later assessed as doomed and fruitless efforts to persuade his American and German colleagues of the follies inherent in their pieties, given his deep misgivings about the Germans' overly developed respect and enthusiasm for military power.

He had willingly allowed the widespread use of his prayer by the American army in Germany during the war and the postwar occupation. But he never knew about the prayer's Swabian life in the divided, peacetime Germany; he was unacquainted with its renown in the upper reaches of the Federal Republic, a state that officially honored him only a few years before his death, when his old friend and ally the Social Democrat Willy Brandt became chancellor. This was after years of government by Christian Democrats, who had inherited and still espoused so much of the conventional German worldview that American Niebuhrs had been opposing for three generations. The West German republic was one whose spirit my father found dangerously flawed by the same pious

---

★It's not the right version, or a good translation, of Pa's prayer. It should, properly, read: "Gott, gib uns die Gnade, mit Gelassenheit Dinge hinzunehmen, die sich nicht ändern lassen, den Mut, Dinge zu ändern, die geändert werden sollten, und die Weisheit, das eine vom anderen zu unterscheiden."

hypocrisies he had deplored all his life; East Germans, meanwhile, were showing equally dangerous, equally pious German tendencies to cede moral authority to the state and thereby compromise their freedom.

We still have the German Bible that Reinhold Niebuhr was given by his German schoolteachers in Illinois when he graduated in 1910, inscribed to a "truly good German." And I still have the King James English Bible he gave to me when I was confirmed, and the books of American history in which he wanted me to study the Founding Fathers. A bust of Abraham Lincoln in his study reminded us always of his profound admiration for this Middle Western biblical democrat who, if ever a political leader did, understood the perils and dangers of righteous indignation, and who truly had the wisdom to distinguish what had to be changed from what could not be changed. The Niebuhrs may have started out German, but they had become very American indeed, and proudly so. If they had any influence on their country's public and spiritual life—and I believe they did—that would have gratified them: better far than a stone monument.

A decade ago or so the state of Missouri honored my father as a distinguished native son, and his bust stands in the state house rotunda along with those of General Omar Bradley and the fine rags composer Scott Joplin, the novelist Pearl Buck, and wonderful Charlie "Bird" Parker; he's opposite Josephine Baker and just around the corner from President Truman. This might have pleased but would have embarrassed him—he thought such memorials only showed the vanity of the eternal human wish to claim immortality, and he had an instinctive dislike of graven images. On his daily walks with our sinful poodles, he would observe the old stone and bronze statues of now forgotten military heroes that decorated Riverside Drive. "See what I mean?" he'd exclaim to his class in Christian ethics. "Look at that fellow across the street whom you pass every day on the way to International House. Do you know who he is or why his statue is there? I ask you, Who the hell is Butterfield?" (This was considered surprisingly blasphemous for a "Rev" to say.)

And yet, he was happy to have his prayers used in whatever context people wanted or needed them, and he respected the intense gratitude that AA members expressed for the Serenity Prayer. I'm sure he'd have respected the quite different phenomenon of the Bundeswehr's enthusiasm for it: after all, Germany has changed. Still, though he might demur, I prefer the idea of that memorial in Jefferson City, Missouri, to the falsified German route by which his wonderful words ended up carved on a tablet for the cadets in Koblenz.

MY FATHER'S STORY came to an end, and the story of the remarkable generation of men and women with whom he worked and prayed—that came to an end, too. But their example taught me the obvious truth that the story of a prayer has no ending at all—it must continue into the future. The story of the Serenity Prayer has no final cadence.

It was painful for Pa and his friends to observe their work being negated or traduced. But my mother would remind me how wrong it was to try to calculate the value of a life or career by measuring whether or how much in it endured. It is not for us to make this accounting.

My father wrote:

We live our life in various realms of meaning which do not quite cohere rationally. Our meanings are surrounded by a penumbra of mystery which is not penetrated by reason. . . . All known existence points beyond itself. To realize that it points beyond itself to God is to assert that the mystery of life does not resolve life into meaninglessness. . . .

You must remember, my mother continued: "Consider the lilies of the field, how they grow, they toil not, neither do they spin; yet I say unto you that even Solomon in all his glory was not arrayed like one of these." The greatest wisdom of the Gospels lies in that verse, she said. One can only live fully by opening one's being to the present, living each new day as if it were the last. Dietrich and Klaus Bonhoeffer understood this. As Dietrich wrote, "One learns to have faith only in the complete this-worldliness of life. When one completely renounces making something out of oneself . . . then one throws oneself completely into God's arms; then one does not take one's own suffering seriously . . ."

My father and Uncle Will and all the others knew this, of course. They submitted their lives to this permanent and ever present judgment. My father prayed, "We acknowledge Thee, O Lord, to be our Lord, our judge and our redeemer. Grant us grace in all of our life constantly to stand under Thy judgment. Remove from us all pretensions of righteousness and goodness and wisdom on our own account. Destroy our self-esteem. Wound us in our pride. . . ."

Can we understand that prayer today? In an inanely amoral, frivolous, and profit-driven world, we are urged to fill ourselves with pride and self-esteem and to armor ourselves with pretensions. We may lose the ability to hear such a prayer. Solemn rebuke from self-important priests would then fall appropriately on deaf ears. But the prayer is not grim, and it came from a free heart, from someone who trusted that the joyful life of attentive, listening, awe-filled, loving people must go on. The Serenity Prayer was meant for them.

Buoyant, even hilarious high spirits marked the public and private behavior of my father's friends and associates, and you knew their gaiety sprang from serious, dedicated hearts. They worked so hard. They were so very loving. And their labors were informed, in the end, by the humble recognition that it is not within our human powers to understand the final tally.

When my father died, he was buried in Stockbridge, which is famous in American history as the town where the great Jonathan Edwards—an eighteenth-century Protestant giant if ever there was one, another of my father's heroes, and about as different from a Swabian Pietist as you can get—preached to a tiny congregation of frontier people and Indians. Edwards took the daily themes of the moral life as his central subject. The stringent clarity, the passionate ascetic power of America's first and in many ways greatest theologian shines as clearly today as it did when he wrote about this eternal work of the present tense:

> Gracious and holy affections have their exercise and fruit in Christian practice. I mean, they have that influence and power upon him who is the subject of 'em that they cause that [it] should be the practice and business of his life. This implies . . . that he persists in it to the end of life; so that it may be said not only to be his business at certain seasons, the business of Sabbath

days, or certain extraordinary times, or the business of a month, or a year, or of seven years, or . . . under certain circumstances; but the business of his life . . . which he perseveres in through all changes, and under all trials, as long as he lives. The necessity [of this] in all true Christians is most clearly and fully taught in the Word of God.

So we must persevere under all trials. We shall probably never have enough courage to change what must be changed. The grace to accept with serenity that which cannot be changed will not easily come to us. And the wisdom to discern the one from the other takes more than our lifetime to acquire.

In a fine riff on the great central Christian text from Second Corinthians about faith, hope, and charity, my father wrote:

Nothing worth doing can be achieved in a lifetime; therefore we must be saved by hope. Nothing that is true or beautiful or good makes complete sense in any immediate context of history; therefore we must be saved by faith. Nothing that we do, however virtuous, can be accomplished alone; therefore we are saved by love.

Acknowledgments

The story of the Serenity Prayer occurred mostly before I was born, and although as a child I knew the people whose works and acts are my subject here, I needed plenty of books to get at the essence of the story. First came books by and about Niebuhrs: my father's *Does Civilization Need Religion?*, *Leaves from the Notebook of a Tamed Cynic*, *Moral Man and Immoral Society*, *Beyond Tragedy*, *The Nature and Destiny of Man*, *The Children of Light and the Children of Darkness*, and *The Irony of American History*, among others; my uncle's books, especially *The Social Sources of Denominationalism* and *The Kingdom of God in America*; my mother's compilation of some of my father's lectures, sermons, and prayers, *Justice and Mercy*, and of his letters and diaries, *Remembering Reinhold Niebuhr*; Charles Brown's valuable *Niebuhr and His Age: Reinhold Niebuhr's Propehtic Role and Legacy*; also *The Essential Reinhold Niebuhr: Selected Essays and Addresses*, edited and introduced by Robert McAfee Brown; William Chrystal's interesting biography of my grandfather, *A Father's Mantle: The Legacy of Gustav Niebuhr*; and Langdon Gillkey's *On Niebuhr: A Theological Study*.

Various biographical and autobiographical sources were vital, chiefly Eberhard Bethge's massive *Dietrich Bonhoeffer: A Biography*, as well as the remarkable little volume edited by Eberhard and Renate Bethge, *Last Letters of Resistance: Farewells from the Bonhoeffer Family*; Peter Clark's *Stafford Cripps*; Father George Barry Ford's memoirs, *A Degree of Difference*; Harry Emerson Fosdick's *The Living of These Days: An Autobiography*; an invaluable, also charming, collection of memoirs entitled *Felix Frankfurter: A Tribute*, edited by Wallace Mendelson, and *From the Diaries of Felix Frankfurter*, with a biographical essay and notes by Joseph P. Lash; Myles Horton's *The Long Haul: An Autobiography*; Margaret Stansgate's *My Exit Visa: An Autobiography*; Ross Sherrill's *R. H. Tawney and His Times*, as well as Tawney's own works (I treasure *The Attack and Other Papers*); and Marion and Wilhelm Pauck's *Paul Tillich: His Life and Thought*.

Diverse historical documents and studies reminded me of essential themes and introduced me to many new facts; these included *Against the Third Reich: Paul Tillich's Wartime Radio Broadcasts into Nazi Germany*, edited by Ronald H. Stone and Matthew Lon Weaver; Heather Warren's *Theologians of a New World Order: Reinhold Niebuhr and the Christian Realists, 1920–1948*; William Temple, *Christianity and the Social Order*; Arthur Schlesinger's great *Age of Roosevelt*, especially the first volume, *The Crisis of the Old Order*, which is dedicated to my father; A. J. P. Taylor, *English History 1914–1945*; and Roy Jenkins's *Nine Men of Power* and *Churchill*.

I mightn't have known Edna St. Vincent Millay's poem "Justice Denied in Massachusetts" were it not that other summer experiences after Heath took me to an island off the Maine coast where she once lived and worked—reason enough to explore her fascinating poems, including this one. I thank her estate for permission to reprint lines from it. The letter written in 1906 by Max Weber was brought to my attention by my husband, who first translated it for me, and it is to him that I also owe the excerpt from Denis de Rougement's diaries. I am especially indebted to Susannah Heschel and her mother, Sylvia Heschel, for their continuing friendship and support; Susannah's and my occasionally parallel explorations of our fathers' work and friendship has been a joy. Edward Mendelson's impeccable administration of the W. H. Auden estate is a model for all scholars and literary executors to follow, and he is a wise counselor, to boot. My friend Hugh Van Dusen imparted invaluable information, gave me badly needed moral support, and loaned me Fosdick's memoir; all were essential.

I owe thanks to the staff of the Manuscript Division of the Library of Congress, and especially its director, David Wigdor, who generously helped me in my explorations of its holdings, including the papers of my father and my mother, which are deposited there, and of Felix Frankfurter. Additional unpublished sources have included memoirs and notes that were among my mother's papers, which my brother, Christopher, and I sorted through after her death. I also thank the estate of Sir Stafford Cripps for permission to reproduce the photograph of him and his wife, and to quote from his letters. And thanks to Alfred Eisenstaedt, who took the picture of my father on page 329 and gave it to him.

I had not visited Heath since our departure from it in 1955 until I returned with my husband for a visit in the fall of 2002. When my friends in the Landstrom, Burrington, Dickinson, and Stetson families welcomed me warmly despite an absence of forty-seven years, I felt it proved that my memories of their generosity of spirit were not at all exaggerated. Thanks also to David and Margaret Howland, and to Hazel Porter and Alastair Maitland, for their kindnesses to me and my husband during that all too brief trip, and for their introducing me to new residents of Heath who love and care about the place as much as we Niebuhrs ever did.

Other friends have given kind and wise counsel, encouraging me at moments when I feared my efforts might be entirely daft. They may not even remember that they did so, but I would like to thank especially Daniel Aaron, Daniel Bell, Marshall Cohen, Andrew Delbanco, Nicholas Lemann, Wilfred McClay, Judith Moore, the Right Reverend Paul Moore, Victor Navasky, Richard Parker, Marion Pauck, the Reverend F. Goldthwaite Sherrill, and David Steinberg for sometimes general, sometimes specific advice and information.

I probably would never have written about the Serenity Prayer at all if it had not been for Hans-Jochen Vogel, whose political memoirs, *Nachsichten: Meine Bonner und Berliner Jahre*, included a quotation of the prayer as it is erroneously known in Germany; when I told him the real story of its composition, he encouraged me to write it up. J. D. McClatchy, whose *Yale Review* published an essay on "The Serenity Prayer" in 1998, and Leon Wieseltier were kind enough to read and comment on my first efforts with this material, and I thank them for their encouragement. A somewhat expanded version of my initial essay, *Das Gelassenheitsgebet*, appeared as a book in Germany in 2001, thanks to Michael Krüger of Carl Hanser Verlag, and to Hartmut von Hentig, who translated it. Thereafter, the fate of my efforts was strongly influenced by the magnetically benign force of Gloria Loomis, my friend and literary agent, and

Robert Weil, an astute and resolute editor; to both of them my eternal thanks.

My sons, Sam, Toby, and John, each in his own way a true grandson of his grandfather, have given me invaluable support, as have my dear cousins Richard and Gustav Niebuhr. Most of all my husband, Fritz Stern, guided me on my adventure; I owe him the most—more than he can ever know—for the love and patience with which he strictly insisted on my adhering to Ranke's mysterious injunction to show it as it actually was.

ENS

February 2, 2003

Index

Page numbers in *italics* refer to illustrations.

McCarthy, Joseph R., 306, 313, 315, 325, 328, 332

McCarthy, Mary, 37–38

McCloy, John, 284

McConnell, Francis, 55–56, 58, 93, 119, 129–30, 171, 195, 258, 317, 332

MacDonald, Ramsey, 200

MacLeish, Archibald, 70

Malone, Dana, 73, 76

Mandela, Nelson, 341–42

Manhattan Project, 286

Man Is Not Alone (Heschel), 334

Mann, Thomas, 225, 263–64

Mark, Saint, Gospel of, 109–10, 131

Marshall Plan, 331

Martin, Kingsley, 194

Marx, Karl, 149

Marxism, 27, 58, 132

Mary, Queen of England, 197–98, 203

Massachusetts, 64, 91–93, 95, 101, 188–89, 327

Matthew, Saint, Gospel of, 105

Mazzini, Giuseppe, 175

Mediation Commission, 40, 41, 43

Melville, Herman, 327

Menace of Fascism, The (Strachey), 201

Mennonites, 96

Methodism, and Methodists, 31, 55, 56, 93–94, 333

Methodist Federation of Social Service, 332

"Mighty Fortress is Our God, A," 179

Millay, Edna St. Vincent, 50–51

Miller, Perry, 88

Miners' Federation, 193

Minnesota, University of, 54

Missouri, 13, 34, 37, 38, 40–41, 114, 345

Missouri Synod of the Lutheran Church, 96–97, 101

Molotov, V. M., 249, 250

Molotov-Ribbentrop pact, 133, 223, 226, 230, 249, 250

Moors, Ethel Paine, 43–48, *44,* 49–50, 63–65, 69, 72–73, 140, 167, 192, 298

Moors, John Cabot, 44–48, *44,* 50, 64

Morgan, J. P., 60

Morgenthau, Henry, 284

Morrison, Clayton C., 133–34, 152

Moscow show trials, 132

Mosley, Oswald, 200

Mount Greylock, 66, 252, 288, 291

Moyers, Bill, 148–49

Muilenberg, James, 169

Mumford, Geddes, 278

Mumford, Lewis, 266–67, 278

Murray, John Courtney, 206

"Music Is International" (Auden), 319

Muslims, 22, 33, 83, 84, 97, 105, 108

Mussolini, Benito, 192, 200, 204, 210, 229, 275, 281

"My Brother Hitler" (Mann), 263

Nagasaki, bombing of, 286–88

Namier, Lewis, 259

Nation, The, 243–44, 257, 262–63, 282–83

National Conference of Christians and Jews, 59, 256

National Socialism, 29, 117, 118, 133, 137, 140, 160, 212, 216, 232–33, 260, 265, 284

Nature and Destiny of Man, The (R. Niebuhr), 226–27

Neubauer, Reinhard, 343

Neutrality Act, 215, 242

New Deal, 25, 45, 76, 153, 154, 306, 312, 325

New Party (U.K.), 200

New School for Social Research (New York City), 162

New Testament, 26, 71, 107, 119–20, 151, 158, 161, 219, 237

see also Gospels

New York City, 34, 37, 58–59, 63–64, 69, 70, 91, 113, 129, 132, 147, 174, 257

New York Times, The, 256, 259

Niebuhr, Christopher (son), 36, 166, 216, 273, 275, *276, 286,* 323

Niebuhr, Gustav (father), 26, 34, 53, 75, 96, 97, 111–12, 113–14, 115–16, 120

Niebuhr, Helmut R. (brother), 26, 92, 97, 119, 123, 133, 159

works of, 120, 122, 124

Niebuhr, Lydia Hosto (mother), 36, 51, 72, 74, 79, 82, 113–14, 133, 246, 297

About the Author

Elisabeth Sifton was born in New York City in 1939. A graduate of Radcliffe College, where she earned a degree in history and literature magna cum laude, she attended the University of Paris for a year and then worked in the U.S. State Department (1961–62). Moving back to New York, she joined the staff of Frederick A. Praeger, Publisher, where she worked until 1968, becoming a senior editor there. From 1968 until 1987, her publishing locus was at The Viking Press, where she was, successively, editor and editor in chief; in the amalgamated company of Viking Penguin, she directed her own imprint, Elisabeth Sifton Books, 1984–87. An executive vice president of Alfred A. Knopf in 1987–92, she joined Farrar, Straus, and Giroux as senior vice president and publisher of Hill and Wang in 1993. She is the mother of three sons, and is married to the historian Fritz Stern.